THE SIZE OF OTHERS' BURDENS

THE SIZE OF OTHERS' BURDENS

Barack Obama, Jane Addams,
and the Politics of Helping Others

ERIK SCHNEIDERHAN

Stanford University Press
Stanford, California

Stanford University Press
Stanford, California

© 2015 by the Board of Trustees of the Leland Stanford Junior University. All rights reserved.

Printed in the United States of America on acid-free, archival-quality paper

Library of Congress Cataloging-in-Publication Data

Schneiderhan, Erik (Professor of sociology), author.
The size of others' burdens : Barack Obama, Jane Addams, and the politics of helping others / Erik Schneiderhan.
    pages cm
Includes bibliographical references and index.
ISBN 978-0-8047-8917-2 (cloth : alk. paper)
1. Addams, Jane, 1860-1935. 2. Obama, Barack. 3. Social reformers--Illinois--Chicago--Biography. 4. Charity--Political aspects--Illinois--Chicago--History. 5. Individualism--Illinois--Chicago--History. 6. Charities--Illinois--Chicago--History. 7. Community organization--Illinois--Chicago--History. I. Title.
HV99.C39S36 2015
361.973--dc23

                            2014044564

ISBN 978-0-8047-9495-4 (electronic)

Typeset by Bruce Lundquist in 10.75/16 Adobe Garamond Pro

For M. P. Stevens
Who helped me leave the sequestered byway

We are learning that a standard of social ethics is not attained by travelling a sequestered byway, but by mixing on the thronged and common road where all must turn out for one another, and at least see the size of one another's burdens.

Jane Addams

There's always been a tension in this country between the desire for liberty and self-reliance and individualism, and the desire for community and neighborliness and a sense of common purpose.

What I am constantly trying to do is balance a hard head with a big heart.

Barack Obama

Table of Contents

THE SIZE OF OTHERS' BURDENS

CHAPTER ONE

An American's Dilemma

IN THE DEPTHS OF CHICAGO WINTER, a young community organizer sat listening to appeal after appeal for help from people who had lost their jobs. It was the same story every time: Good-paying jobs were few and far between, and the government provided little support for those who were not working. In a climate of "pull yourself up by your bootstraps" and individual responsibility, there were few places to turn for help. Community organizations in Chicago tried to fill the gaps, but funding was tight, there were not enough resources to help everyone, and the economy showed no signs of improving. Each person appealing to the organizer was looking for the same thing: a way out of his or her struggles. But the organizer had very little to offer beyond the motto "a helping hand, not a handout."

One plea was particularly hard. The organizer knew the man standing there, hat in hand. They lived in the same neighborhood, and the supplicant, who had been fairly successful in shipping until he was laid off, did not know what to do or where to turn. The organizer's instructions were clear—no handouts until all other options had been exhausted. Had the man looked for work elsewhere? Yes. Well, the organizer did know of temporary work on one of the city's public works projects. The man protested: He had been working a desk job and would not survive hard physical labor outside in the dead of winter. The organizer was torn but remained firm, and the man walked away with details for contacting the project supervisor. The next day the former shipping clerk grabbed a shovel and joined the public works crew, excavating a drainage canal. He worked for two days in the winter cold before he contracted pneumonia. A week later, the man was dead.[1]

This book is, in part, about the community organizer in this story—one of America's greatest figures—whose list of accomplishments should sound familiar: Chicago activist, University of Chicago lecturer, gifted orator, politician and elected official, crusader against discrimination, winner of the Nobel Peace Prize, and author of one of the most-read autobiographies in America today. Why didn't this story come up during the 2008 or 2012 presidential elections? Because it happened in 1893, and the Chicago community organizer is Jane Addams.

Addams is best known for founding Hull-House, the celebrated American "settlement house" that served as the incubator for many ideas that would become the foundation of modern social work. How we help people in the United States today is in large part due to Addams's efforts and thinking in the late nineteenth and early twentieth centuries. In simple terms, the settlement was a building, situated in a poor neighborhood, which served as a center for helping people. But it was more than just a physical space. Addams summed up what *she* viewed as the overall logic of the settlement: "It aims, in a measure, to develop whatever of social life its neighborhood may afford, to focus and give form to that life, to bring to bear upon it the results of cultivation and training." Young men and women, called "residents," provided services in the neighborhood, serving as visiting nurses, educators, childcare providers, and advocates. Also, neighbors used the resources of the settlement house, and it was a research center; residents gathered data on social problems with the goal of bringing about social change. Many of the reforms that Hull-House and other settlement houses initiated were geared toward improving the lives of working-class immigrants who shouldered the bulk of the burden of capitalism's explosion.[2]

Robert Hunter—a sociologist, author, charity organizer, and contemporary of Addams—believed that settlement residents were wired differently. They had, he said, different "habits of their minds," and the "work of their lives is incited by entirely different stimuli," like travel, deep introspection, or the influence of strong mentors. Through the settlement movement, Addams and other American women would alter the trajectories available to them and create new paths forward, satisfying their desire for individual growth and their aspiration to help others, and earning them the moniker "Spearheads for Reform."[3]

Neighborhood Guild, the first U.S. settlement house, was established in 1886 on the Lower East Side of Manhattan. Including Addams's Hull-House, founded in 1889, only four settlements were founded in America before 1890. By 1900 there were approximately a hundred in operation, and by 1910 there were about four hundred. Chicago was home to sixteen at its peak, most notably Hull-House and Graham Taylor's Chicago Commons.

The American settlement movement also had a strong religious impetus but was not affiliated with any particular faith. The settlement was a church of sorts, allowing residents to worship God through acts in the real world. However, such general descriptions must be used cautiously, as settlement houses were not all the same. Similarly, it would be easy to romanticize the settlement movement and characterize it with more uniformity than it actually possessed; some operated more as religious convents, particularly in smaller cities, while others were closer to the Hull-House model, pursuing social morality in the spirit of the Gospels and of the emerging and distinctly American philosophy of pragmatism.[4] There are still settlement houses in operation today. While they do not have the coherence of a social movement, they are in some places still important outlets for our efforts to help in the community. They serve as lighthouses that draw people in need to safety and support.

The struggle between promoting individual responsibility and helping others in the community was as pressing in Addams's time as it is today. Resources were equally scarce. For over a hundred years, Americans like Addams have worked to balance the requirements of these competing ideals. Many citizens, then and now, have wondered how to preserve their livelihood, provide for their families, and validate their *own* hard work, while also addressing the urge—even the moral imperative—to help people less fortunate. For some, like Addams, the answer to this dilemma lies in getting involved in the community and even politics.[5] Indeed, Addams went on to successfully work front stage and behind the scenes in municipal, state, federal, and international politics. But becoming political often requires revisions and compromise in order to get things done. And, certain paths are not always open to particular categories of people in certain historical contexts. Biographies rooted in race, gender, and class (to name but a few) interact with the times to open certain ways and close down others.

This was the case for Addams in the late nineteenth century, just as it was for Barack Obama in the late twentieth century. The parallels between their lives are remarkable. They both moved over and against the limits placed on them by society because of their particular identities. They both began their careers as community organizers and activists in Chicago. Addams settled in the Nineteenth Ward and founded Hull-House, while Obama worked on the South Side of Chicago as a community organizer for the Developing Communities Project. Both became frustrated with the inability to make change outside the political system, got involved in politics, and ran for and won public office. And, as they became political, both Addams and Obama ended up revising their earlier ideals and moving away from their earlier creative work so that they might effect change on a larger scale.[6]

Addams had founded Hull-House as an alternative to the dominant, hard-nosed approach of existing charities. But as she became political, she ended up working closely with these existing groups, moving away from her own more experimental and neighborhood-based roots. She created ties to government officials and Chicago elites, and with these ties came reciprocal demands. They scratched her back, and she had to scratch theirs in turn. She had to be sensitive to and cooperative with one-time adversaries, lest she lose her hard-earned support. At the same time, she felt the pull of the changing times, as women struggled to find their own political voices, independent of men. And, Addams needed to tend to the needs of her family and her own poor health. Not to mention that she had individual yearnings—to read, travel, and enjoy the company of her friends.

For his part, Obama was first elected to public office as an Illinois state senator in 1996. His compromises are better known. In particular, his U.S. Senate campaign in 2004 and his 2008 presidential campaign were full of promises; those who elected Obama did so because they had the hope and craved the change his campaign trumpeted. But quickly, the demands of working with Congress, appeasing donors, and navigating increasingly tumultuous economic waters left many supporters feeling Obama had moved away from—even abandoned—his goals and principles. This showed at times in his successful reelection effort in 2012. But the revisions he made *prior* to running for office are equally important in understanding his life's trajectory. Obama worked hard to provide South Side Chicagoans with a voice in the city. But, like Addams, as he worked closely with city officials and elites, he gradually moved away from his more radical and experimental efforts. He was convinced he could not be effective without further education, so he went back to school, then returned to Chicago. All the while, Obama struggled to find his bearings; as a man of mixed racial heritage, the way forward in the post-Civil Rights era was not readily apparent. He had to make his own way.

The shared successes and struggles of Addams and Obama are the subject of this book, but this is not a book *just* about them. Their stories are instruments to help answer questions about American social life: How do Americans act in the face of competing social pressures when trying to help others in their communities? What happens when Americans become political and partner with elites as part of their efforts to move forward? The conflicting social demands of individualism and community assistance comprise a challenge that many face— it's the American's Dilemma. Well-meaning people are torn, akin to Goethe's Faust who bemoaned having two souls beating in one breast. Whether the president of the United States, a registered nurse, or a university student, at some point most Americans wonder how to help others while still working toward the American Dream, how to lend a helping hand and still be a bootstrapping success. We are asked by society to be good workers, to be good consumers and "buy American," to be healthy, to be good parents, and to be good friends. We also have our own drives, from wanderlust to sitting down on the couch to spend an hour with a good book. Obama and Addams, like ordinary Americans, felt the pull of all these competing urges.

Americans have a fierce spirit of individualism dating back to the nation's founding. In public discourse and in the home, most Americans hold dear the notion that (for better or worse) each should be left to sink or swim. The United States was built on the idea of classical liberalism, which emphasizes individualism and freedom. The idea of doing it yourself, whatever that may be in practice, is reinforced from every direction by social institutions, including the media, schools, and workplaces. Still, Americans also like to help people. In America's national culture, there are certain norms that shape social behavior. Most world religions encourage the helping of others in one way or another, and the idea of doing good works is tied to individual transcendence. The engine of faith has driven much of community helping in America. In fact, we will see that both Addams and Obama were influenced by religion. It is also clear that the idea of lending a helping hand is part of the myth and legend of the nation's founding. Whether the story is of Native Americans helping pilgrims to survive the cold

New England winters or of neighbors helping neighbors in the wake of a tornado in Oklahoma, Americans believe that, in a pinch, they will help their neighbors and their neighbors will help them. Sometimes it is hard to adjudicate between the competing spirits of individualism and community. They are, at times, incommensurable.

We are influenced in our decisions about how to be a social citizen by what our parents did—maybe they provided money or time to help people in their community, on their own or through a local church. Or maybe the parents did little community work—they were working too much or didn't think it was their responsibility. Friends and mentors will have an influence, too. "Make a difference! Get involved!" All this exposure to new ideas can generate excitement, leaving one feeling as if one can do anything with the right attitude. This spirit is captured by the Margaret Mead quote that pops up in greeting cards and on inspirational posters: "Never doubt that a small group of committed people can change the world. Indeed, it is the only thing that ever has."

Still, it is easy to be overwhelmed with the problems of the world. They can leave a person feeling small and ineffective, confused about where to start and fatalistic about what an individual person can actually do. The problems are just so monumental! Admiring and emulating Margaret Mead are different things when there is a paycheck to earn, rent to be paid, or diapers to be changed.

All of this equivocating is part of the American's Dilemma. It has been with us since our nation's founding, and, as a society, we have had plenty of time to think about the answers. Often, though, Americans have let such uncomfortable ideas go quietly ignored. The idea of America as a place of incommensurable dilemmas is not new. We are put in difficult positions by competing, but core, American values: "Americans help each other" and "I am responsible for my own success." The choices we make for moving forward when these values conflict define us as individuals and contribute to our moral development, both individually and socially. What we do is important not just for our own lives, but also for our community values. The most promising social "place" to experiment with ways to accommodate our conflicting values is in relations with others in our neighborhoods.[7]

We all deserve to receive help in times of need, and we may be in a position to help someone else in another moment. Maybe we do it through an organization or on our own. But this help is about on-the-ground, face-to-face relations. It is a back-and-forth process with no end. In a sense, we are building roads that we travel together, and we are acknowledging that there is no destination but a better society. Perhaps this sounds a bit pie-in-the-sky.[8] But Addams and Obama show us that it is possible. They demonstrate that sometimes we get stuck and cannot move forward in the direction we want to go. Limitations made each choose a different path, entering into politics. Rather than continue their initial community work, Addams and Obama revised and scaled up their efforts. Surely, they also left something behind.

This book tries to bring together some of the best thinking on how we might conceive of and practice helping in our own communities. It might help readers move forward from ambivalence, equipping each to solve his or her own American's Dilemma. And from the ideas in this book, we can think through and critically examine the stories of Jane Addams and Barack Obama in their communities. Facing the same questions most Americans face, Addams and Obama made choices about involvement with their communities and politics; those choices had consequences. Studying the roads each traveled—their wrong turns, the roadblocks they faced, and the places they stopped in their respective journeys—holds instructive potential. If we want to solve the social problems facing our communities, it is helpful to understand the pitfalls that might lie ahead. The cases of Addams and Obama help us understand how our dilemmas come to be, and how we might work through them.

While Addams and Obama were both inspirational activists who brought about real change, they faced different challenges. Addams could not turn to government and the welfare state for support, as there were virtually no public funds available for the kind of work she did at Hull-House. So, she used her own money and raised more from other wealthy individuals. Although the lack of state resources was problematic, it also meant freedom from state oversight—essentially, Addams could do whatever she wanted, within reason. Obama, on the other hand, worked in a period of relatively high state support for public welfare provision, and that was accompanied by significant regulation and a need for political maneuvering. Held up together, the cases show the value of combining today's state resources with the innovation and flexibility of Addams's time. The stories show the value of looking to the past to understand the present.

A caveat: This book may be many things, but there are many it is not. For instance, though I will talk about the compromises Addams and Obama had to make as they waded into politics, this book is not an indictment of either. Nor is it meant to be yet another adoring biographical treatment of how each dramatically changed the landscape of American society. It is not about citizenship and the welfare state or whether the United States is "going in the wrong direction," is politically divided, or requires balance. It does not indict the Right or valorize the Left. Rather, this book is a social diagnosis based on historical evidence. This evidence comes from data collected during my own archival research and gleaned from a treasure trove of secondary sources. My hope is that this evidence will provide a platform for helping us better understand the United States of America and offer ideas for how to move forward and help others when faced with our own moments of dilemma.

It is probably obvious that there is a strong normative element to this text. In it, I take the position that good social science is not just about adding to existing literature but also about "making a difference" in our world. American philosopher William James talked about the "cash-value" of ideas for society, asking "What difference would it practically make to any one if this notion rather than that notion were true?" Ideas that do not impact how we live our lives are of little consequence. One might consider the pages to come a search for what Richard Rorty, another American philosopher, terms "a hint of how our lives might be changed." Not everyone can run for president or win a Nobel Prize. But we can help others without sacrificing their dignity or our principles. Great thinkers of the past and present will give us the ideas and motivation; Addams and Obama will show us how. The hope is that this book will inspire readers to address their own American's Dilemma by connecting to community.[9]

CHAPTER TWO

The Right to Be Heard

All that subtle force among women which is now dreaming fancy,
might be changed into creative genius.

Jane Addams[1]

S HE HAD NOT ANTICIPATED the death of her father. It was August 1881, and Jane Addams had been vacationing with her family when John Addams developed acute appendicitis. He died in Green Bay, Wisconsin, too sick and tired to make the trip back home to Cedarville, Illinois. The family had likely been trying to escape the recent drama surrounding the shooting of President James Garfield on July 2, 1881. (Garfield would die two months later.) The shooter, Charles Guiteau, had close ties to the Addams family. His father had been a long-time friend of John Addams, and the two families had numerous connections.[2]

The escape, however, became a case of out of the frying pan and into the fire, as Jane Addams was forced to consider the loss of her father, one of her closest friends and confidants. In the wake of his death, she was rudderless: "How purposeless and without ambition I am," she wrote two weeks after the funeral.[3] Jane had just graduated from Rockford Seminary—valedictorian with the equivalent of a B.A., but she was a woman without a plan. She wanted to continue her studies at Smith College in Massachusetts in the fall, but her father had said no repeatedly. Now, the main obstacle to Addams attending Smith was gone.

Her remaining family and a number of her father's friends jumped in, offering unsolicited advice. Her brother-in-law advised her in a letter to "live for the world, for humanity, for yourself & for Christ." Reverend Charles Caverno, a family friend who knew about Addams's plans to attend Smith, wrote, "I have wanted all along to enter a pro-tests against your doing that *on account of your health. . . .* Why do I write this to day? Because if my daughter were Father-less I should wish any one to give any advice tending in ~~their~~ his opinion to her happiness or welfare."[4] The particular paternalism of this type of ad-vice is readily apparent, with people stepping in to provide fatherly counsel they believe is desperately needed.

Confounding any decision was the fact that Addams was now a woman of means. Her father had left her with a significant in-heritance, including a farm, land for timbering, bank and railroad stocks, and other income. Addams and her three siblings each re-ceived (in today's dollars) nearly one million dollars as a total inheri-tance. This money would open numerous doors; in Addams's life to come, it would help her make magic in Chicago. It would help her create Hull-House, a place where she could live for the world and help others.[5]

The America in which Addams lived was one of obvious cultural contradictions, particularly along gender lines. Freedom and equality were not the lot of women in 1881. Addams knew this and struggled with it. Her senior essay at Rockford, written several months before the death of her father, reveals the dilemmas she faced at this point in her life. The essay, titled "Cassandra," is about how women can apply their intuition to help others and bring about meaningful social re-form. Addams calls for women to strive for "*auethoritas*" or "the right of speaker to make themselves heard."[6] This is a political call through and through. Addams is searching for a foundation for women to participate in the public sphere and engage in helping others without the constraints of men.

Her "Cassandra" essay was a departure from earlier writing and speeches, showing, as biographer Louise Knight points out, her "conflicted frame of mind." Pulled on the one side toward tradition and family responsibility, and on the other toward a desire to be heard and to free herself from the restrictions of a patriarchal society, Addams eventually found, in Hull-House, a way to move forward. In a sense, then, the settlement movement in the United States emerges as the solution to the seemingly intractable problem of Addams and other white, educated women in the nineteenth century: how to make a difference in society without compromising the right to be heard. Few women had the resources to envision and pursue nontraditional lines of action. How did Addams come to be in such a privileged position for her time and gender?[7]

Addams was born in 1860, on the eve of one of America's greatest divisions: the Civil War. Her father was a staunch Union supporter. He had served as an Illinois state senator since 1854 and was a close colleague of Abraham Lincoln, helping Lincoln with his 1858 U.S. Senate race (at the time U.S. senators were selected by the state legislature) and organizing Lincoln's famous debates with Stephen Douglas. John Addams profited greatly from the war. He had ownership positions in both woolen mills and gristmills, and their products were in great demand for Union troops. Further, millers were exempt from service in the army—a policy that likely saved John Addams's life. In the Reconstruction era, he was a wealthy man with a thriving business as well as one of the most powerful politicians in Illinois.[8]

He was also the single most powerful influence on his daughter Jane. This was due in large part to the death of his wife, Sarah, in 1863. She had fallen while pregnant, and the internal injuries took her life and that of the child. She left behind five children, including three-year-old Jane. For the next five years, until he remarried, John Addams was a single parent, instilling in his children an ecumenical faith and a deep sense of the importance of honesty and helping your neighbors.[9]

For Addams, privilege was cultivated at an early age. She grew up in Cedarville, a small town in the northern part of the Illinois, where her father's wealth and status meant she lacked for little. John Addams was a constant presence in the house and allowed his daughter unfettered access to his extensive library, even providing her an allowance for reading and giving oral summaries of works such as Plutarch's *Lives* and Washington Irving's *Life of Washington*. Perhaps this opened young Addams's eyes to the world. It appears, somewhat surprisingly for someone her age, that she was aware of her privileged life. On a visit to the nearby town of Freeport, Addams had an epiphany:

> Before then I had always seen the little city of ten thousand people with the admiring eyes of a country child, and it had never occurred to me that all its streets were not as bewilderingly attractive as the one which contained the glittering toyshop and the confectioner. On that day I had my first sight of the poverty which implies squalor, and felt the curious distinction between the ruddy poverty of the country and that which even a small city presents in its shabbiest streets. I remember launching at my father the pertinent inquiry why people lived in such horrid little houses so close together, and that after receiving his explanation I declared with much firmness when I grew up I should, of course, have a large house, but it would not be built among the other large houses, but right in the midst of horrid little houses like those.[10]

The seeds of awareness of her social position in society were planted at an early age, and Addams clearly struggled with the distinctions that she saw.

When Addams was a child, settlement houses did not exist in the United States. So, her experience with how people helped others was grounded in the church and local relief organizations. Her father was a devout, interdenominational Christian with Quaker sympathies. Like his friend Lincoln, he belonged to no specific church. But his children attended the nondenominational Union Sunday School each week. Here, Addams would have been exposed to the Gospels of the New Testament, replete with lessons from Jesus on how and why we should help our neighbors. Interestingly, Addams remained unbaptized; her father led the way in eschewing any one denomination.[11]

Whether it was her father's instruction and his library, the Sunday school lessons, or an innate kindness, Addams struggled with how to carry herself in society. She realized her privilege and saw how others were less fortunate:

I constantly confided my sins and perplexities to my father. . . . I can remember an admonition on one occasion . . . as a little girl of eight years, arrayed in a new cloak, gorgeous beyond anything I had ever worn before, I stood before my father for his approval. I was much chagrined by his remark that it was a very pretty cloak—in fact so much prettier than any cloak the other little girls in the Sunday School had, that he would advise me to wear my old cloak, which would keep me quite as warm, with the added advantage of not making the other little girls feel badly. I complied with the request but I fear without inner consent, and I certainly was quite without the joy of self-sacrifice as I walked soberly through the village street by the side of my counselor. My mind was busy, however, with the old question eternally suggested by the inequalities of the human lot. Only as we neared the church door did I venture to ask what could be done about it, receiving the reply that it might never be righted so far as clothes went, but that people might be equal in things that mattered much more than clothes, the affairs of education and religion, for instance, which we attended to when we went to school and church, and that it was very stupid to wear the sort of clothes that made it harder to have equality even there.[12]

This conversation stayed with Addams and is emblematic of her early dilemma as she tried to balance individual desires with obligations to her community.

Addams's childhood did not leave much room for her to satisfy any charitable urges. She was kept busy in the house, particularly after her father married Anna Haldeman in 1868. Anna was more strict and traditional than her new husband in terms of discipline and the role of women in the household. As an adolescent, Addams was now required to clean the house regularly and bake pies on Saturday. Still, housework aside, Anna brought a love of culture into the house and instilled in Addams a passion for literature, music, and art that would serve her in the future as she socialized with the elites of Chicago.[13]

Addams also learned from a young age to be at ease with the rich and powerful. Famous men would occasionally visit her father at home. Ulysses Grant, celebrated general and future president, the governor of Illinois Richard Oglesby, and Senator Lyman Trumbull (coauthor of the Thirteenth Amendment to the U.S. Constitution) all called on John Addams in Cedarville. Jane Addams later said: "Even as a little child I was dimly conscious of the grave march of public affairs in his comings and goings at the state capital." But more important, she became comfortable with this world and her own place in it. She was slowly and surely engaged in embodying both privilege and ease in elite American society.[14]

Addams was also experimenting with and learning about the value of connecting with others. In her last year of high school, she created the Capenic Society of the West. The idea was to bring together people who were interested in the work of John Capen, a phrenologist who worked in Philadelphia. Addams had visited his practice during a family trip to the Centennial Exhibition in Philadelphia. There, she had become intrigued by phrenology's premise that it is possible to understand individual personalities by "reading" head shape and size. While admittedly a bit odd as a first venture into social connections, the idea of a young woman in nineteenth-century America organizing a social club of any kind is noteworthy.[15]

To be sure, life was still a bit provincial for Addams. When she started school at Rockford Seminary in September 1877, it was more out of duty than any sense of stepping onto a new and exciting road:

> As my three older sisters had already attended the seminary at Rockford, of which my father was trustee, without any question I entered there at seventeen, with such meager preparation in Latin and algebra as the village school had afforded. I was very ambitious to go to Smith College, although I well knew that my father's theory in regard to the education of his daughters implied a school as near at home as possible, to be followed by travel abroad in lieu of the wider advantages which the eastern college is supposed to afford.

Rockford's was an ascetic lifestyle. Students were responsible for keeping their rooms clean, making their own fires, and fasting one day each month. Religion was ever-present, particularly on the Sabbath:

> Sunday morning was a great clearing up day, and the sense of having made immaculate my own immediate surroundings, the consciousness of clean linen, said to be close to the consciousness of a clean conscience, always mingles in my mind with these early readings. I certainly bore away with me a lifelong enthusiasm for reading the Gospels in bulk, a whole one at a time, and an insurmountable distaste for having them cut up into chapter and verse, or for hearing the incidents in that wonderful Life thus referred to as if it were merely a record.

Addams's enthusiasm for the Gospels is telling: It marks the cultivation of a deep sense of the importance of helping others.[16]

If her home life helped Addams carry ease and privilege, Rockford, an all-women's seminary (though not, at the time, a college), helped her develop a sense of the true limits placed on the education of women. The school's goal (and motto) was to turn its students into "cornerstones polished after the similitude of a palace." Being a cornerstone, likely for some man's building, was not necessarily the ultimate expression of personal development in the minds of the female students, but there just were not many other options for women to further their education. A group of students, Addams among them, pushed for Rockford's installation as a college. Addams recalled:

> The opportunity for our Alma Mater to take her place in the new movement of full college education for women filled us with enthusiasm, and it became a driving ambition with the undergraduates to share in this new and glorious undertaking. We gravely decided that it was important that some of the students should be ready to receive the bachelor's degree the very first moment that the charter of the school should secure the right to confer it.

One Rockford teacher in particular tacitly encouraged her students through teachings on history and literature to become assertive, engage in oral debate in class, and consider the potential for independence and original thinking in life. As such, the Rockford classroom was at times a place of tremendous cultural contradictions, challenging women to focus on how they might better themselves socially and intellectually, while also asking them to help others in the tradition of the Gospels. Addams showed an increasing awareness that she was being pulled in two directions. She needed to balance her individual and community-oriented action.[17]

In pursuit of her individual goals, Addams tried several times to transfer to Smith, but she eventually, and somewhat grudgingly, gave up and prepared to graduate from Rockford. Her focus at the time was on preparing to practice medicine, but because Rockford was a seminary, the push was for students to pursue a career in religion. Jane resisted:

> So curious, however, are the paths of moral development that several times during subsequent experiences have I felt that this passive resis-

tance of mine, this clinging to an individual conviction, was the best
moral training I received at Rockford College.

In other words, this resistance was a crucible in which Addams forged
a sense of self. It would take her on a different, nontraditional road.

In her final year at Rockford, Addams asserted herself, becoming
editor-in-chief of the *Rockford Seminary Magazine*, where she even had
her own office—quite a luxury for a student. Perhaps it was this success that led her to seriously consider trying one more time to open
the road to Smith, as she wrote in a letter to her friend and former
classmate, Ellen Gates Starr: "This year is a solid dig to make up all the
odds and ends for Smiths; such little things as spherical trigonometry
and the Memorabilia."[18]

Her editorials for the magazine reveal her dilemmas. She wanted
to go to Smith and eventually become a doctor. But she also celebrated the idea of keeping multiple lines of action open in life, as
it was hard to know "what niche in the world has been left for us to
fill." Counter to her acts of resistance, she wrote an editorial celebrat-
ing "submission to rightful authority," calling it "one of the most
useful habits of life." Dealing with resistance and submission, these
writings show plainly the contradictory discourses that coexisted in
American culture.[19]

The road less traveled was appealing in the abstract, but in practice the route was unclear. Addams, for all her privilege, was not very
worldly in a practical sense. When she received her inheritance, the
only thing she was certain of was that she wanted to give to Rockford:

> The first gift I made when I came into possession of my small estate the
> year after I left school, was a thousand dollars to the library of Rock-
> ford College, with the stipulation that it be spent for scientific books.[20]

Addams was still focused on the idea of pursuing studies in medicine
(note that she specified the Rockford library acquire scientific books),

but everything was uncertain in the Addams household in the wake of her father's death.

A plan quickly emerged: Addams's stepmother Anna would close up the Cedarville home and move to Philadelphia, where she had family. Though Addams was now financially independent and free to make the leap to Smith, she complied with Anna, who insisted Addams was too "frail" to go off on her own. It was an all-too-common occurrence; young women were stymied by claims of frailness or mental instability mapped onto them (usually by men). Rather than head to Massachusetts, Addams enrolled for the fall term at the Woman's Medical College in Philadelphia. Though it was one of the top medical schools in the nation, in a somewhat ironic twist, Addams's health quickly deteriorated. She was depressed and had terrible back pains. She battled for four months before being admitted to the hospital for treatment of neurasthenia (exhaustion of the central nervous system).[21]

In essence, the entire frame for her illness was one of psychological failure and selfishness. Addams, the medical community seemed to concur, could be better if she *wanted* to, and the treatment (which included electric shocks) was designed to be so unpleasant as to motivate recovery. Needless to say, Addams's focus now was very much on her own personal health and well-being. There was no time or space to look at the larger world.[22]

Addams continued to convalesce, returning with the family to Cedarville. In June 1882 she received a much-needed boost when Rockford announced it was becoming a college and formally awarded her a bachelor of arts degree. Addams visited Smith College with a friend on the way back from Nantucket Island in Massachusetts. "Going to Smith College to start fresh," she wrote in August. But again, the plan derailed when Addams's brother Harry, also studying medicine, convinced her to try a revolutionary new operation for her back problems. The procedure was ghastly; a surgeon used hot wires to fuse the damaged portion of her spine (twisted because of childhood tuberculosis).

Rather than spending the last two months of 1882 in Northampton, home of Smith, Addams was in bed in Cedarville, despondent. The procedure appears to have worked to some degree, but this was hardly the vision Addams had held for that fall.[23]

The next five years were ones of stasis and "perplexity," the term Addams used to describe a moment when habits or traditional ways of action break down. How to move forward? There was a great deal of family upheaval, which certainly put pressure on her to focus inward, rather than on her own future and on helping those outside the family. She spent the first half of 1883 convalescing in Iowa, at the home of her brother Weber, until he was declared insane and committed to the Illinois state mental hospital. Another setback for Addams.

She returned to Cedarville with a sense that she needed to get away. A speech to the Rockford Female Seminary Alumnae Association on June 20, 1883, reveals her turmoil, what she calls "the uncomfortableness of transition." While ostensibly talking about Rockford, there is a subtext to her address to her female peers:

> We are uncomfortable and uncertain because we are dimly conscious of sham and unfairness, because we bear a name which we do not duly represent and have raised vague expectations which we cannot fulfill.

Uncertainty was a hallmark of this time in Addams's life. As a response, she fell back on the expected and began planning a trip to Europe with her stepmother in the summer of 1883. Such a Grand Tour, as it was called, was common for privileged women of Addams's age. It was seen as a way to become cultured and to learn about the larger world. Addams left the United States in August and would not return until June of 1885. She toured all the major sites of Europe and spent several months living in Dresden, Berlin, and Paris.[24]

There are signs that, during her extended travels, Addams's was brought face-to-face with situations outside her comfort zone. Most notably, when Addams was in London, she visited the East End and was shocked and appalled by its poverty and squalor. Upon reflection, Addams viewed this encounter as formative, and it would percolate in her mind as she began to converge on the idea of Hull-House. A letter written by Addams two days after her visit reveals her struggles to absorb what she saw in the East End:

> We took a look down into dingy old Grubb St. It was simply an outside superficial survey of the misery & wretchedness, but it was enough to make one thoroughly sad and perplexed.

She would later recall people clamoring to buy castoff vegetables from the local market:

> . . . we saw two huge masses of ill-clad people clamoring around two hucksters' carts. They were bidding their farthings and ha'pennies for a vegetable held up by the auctioneer, which he at last scornfully flung, with a gibe for its cheapness, to the successful bidder . . . [the people] were huddled into ill-fitting, cast-off clothing, the ragged finery which one sees only in East London. Their pale faces were dominated by that most unlovely of human expressions, the cunning and shrewdness of the bargain-hunter who starves if he cannot make a successful trade, and yet the final impression was not of ragged, tawdry clothing nor of pinched and sallow faces, but of myriads of hands, empty, pathetic, nerveless and workworn, showing white in the uncertain light of the street, and clutching forward for food which was already unfit to eat.[25]

Addams had never seen anything like it. Surely, this made her personal struggles and concerns seem trivial by comparison.

During this trip, Addams was also thinking more deeply about the need to connect with others. She wrote in a letter to her stepbrother George: "I am more convinced all the time of the value of social life, of its necessity for the development of some of our best traits."[26] But her experience in the East End and her growing conviction of the importance of the social did not crystallize into a plan of action. Consequently, Addams found herself back in Cedarville in June of 1885, better informed but still a bit adrift.

Addams threw herself into reading and reflection, recalling later, "The two years which elapsed before I again found myself in Europe [in 1888] brought their inevitable changes."[27] Why? The inevitability of events is not apparent, but there is no question that some critical shifts occurred in her thinking. In this period, Addams resided for some time in Baltimore, Maryland, with Anna, and for the rest at the family home in Cedarville. She read widely and became inspired by Leo Tolstoy's book *What to Do?*[28] In it, Tolstoy was concerned with the role of science in helping others. He was clear that it was not enough to give money; one must act and connect:

> [People] should . . . enter into relations with the people who are in need of assistance, and labor for them. . . . Money is not needed. What is needed is self-sacrificing action; what is needed are people who would like to do good, not by giving extraneous sin-money, but by giving their own labor, themselves, their lives. Where are such people to be found?[29]

Addams also read *The Subjection of Women*, by John Stuart Mill, in which he makes a call for gender equality based on utilitarian philosophy. It is likely that this influenced her decision to refuse a proposal of marriage from her stepbrother George in May 1887. While closing down one possible future, that refusal also opened up another line of action: that of an unencumbered single woman.[30]

Somewhat surprisingly, Jane also decided to become a Presbyterian and was baptized:

> At this time there was certainly no outside pressure pushing me to-wards such a decision, and at twenty-five one does not ordinarily

take such a step from a mere desire to conform. While I was not conscious of any emotional "conversion," I took upon myself the outward expressions of the religious life with all humility and sincerity. It was doubtless true that I was "Weary of myself and sick of asking What I am and what I ought to be."

Addams's quotation of Matthew Arnold's poem "Self-Dependence" is telling. She is clearly trying to figure out what actions might arise from fixing on a stronger sense of self. Religion offered some concrete appeal, providing a channel for some of the enthusiasm she felt for Tolstoy's ideas.

In thinking through who she "ought to be," Addams did try to change some practical dimensions of her life. She felt terrible about collecting rents from farmers on the land she inherited from her father, so she experimented by investing in a cooperative sheep farming venture, rather than accumulating the capital. The plan was a failure, but her efforts are worth noting: She had clearly rejected the expected framework and tried to find a way to eke social benefit from her capitalist activities.[31]

Addams was thinking hard about how to do things differently in her life. At some point during the summer of 1887, Addams picked up the May issue of *Century* magazine, which contained a letter from R. R. Bowker, who had visited what he termed "an interesting social experiment" in the East End of London, the very site of Jane's memorable encounter with the depths of poverty. This social experiment, the letter described, was conducted by

> . . . fifteen or twenty men, most of them graduates of Oxford or Cambridge, some of them busy in the city, others men of leisure and wealth, all of them giving more or less of their time to the work of making the lives of the East End poor more wholesome and beautiful than they could be without such help. The hall is named after Arnold Toynbee, one of the scholars of Balliol College, Oxford, who had interested himself deeply in social questions.[32]

Most likely, her reading of this letter prompted the settlement idea. Looking back, she wrote: "It is hard to tell just when the very simple plan which afterward developed into the Settlement began to form itself in my mind. It may have been even before I went to Europe for the second time."[33] The foundations were certainly there: a commitment to social connections, a passion for helping others, a rejection of the inevitability of abject poverty, and finally, a sense that, even though she did not have all the answers, she might try to make a difference.

Beginning in January 1887, Addams had begun making plans to return to Europe with her friend Ellen Gates Starr. At least there, Addams had been stimulated to think beyond her life in Cedarville. But the Toynbee letter provided a bit of focus. It was a liberating moment when, on December 14, 1887, Addams set sail, again for England. Her friend Sarah Anderson, on the faculty at Rockford, accompanied her; Starr, chaperoning other two young women on their first Grand Tour, would meet them later in the trip.[34]

Addams's second Grand Tour was as long and winding as the first, taking nearly eight months. Biographers make much of this trip, in particular focusing on an epiphany Addams had at a bullfight in Spain:

> It was suddenly made quite clear to me that I was lulling my conscience by a dreamer's scheme, that a mere paper reform had become a defense for continued idleness, and that I was making it a raison d'etre for going on indefinitely with study and travel.

In the days that followed, Addams and Starr began to talk in earnest about what they called "the scheme." Soon after, she recalled, "the scheme had become convincing and tangible although still most hazy in detail." Within a month, Addams had made her way back to England:

> . . . in June, 1888, five years after my first visit in East London, I found myself at Toynbee Hall equipped not only with a letter of

introduction from Canon Fremantle, but with high expectations and a certain belief that whatever perplexities and discouragement concerning the life of the poor were in store for me, I should at least know something at first hand and have the solace of daily activity.

With this visit, Addams found a way to make her vague plans concrete.[35]

Founded in 1883, Toynbee Hall was situated in one of the poorest urban neighborhoods of East London. The settlement's residents lived right alongside the poor. Their primary task, as she mentioned in a speech she gave in 1891, was to provide education and culture to their less fortunate neighbors, as a sort of "university for working people." Further, Toynbee pursued an agenda for reform that included higher wages, job training, public health services, and better working conditions. In a letter to her sister dated June 18, 1888, Addams mentions this second visit to Toynbee:

> It is a community of University men who live there, have their recreating clubs & society all among the poor people yet in the same style they would live in their own circle. It is so free from "professional doing good" so matter of factly sincere and so productive of good results in its classes and libraries that it seems perfectly ideal.[36]

The philosophical grounding of reform effort at Toynbee was inspired in large part by Matthew Arnold, who harbored the "hope of transforming England into a nation of 'sweetness and light.'" This transformation would, Arnold believed, take place through the Victorian middle-class's participation in social provision. T. H. Green, a philosopher at Balliol College of Oxford University, and Benjamin Jowett were also major influences. Samuel Barnett, the warden of Toynbee Hall, was taught by Jowett and Green and was shaped by Green's ideas on the importance of community and individual connection, as well as his emphasis on action rather than simply ivory-tower discussions. Equally important, Toynbee Hall emphasized the reciprocal nature of relationships between residents and their neighbors. Taken together, these principles (and their manifest practices) can be understood as providing a sort of blueprint for Addams's approach at Hull-House. An early visitor, in fact, called Hull-House "a Toynbee Hall experiment in Chicago."[37]

There are also important limitations to Toynbee Hall's influence on the creation of Hull-House. Most notably, Toynbee had close ties to the London Charity Organization Society. Charity Organization adherents had completely different ideas about helping people, and they were far from both Tolstoy's philosophy and Addams's personal inclinations. Barnett had helped establish a Charity Organization committee at his first parish, and his wife had once worked closely with Octavia Hill, a Charity Organization supporter (and successful rent collector for London landlords). Given the amount of time Addams spent at Toynbee Hall, she was likely aware of—and possibly wary of—its ties to the London Charity Organization Society.[38]

Another limit to the Toynbee model's influence on Addams lies in dispositions: The initial residents at Toynbee Hall were male graduates of Oxford. To quote Robert Woods:

> Toynbee Hall is essentially a transplant of [male] university life in Whitechapel. The quadrangle, the gables, the diamond-paned windows, the large general rooms, especially the dining-room with its brilliant frieze of college shields, all make the place seem not so distant from the dreamy walks by the Isis or the Cam.[39]

Provided with such a strong image of male privilege, it is not difficult to imagine that, for Addams, the relationship between residents and neighbors might have looked imbalanced, not only in terms of gender but also of class. While the residents of Hull-House would also be well educated and occasionally of means, they were by no stretch the elite of American society. Further, the gender dimensions of Toynbee Hall's early years no doubt influenced the type of relationships residents were able to develop with their neighbors. The men of Oxbridge were un-likely to have had much appreciation for the particular needs of women trying to balance the challenges of raising children, doing household work, and participating in the labor market.

It is clear from her letters and later recollections that this second European trip was a personal crossroads for Addams. Whatever resistance she had gave way to the excitement of creation. Returning from her travels at the end of the summer of 1888, Addams was energized; her letters show that she was filled with a new sense of purpose. In this critical moment, she was ready to upend her comfortable life as an educated, upper-middle-class woman in Illinois. She had come face-to-face with a way of helping that was new to her. During the next year, she spent her time formulating "her convictions" into a "plan of action." Addams would later characterize this as the moment her "period of mere passive receptivity had come to an end."[40]

Addams and Starr had begun to plan in Europe, and they determined to try to get something started in Chicago, where Starr had been working as a teacher. These women were not the first to resolve to help others in Chicago, of course. Since the city's founding in 1833, neighbors had worked to help one another, changing their approaches over time. In many ways, the story of Chicago is the story of all of urban America; looking at its past and getting a sense of its history can reveal the challenges Addams faced and how they relate to the American's Dilemma. Addams's Hull-House and its settlement programs emerged *in relation to* other Chicago organizations. Addams set out to try something totally new, an approach that was different from what charity programs were already attempting in Chicago (and what she saw wasn't working). As a woman, she also needed to create a place that would allow for her fullest expression as a person, her full potential. Addams consciously created Hull-House to seek effectiveness without sacrificing the dignity of those she wanted to help.[41]

.   .   .

In the mid-nineteenth century, Chicago was still a fairly small city. By the end of the 1800s, it experienced a period of unparalleled post–Civil War growth. Its population doubled between 1880 and 1890 as massive immigration—in part a response to increased demand for workers—caused cities across the United States to expand rapidly. There was also the push factor of recently freed slaves and unemployed whites looking to escape the economically (and socially) devastated South. As people moved from rural areas to urban centers, leaving farms and self-subsistence behind, more workers came to rely on the factory system for employment. These workers became increasingly vulnerable to the ups and downs of the market. A drop in demand might mean steep cuts in production and fewer hours and take-home pay for workers—even layoffs. For workers who were already paid little and had virtually none of the workplace protections we expect now (from breaks to weekends off, let alone safety standards), any serious economic downturn, like the 1893 depression, was sure to be devastating.[42]

There was little state welfare support as we know it; public resources for social provision were scarce and provided reluctantly. Community-based helping was like a patchwork quilt, with lots of different types of organizations and strategies. Much of the work was gap-filling, in which volunteers in Chicago and elsewhere tried to address massive unmet needs through "indoor" and "outdoor" relief programs. (Think of indoor relief as getting a place to stay—the poorhouse made famous by Charles Dickens and other nineteenth-century writers—and outdoor relief as receiving help in your own home, in the form of a meal, household items, or advice.) In Illinois, the brunt of the burden for helping those in need was carried by private organizations such as churches and relief societies, with limited coordination by the state and county boards of charity.[43]

Wealthy Chicago women, commonly and collectively known as Lady Bountiful, began to find an outlet in asylum work, but most people did not want to associate directly with the poor. In particular,

Chicago's elite felt threatened by a constant barrage of the poor literally knocking on their doors seeking help. So, they began to retreat behind both literal and figurative walls; they gave money in order to maintain distance. The state *could* not help people, and most private individuals *would* not help. Charitable organizations did their best to fill the gaps, but they were overwhelmed. They did not have the capacity to respond adequately to the needs of the day, and what they did do was not particularly effective.[44]

One of the "gap-fillers" in Chicago charity was the Chicago Relief and Aid Society (CRAS).[45] The organization was not (at least in financial terms) a significant player in the city's social provision until 1871. In fact, there does not appear to have been *any* organization that played a significant, citywide role between 1857 and 1871. Individual churches picked up some slack, but the efforts varied by congregation. This lack of organizational activity may have been due to the impact of the Civil War on the capacity of civil society to create alternatives—there just wasn't enough financial or human capital available to meet what were surely great needs. Wage labor was inadequate and dangerous, and many families had lost members or seen casualties from the war. While economic booms and busts passed, poverty was endemic.

When Chicago's Great Fire happened in October 1871, the patchwork helping system could not handle the aftermath. More than a third of the city's residents were left homeless. Including the *entire* downtown and business district, 18,000 buildings were destroyed. No one was prepared for this devastation, and the government had to turn to the private sector.

Mayor Mason gave the Relief and Aid unprecedented authority to administer the aid funds pouring in from all over the world. An official statement shows the Mayor's confidence:

> I have deemed it best for the interests of the City to turn over to the
> Chicago Relief and Aid Society all contributions for the suffering

people of this City. This Society is an incorporated and old established organization, having possessed for many years the entire confidence of our community, and is familiar with the work to be done.

Almost overnight, the Relief and Aid grew from a small organization into the most significant charity provider in Chicago, if not the nation.[46]

The Relief and Aid handled nearly $5 million (about $80 million today) during the relief effort, and it helped approximately 157,000 people. It used the money primarily to provide relief in the form of supplies, but in 1873, when it concluded its Great Fire relief effort, it still had $600,000 on hand—nearly $10 million in today's dollars. The group used part of the money to purchase a lot and erect a building that would become its headquarters in 1874.[47]

How are the Great Fire and the Relief and Aid part of Jane Addams's story? To understand what Addams did, one needs to understand the field she entered into. Chicago had made the Relief and Aid the standard-bearer of relief efforts after the Great Fire, and the organization was able to dictate the terms of how it helped people in Chicago. Its way of doing things was dominant. More broadly, by controlling relief funds, the Relief and Aid was able to pick winners and losers in the pool of community organizations, funding those it liked and ignoring those it did not. This is not to say that the organization did not do real and meaningful things to help people. It is a matter of considering *how* they helped and what this particular way of helping might have done to perpetuate the existing power structure. But it should not be surprising that many of the organizations helping people in Chicago held philosophies that hewed closely to that of the Relief and Aid: They emphasized help for the "worthy" poor. The noblesse oblige of the middle and upper classes was real and impacted people's lives. Clergy preached the Social Gospel from pulpits across the city, and the call for good works was no doubt heard. However, the impulse to do good and any actual help given were usually conditional.

Soon, rich people knew that, when disadvantaged and struggling people knocked on their doors, they should refer all such appeals to the Relief and Aid. There, agents and volunteers would assign case numbers and investigate to see that applicants had not previously received aid and, more importantly, were truly unable to work for "honest wages." Someone might be sent to the supplicant's house to verify the depth of need. The Chicago Relief and Aid Society's Annual Report from 1875 describes the likely candidate for receiving help:

> Only the Sick, Aged, and Infirm, or widows with families will be regarded as proper subjects of relief, unless it shall appear that there are old people or an unusual number of small children dependent upon them, or in cases of temporary disability not included in the above.[48]

Data show that the "worthy" poor in Chicago did receive Relief and Aid help, as evidenced by two examples excerpted from its annual reports:[49]

> No. 32796. A neighbor made application for a Swedish woman with two small children and a husband in the Bridewell for drunkenness and cruelty to his wife. For a long time she had been obliged to support herself and children by washing, but the children were both sick and the mother worn out. The rooms were clean, and the neighbors spoke well of the woman. Some ladies from Clybourn Avenue Mission had brought food. She was aided once, and has not applied again.

> No. 32718. An American family with four children was brought to the notice of the Relief [sic] by the Humane Society. The man was a cook and had always supported his family, but had been very ill for three weeks, and had lost his voice. The children had all been sick, and the mother was not well. They had received help from the Western Avenue Presbyterian church. This family was aided by this Society eight times before the man was able to resume his work.

These accounts—perhaps not coincidentally, since annual reports are nothing if not marketing pieces—illustrate the benefits of a helping hand, as opposed to a handout. But if one were to rely solely on publications and meeting minutes of the Relief and Aid for information, it would appear that the majority of those seeking help were revealed to be unworthy. For example, Ms. Catharine Beardsley applied for admission to the Old People's home. The Relief and Aid board decided:

> . . . the applicant had not been a resident of this community long enough to entitle her to the benefits of that charity, but that the support should devolve upon those with whom she has spent nearly her entire life, and that this society might properly aid her in reaching those friends.[50]

Simply put, Beardsely deserved a place in the Old People's home, but her family and friends should pick up the tab.[51]

Again, none of this should be read as an indictment of the Chicago Relief and Aid Society. It is how the organization worked, and it provided real help. It supported various organizations—notably, hospitals—and gave direct relief to thousands who suffered in the wake of the Great Fire. It coordinated relief provision, which rendered the process of helping much more effective. And it served as a beacon of hope when Chicago was reeling from both war and urban disaster. Although the Relief and Aid Society's standard practice was perhaps stingy and limited, it was still *help*.

At around the same time, a new type of social provision was emerging in the United States: the "charity organization." Although the charity organization had roots at least as far back as late-eighteenth-century Hamburg, Germany, it did not take hold in the United States for another hundred years. Between 1877 and 1900, charity organization societies proliferated, spreading from America's larger cities to smaller population centers. The charitable organization movement was partially a reaction to the widespread belief that outdoor relief, including efforts by organizations like the Relief and Aid, had failed to alleviate poverty.[52]

The charitable organization saw itself as a new approach to the problem of poverty. Unlike what would occur at the settlement house, there was little effort to articulate the importance of maintaining dignity and opening up the potential for reciprocity. Instead, the approach was much more clinical and cold, with its intellectual influences in Malthusianism and Social Darwinism. In other words, let the fittest survive in a world with ever-shrinking resources. Polite society should prevent poor people from reproducing both their immoral habits and their burdening fast-growing populations. If the poor were allowed to simply rise to their own levels of incompetence and immorality, their numbers would dwindle naturally.

The charitable organization movement also had strong practical and philosophical ties to business, grounded in the idea of the self-made man. The "business idea" underpinned its efforts. The boards of most charitable organizations included prominent members of the important elements of the economy, including banking, steel, textiles, and railroads. One movement leader summarized the situation: The "same wisdom which has given this generation its wonderful industrial capacity will preside over the administration of charity."[53] More cheekily, Boston poet and reformer John Boyle O'Reilly wrote a rhyme that was understandably popular:

> Organized charity scrimped and iced,
> In the name of a cautious statistical Christ.[54]

The thought of Christ cautiously using statistics to decide who might receive help just feels plain wrong, which is precisely the point.

The charitable organization was meant to be the central node of a network of associations, serving as a clearinghouse for charity. Its methods were very influential in shaping the practice of social work decades later: It tracked relief recipients with a central registry and used what it termed "friendly visits" to diagnose individuals in need. Most community organizations dealing with urban poverty, including churches and relief societies, sent relief applicants to the appropriate charity organization district office. The district office then sent an employee to call on the applicant at home and report to the district committee, which determined need. If the applicants were deemed worthy of help, the visitors—usually wealthy female volunteers (recall Lady Bountiful)—were paired with applicants (and their families), and tasked with overseeing progress toward self-sufficiency. Visitors were not to judge, but to provide advice—from how to spend relief dollars, to how to manage personal hygiene, to whether to relocate to a more respectable neighborhood—and ensure that applicants followed it. A publication from 1886 sums up the process of the friendly visit, at least from the point of view of the charity organization:

> The Volunteer Visitor's duty begins when that of the agent ceases, *i.e.* when the case has been investigated and relief, if necessary, secured. Then to assist the poor family as its friend, to guide, advise, sympathize, encourage, to avert need of further aid, to watch over and influence into ways of independence, such is the work of the Friendly Visitor.[55]

In abstract it sounds wonderful. Through the mechanism of the visit, it would be possible to curtail the wanton provision of unnecessary help. With a finite amount of resources available, it made good sense.

However, because of the primacy of the Chicago Relief and Aid Society, the charity organization movement had difficulty taking hold in Chicago. In 1883, the Chicago Charity Organization Society was founded by S. Humphreys Gurteen, but it didn't get much done in its first few years, mainly because Gurteen quit after just a year. It only managed to set up a wood yard where "tramps" could do some "honest work" in return for help. Alexander Johnson, who took over as superintendent in 1886, lamented that the Chicago Charity Organization Society had bitten off more than it could chew and often had to compromise principles to deal with realities:

> The pressure of the numerous cases so many more than the staff has time and strength to do more with than to investigate and relieve; the ever insistent need of *some* relief in many if not in most cases: the fatal facility of disposing of importunity by relief; above all the difficulty of convincing our subscribers, directors, agents, clients—even ourselves, that service means more and is worth more than relief . . . all these together were too strong to be resisted.[56]

The "statistical Christ" of the charity organization did not always offer guidance in dealing with the on-the-ground realities in Chicago. But in spite of his experiences and his position at the head of the Charity Organization Society, Johnson remained convinced that relief was *not* what the poor needed.[57]

The Charity Organization continued the process of "rooting out fraud." Superintendent Johnson remembered an occasion when a member of the Relief and Aid board called late one night (the Relief and Aid kept gentleman's hours, while the Charity Organization's main office stayed open until at least 10:30 p.m.) to ask for help with a woman at his door, claiming that her children were starving. Johnson details his response:

> I told him to give her car-fare and that our agent would be there before she could arrive as we were two miles nearer her alleged location; that we would give immediate emergency aid if it seemed necessary and take up the case thoroly [sic] on Monday. I sent a boy with explicit directions, who soon reported by phone that there was no such number on the street. I knew the neighborhood as one of the thrifty middle class ones and was quite sure it was a false address; however I told my agent to enquire at the corner drug store and any other place

he could reach. I then called up the gentleman and reported the result of the search; he was evidently dissatisfied but being a sincerely benevolent man, he spent Sunday morning hunting thru the district and convinced himself that my report was justified. On Tuesday, he sent a check for $50, with a note acknowledging the need and value of C.O.S. [Charity Organization Society] methods.[58]

Notice the valorization of the "thrifty" middle class. And the extreme suspicion is particularly fascinating, because there is no compelling evidence that deception or fraud were particularly widespread in Chicago at the time. In any urban society lacking basic social services, there are bound to be individuals who will resort to theft or fraud out of desperation—the con man can be found in historical accounts going far back in time. But here, it is almost as if Dickens's Ebenezer Scrooge was informing the Relief and Aid and the Charity Organization Society.

In Chicago in 1886, over 20 percent of "resident" applications to the Charity Organization Society were rejected because the applicants were deemed "not needy," "unworthy," or "ineligible."[59] Another 20 percent were assisted in finding employment. The rest—60 percent—were referred to various institutions or private individuals for assistance. Of "non-residents," one-third were rejected. Most of the remaining two-thirds of non-residents were referred to the Charity Organization's wood yard for work. Across the meeting minutes of the Relief and Aid during the 1880s and early 1890s, the same story plays out. It referred most applicants to its work department, established in 1868 to provide men with a chance to work at a wood yard in return for room and board, but a significant portion of applicants was turned away as unworthy.

Non-residents, typically referred to as "strangers," received almost nothing from the Relief and Aid. Instead, it had long facilitated the process of removing the non-resident needy, helping railroad companies provide "charity tickets"—one-way tickets to anywhere outside Chicago for those with family elsewhere.

This system of difference can be seen in the story of a group of Cherokees who "had come to the city with a view of giving concerts in Churches, but who had utterly failed in their expectations and were now in the city, entirely stranded and unable to return to their homes." The Relief and Aid board voted to allocate $50 to help them, "provided that sum would enable them to leave the city and reach their homes." The minutes do not say from whence the Cherokees came, but they were sent somewhere by the Relief and Aid. As the minutes indicate, "the Indians were sent home (with considerable difficulty)." After reporting on the deportation, the meeting's minutes go on to report that the superintendent moved on to a discussion of the merits of purchasing "brass plates with suitable subscriptions, to be placed on the portraits of the various deceased directors."[60]

The notion of the stranger is important—it shows a nativist element in the practice of helping. That is, the methods undertaken by the Relief and Aid and the Charity Organization valued some people (here, people from Chicago) over others. These kinds of distinctions were part of a system of meaning created by people and organizations in the business of helping. Given the similar work of the Chicago Relief and Aid Society and the Chicago Charity Organization Society, it makes sense that the two organizations merged in 1888. But it was not a merger of equals; political maneuvering resulted in the Relief and Aid generally continuing its work, with the added benefit of new district offices and a new donor list.[61]

.   .   .

Such was the state of things in Chicago as Addams's plans were coming together: The Chicago Relief and Aid Society was dominant, thanks in large part to the support of the mayor immediately after the Great Fire, while the Chicago Charity Organization Society was important, affiliated with the Relief and Aid, and similarly stingy with actual, direct relief. Between 1871 and 1889, when Addams started Hull-House, any aid organization was essentially with or against these two overwhelmingly male groups and their logic. From her gender to her philosophy and practice, Addams would open Hull-House in opposition to existing ways of helping others in Chicago. Choosing neither relief nor charity organization, Addams struck out in a new direction, grounded in the idea of the social settlement led by women.

Addams's new direction, the "scheme," did not come together easily. Her family—-her stepmother in particular—made clear their desire for Addams to occupy a traditional role and devote more time to family. The family also refused to provide any financial support for her new ideas. On the other hand, Starr, filled with energy and enthusiasm, urged her friend Addams to embark upon the new project in Chicago. Addams chose to venture into the unknown. The plan was set into motion by Addams moving to the city six months after she returned from Europe. She and Starr began to make the rounds, presenting the idea of a settlement house to other community-based organizations and in the press. They started by attending a Rockford alumnae gathering in late January 1889. Their efforts to make connections were helped by the Chicago Women's Club, which they joined in April 1889. By this time, Addams knew what her work in the settlement house was really going to be about: reciprocal relations like those she saw at the heart of Toynbee Hall's philosophy. Chicagoans who heard about their idea loved it.[62]

In an interview with the *Chicago Evening Journal* in June 1889, the author wrote of Addams's attachment to the idea of neighbors helping one another:

> One of these smooth talkers [Starr or Addams] let fall the astonishing proposition that there are many educated and society girls and ladies who need the tasks a great city offers as much as the humbler classes

need the intervention of high circles. "They need the poor as much as the poor need them"—a proposition that no one will hasten to deny.[63]

This is a very different idea from the one that motivated the Relief and Aid, and it is telling that Addams did not create any strong ties to the organization when she first moved to Chicago. She was doing things her own way, unfettered by anyone else's ideals.

But they needed a physical space. During the spring of 1889, Addams and Starr had, indeed, looked around for a place to "settle," looking at a number of "slums" before deciding on a rundown mansion on Halsted Street, inherited by Helen Culver from her late uncle Charles Hull. The house was a warrior—just over thirty years old and a survivor of the Great Fire. It was a perfect setting, given its location in the Nineteenth Ward, a neighborhood full of poor European immigrants working to support the city's booming industry. Culver was a generous landlord for what was to be called Hull-House. Addams and Starr signed a lease in May, renting the bulk of the house (some would remain storage space for a school furniture factory). Addams paid a thousand dollars out of her own pocket to renovate the second floor. Eventually, Culver would become a patroness, allowing the settlement to occupy the entire space rent-free and providing thousands of dollars in funds to keep the house running and support its expansion. With the help of another independent, wealthy woman, Addams began to blaze a new trail in the charity landscape.[64]

Addams was limited by a society that relegated women to the sidelines: Women of her time just didn't *do* what she did at Hull-House. As she recalled,

> Whatever may have been the perils of self-tradition, I certainly did not escape them, for it required eight years—from the time I left Rockford in the summer of 1881 until Hull-House was opened in the autumn of 1889—to formulate my convictions even in the least satisfactory manner, much less to reduce them to a plan for action.[65]

It took some time, but Addams would not allow others to control the construction of her social self. She could not completely throw off the mantle of her social world (no one can), but she was able to modify or move around barriers. It was remarkable for a woman of her time. She created her new way forward through the idea of the social settlement. She had found her voice at last.

CHAPTER THREE

The Chicago Scheme

A woman named Jane Addams fed the poor

and helped them find jobs.

She opened doors and gave people hope.

She taught adults and invited children

to play and laugh and let their spirits grow wide.

Barack Obama[1]

J ANE ADDAMS mentions the opening of Hull-House with a one-line entry in her diary: "Came into residence Sept. 18, 1889."[2] What excitement and trepidation she must have felt as the scheme finally came to fruition.

Addams and Starr had moved into one of Chicago's poorest neighborhoods. They knew almost no one. So, they started by connecting with their neighbors, particularly with children, as Addams recalled to her sister in a letter shortly after Hull-House opened. Perhaps understandably, adults in the neighborhood were more wary: Why would two rich women move to *this* neighborhood? But the children were excited to visit a fancy house run by well-to-do women.

Addams and Starr immediately organized two boys' clubs that met every Tuesday evening. They also started a kindergarten class for twenty-four children (with an additional seventy on a waiting list). Starr was the teacher, and class hours were from nine to noon each weekday. Jenny Dow, a former student of Starr's, soon moved into

Hull-House and took over the kindergarten. Dow wrote that, early on, neighborhood relations—what Addams later called "propinquity" (essentially, nearness)—were the key to success:

> The most interesting put of the work cannot be written about. It is the simple and natural way in which the neighbors bring their joys and sorrows to this hospitable home. Indeed, one feels not that Miss Addams and Miss Starr have given up anything to live there, but that their lives are richer and better for these demands on their sympathies.[3]

The sketches of a successful roadmap were already emerging—connect with neighborhood parents through their more receptive children and prioritize person-to-person relations.

Inexperience wasn't daunting for Addams: She was more than willing to pitch in and help with direct care, even with children, though they were relatively unfamiliar to her. Florence Kelley, a resident of Hull-House, recounted that when she first arrived, Addams greeted her at the door, "holding on her left arm a singularly unattractive, fat, pudgy baby," while at the same time "hindered in her movements by a super-energetic kindergarten child left by its mother while she went to a sweatshop for a bundle of cloaks to be finished."[4]

It didn't take long for Addams to figure out that most of the children were hungry and malnourished. Most neighborhood mothers worked during the day, so their children frequently missed lunch unless they could manage it on their own. Practical Addams quickly dreamed up a meal plan for children. Mothers (though not fathers) who worked during the day could buy an inexpensive meal ticket for themselves and their children to be fed at Hull-House. Even better, Addams and the principal of the nearby Polk Street School realized that linking school attendance with the meal program meant children would be more likely to attend school. So Addams's meal ticket worked almost like "a truant officer in keeping them at school, for no school implies no dinner." Working mothers also had the option of leaving their younger children in the newly created Hull-House daycare, eventually called the "crèche." Each morning, twenty-five children were dropped off on Hull-House's doorstep: For a small fee, their mothers could go to work knowing their child was going to get a snack, toys, a nap in a bed, and even a bath.[5]

A perennial obstacle to labor force participation was (and still is) access to childcare. Addams identified this key problem and found a way to meet the need in short order. But Hull-House was not simply a daycare center, a kitchen, or a kindergarten. The seemingly indefatigable Addams also emphasized the vocational and practical dimensions of activities for children, pointing out "girls are put into kitchen-garden, house-keeping, cooking and sewing classes, and are allowed the range of the house to teach them what it may." When the Tuesday "Schoolboys' Club" met, the boys chose books from the "circulating library" at Hull-House (a rotating selection of books from the Chicago Public Library), which they then read aloud. There were a number of instructional classes for boys each evening, ranging from "what to do in emergencies [to] simple chemical experiments." Addams had not yet fully shed the gendered norms of her time, but that she was encouraging poor immigrant girls to develop any skills at all is quite remarkable. Further, she was breaking down gender norms by example, showing these girls that women could lead and make a difference.[6]

This initial focus on children did not mean that Addams and the other residents of Hull-House ignored the needs of the neighborhood's adults. In fact, the connection with children seems to have given Addams and Starr access to adults, and the two women began to visit neighborhood homes. Daytime visits were disruptive for women in the midst of housework (if, in fact, they weren't away at work), so Addams and Starr usually went in the evenings; they also tried to bring along a male volunteer, helping to set the men of the houses at ease.

It was likely during these visits that they began to learn about some neighborhood household needs, for Hull-House soon began to share its laundry facilities with women who needed them.[7]

Addams and Starr saw, too, that the neighborhood needed a social space for talking through problems and making sense of the world; a weekly Social Science Club (attended mostly by men) soon provided a forum for taking up a political or social issue of the day. The club talked about socialism in Europe, taxes, the Haymarket riots, and the challenges of collective action. College extension classes for adults were offered in the evenings; like many of the programs at Hull-House, they were casual and a bit hodgepodge at first. Addams recalled:

> . . . the college extension courses grew . . . from an informal origin. The first class met as guests of the residents. As the classes became larger and more numerous and the object of the newcomers more definitely that of acquisition of some special knowledge the informality of the social relation was necessarily less.

In other words, the impulse for more education and a program to meet this demand emerged out of relations between Hull-House residents and neighbors. The neighborhood demand for knowledge may have also contributed to the idea for a summer program for women at Rockford College in Illinois. The program, started in 1891, took place over four weeks at Rockford's Seminary, and it offered a liberal arts curriculum to working-class women who took extension classes at Hull-House. Over 90 women attended during the first two weeks, supported by funds raised from Rockford, Illinois residents.[8]

The spirit of helping that infused the programs at Hull-House grew out of personal interactions with the neighbors Addams and the other residents wanted to help. The reciprocal relations Addams most likely witnessed at Toynbee Hall were her guides. To be more concrete, we can look at an example provided by Addams. Writing about an encounter at Hull-House, she shows the generative potential of relations between neighbors and residents:

> A woman for whom the writer [Addams] had long tried in vain to find work failed to appear at the appointed time when employment was secured at last. Upon investigation it transpired that a neighbor further down the street was taken ill, that the children ran for the family friend, who went of course, saying simply when reasons for her non-appearance were demanded, "It broke me heart to leave the place, but what could I do?"[9]

No doubt Addams's first reaction was frustration that she had found a job for the woman, only to see her throw it away. But Addams also must have understood that obligation and desire to help a neighbor could trump individual needs.

With encounters like this one, it did not take long for Addams to realize how hard it was to participate in the labor market. She described immigrant workers as

> people who are SUNK in toilsome and under-paid labor; who, by the utmost efforts of their undeveloped and inefficient powers, gain but a bare subsistence; the ends of whose day's work leaves them so exhausted of nervous energy that they are gradually sinking in spirit and are worn out long before old age overtakes them.

Addams was also clear about the benefit that these workers would accrue from interacting with those in residence at Hull-House: "[Hull-House would] bring them in contact with a better class of Americans."[10]

This cringe-worthy comment should not take away from the fact that Addams was actively trying to create social relations with people who she knew would change her understanding of the world. The Chicago labor market was brutal for the average worker, and Addams most likely "got it" right away. She also came to see (from the "lesser class") how ties with friends and family came before the demands of the labor market. And these were just a few of the social relations that gave texture to Addams's understanding of the complexity of trying to keep a job in nineteenth-century Chicago. It was not just a simple matter of whether someone was able-bodied and willing to work; and that was a profound realization for Addams and her fellow residents. Those at Hull-House seem to have learned *how* to understand and help their neighbors only through their day-to-day relations *with* those same neighbors. What Addams wrote about the hierarchical relationship between resident and neighbor, expressed in the idea of a "better class," belies the equal exchange of knowledge and understanding that happened every day in her settlement community.

Hull-House distinguished itself in another way: It developed a reputation for helping disadvantaged people across Chicago, particularly immigrants and people of color.[11] In June 1891, Standing Bear, the son of a Sioux chief, came into residence at Hull-House. He had been trying to return home from school and had run out of money. Addams took him in even though he was a "non-resident" (not a native Chicagoan), and he stayed at Hull-House for over six months.[12]

Addams was really trying to do things differently and reach out to those who were falling through the cracks of the current system. It would have been easy to confine her efforts to the white, European immigrants in her immediate neighborhood, but Addams reached out to more and more people through her expanding network of neighborhood relations.[13] As a result, Hull-House grew in terms of its programming and its physical size. It was no longer just a house, but an expression of neighborhood needs. Five public baths were constructed, and they were nearly always in use (most of Addams's neighbors would not have had access to clean facilities, and even public toilets were a rarity). Twelve new showers were added when the new gymnasium was built in 1893, and they, too, were in near constant use. Now the kids were cleaner, but they still needed a place to play. Addams and the other residents were supporters of the idea of "creative play" as articulated by Friedrich Froebel, father of the kindergarten system, but the streets of the neighborhood were too filthy and busy to play in—creatively or otherwise. So Addams shamed a neighborhood slumlord into providing a plot of land (rent-free), demolishing the dilapidated housing on the lot, and building a public playground. Then she convinced the city to assign a police officer to patrol the playground; the officer reported to Addams each day before he made his rounds.[14]

Addams expanded the day nursery program to a nearby cottage; now, on a typical day, forty or more children were dropped off. Again, these ideas were not part of a fully planned program of action that Addams worked though. Rather, she learned of the needs of her neighbors and tried to meet them in an evolving, sometimes piecemeal approach to helping at Hull-House. Her deep connections with neighborhood women, for instance, soon turned Addams's attention to the problem of housing and likely led directly to the "Jane Club," established in May 1892. The Jane Club was a cooperative boarding house that provided room, board, heat, light, and other necessities for three dollars per week, with one month of free rent for female club members.[15]

All this expansion in programs and infrastructure cost money. Addams's inheritance money was the main source for the first few years and helped her create the magic at Hull-House. She was able to capitalize Hull-House and cover most of its operating costs. Some of the Hull-House programs (kindergarten, daycare, classes, and summer school) were self-sustaining, at least breaking even, thanks to nominal user fees. Addams then spent most of the rest of her own money repairing and expanding Hull-House and providing subsidies to residents for their room and board. By the fall of 1893, Addams had spent $15,000—about $400,000 in today's terms—from her own pocket. The financial independence afforded Addams because of her inheritance allowed her to remain free from the influence of Chicago's business leaders, particularly the men of the Chicago Relief and Aid Society.[16] But things were slowly getting out of hand, at least in financial terms. Addams was spending much more than she brought in, and eventually she turned to others for help.[17]

It might be easy to conclude that Addams solved her own American's Dilemma by just giving all her available time and money to helping others. That's not the case. Addams created boundaries. She was frequently ill and took time to convalesce without working, often for months at a time. Further, she did not use *all* of her money on Hull-House; she maintained a standard of living that included well-appointed housing, frequent travel, and exposure to culture through books, fine art, music, and theater. She was very social and frequently entertained or hosted gatherings at Hull-House. And her increasing fame brought her to the attention of the wealthiest people in Chicago, who hosted her in their homes, included her in their social functions, and provided her with a level of intellectual engagement with few parallels in the United States at the time. Jane Addams did not throw away her identity for Hull-House: She did not stop living her own life; she did not give away all of her worldly possessions. She simply created deep ties to her community, learned through those connections, and acted on that knowledge. It was a continual, unending process of connecting, learning, and acting.

In addition to requiring money, the growth at Hull-House required a bit of structure to handle decision making. But once again, even the need for a decision-making framework emerged out of practice. It was not as if Addams sat down on day one and said, "If we are going to do this, we will need a weekly meeting with specific rules of speaking and engagement." As more residents came to live at Hull-House, they needed an inclusive forum for sharing ideas and information.

The residents (for the first three years, all women) engaged in a quite democratic form of collective decision making. Addams served as "head resident," but actively encouraged others to take ownership of the managerial process, and that made it lively. Addams did not surround herself with meek, mild-mannered, or acquiescent women; on the contrary, some of the most formidable, innovative, and energetic women in the nineteenth-century United States were residents at Hull-House. There is very little data on the early residents' meetings, but an examination of what does exist shows that the meetings were a space for deliberation—and contestation—over new ideas. Decisions about who would reside there, the ideal gender composition of the resident group (fifteen women and ten men in late 1893), whether to partner with various social provision organizations, and Hull-House's policy toward relief (it would vary over time) were all routinely taken up by the group. The meetings also served as a forum for residents to get information; there were usually presentations on the goings-on at Hull-House, as well as reports on new charity projects in the city.[18]

This particular form of collective decision making privileged reason (that is, providing justification for one's suggestions) and an ethic of inclusiveness. Philosophers from Aristotle to John Rawls and Jürgen Habermas have written of the importance of this way of communicating, considering it more fair and just than other forums. More recently, social scientific research has shown that the construction of "mini-publics" or spaces for "deliberation" actually lead people to move away from entrenched positions and allow them to consider new ideas; discussion spaces help people let go of long-held views and become ready to think about new ones.

What is remarkable is that Addams and her colleagues developed this type of communication organically. They simply hoped to face the perplexities of communal living and effective action by talking things through, open to any useful ideas for moving forward. Addams even went so far as to recognize the value of deliberating *with* those she was trying to help, including children. She empowered those she was helping by including them in decision making whenever possible. For example, during after-school classes, Addams asked children to be leaders and to decide what these classes "might entail."[19]

Investigation and information gathering made the deliberative sessions more effective. Addams felt one needed to know the situation (among other things) before making decisions. Starting in 1892, the residents kept a "ward book," in which "have been noted matters of sociological interest found in the ward." These "matters" included sanitation problems, sweatshops and child labor issues, wage scales, and population density. In 1895, the data in this book informed the creation of the celebrated *Hull-House Maps and Papers*, an unprecedented effort to "put into graphic form a few of the facts concerning the section of Chicago immediately east of the House." The book, written by Hull-House residents, cemented the settlement's reputation as an organization concerned with defining and addressing the problems of the Nineteenth Ward and the city as a whole.[20]

This all paints a rosy picture of Hull-House: It all sounds so ideal and perfect. The residents figured it out as they went and always did the right thing for the neighborhood. Not quite. Like any well-intentioned people, Addams and her cohort made a lot of mistakes along the way. In 1890, for example, Hull-House simply closed its doors for the summer so that Starr and Addams could visit friends and family and spend the hot months in cooler climes. But the needs of the neighborhood didn't disappear with the seasons.[21]

Another example with more dire consequences comes in the infamous story of the baby with the cleft palate in *Twenty Years at Hull-House*. Addams recounted the situation:

> For six weeks after an operation we kept in one of our three bedrooms a forlorn little baby who, because he was born with a cleft palate, was

most unwelcome even to his mother, and we were horrified when he died of neglect a week after he was returned to his home.[22]

The death of a child is a terrible thing for anyone to experience. It must have been particularly difficult for the residents of Hull-House, given that they had returned the baby to the family with the mistaken impression that he would receive love and care.

A less serious misstep can be seen in Addams's efforts to open a "Diet Kitchen," also known as the "New England Kitchen." Based on the latest East Coast scientific thinking on proper diet, Hull-House's Diet Kitchen provided meals for the sick and for those in need of good nutrition, and it offered cooking classes so that neighborhood women might learn to make nutritious meals. The opening of the Diet Kitchen was celebrated with a dinner for elite Chicago women:

Miss Addams of Hull house opened yesterday the novel little kitchen attached to the place. [It] was filled with members of the Woman's club, who tasted of the delicate palatables cooked on strictly scientific principles. This culinary apartment, which is placed at the rear and adjacent to the coffee house is patterned after the famous New England kitchen which was organized by Mrs. Ellen G. Richards. Mrs. Richards for two years studied the best and cheapest way to cook. She has reduced her principles to a science and cooking utensils have been made for the purpose. There are six Aladdin ovens invented by Edward Atkinson of Boston. These are covered with asbestos on the outside and lined with tin on the inside. The heat comes from a lamp. The sides are about an inch thick. In addition to this there are half-jacket steam kettles, and a steam plant in the yard. The soups are cooked in these kettles and none of the steam escapes. Every atom of nutrition is conserved. . . . The object is to bring nutritious food within reach of those who are not able to pay extravagant prices.[23]

Well, the Diet Kitchen was a failure at first. Nobody liked the food (unsurprising, given that a sample menu appeared to consist primarily of broth, jellies, gruels, and custards). And somewhat surprisingly, the settlement residents did not account for the fact that in a diverse immigrant community, ideas about what tastes good might not match their own. Addams wrote simply:

> We did not reckon, however, with the wide diversity in nationality and inherited tastes, and while we sold a certain amount of the carefully prepared soups and stews in the neighboring factories—a sale which has steadily increased throughout the years—and were also patronized by a few households, perhaps the neighborhood estimate was best summed up by the woman who frankly confessed, that the food was certainly nutritious, but that she didn't like to eat what was nutritious, that she liked to eat "what she'd ruther."[24]

So, shortly after its creation, the Diet Kitchen was converted, with borrowed money, to expand into the profitable cafe that provided both coffee and hot lunches to neighborhood residents. Now Addams saw something new and unanticipated emerging with the coffeehouse:

> If the dietetics were appreciated but slowly, the social value of the coffee-house and the gymnasium, which were in the same building, were quickly demonstrated. At that time the saloon halls were the only places in the neighborhood where the immigrant could hold his social gatherings.[25]

Addams may not have been successful in fostering a healthy diet, but in her revisions, she was able to create a space conducive to conversation and socialization, the very stuff that is the fabric of democracy.[26]

In addition to stumbling from time to time, it seems as if it became harder and harder for Addams to scale up her efforts. She oversaw an incredible period of growth and energy at Hull-House; it was a dynamo station generating energy that moved neighbors to help neighbors. But underneath, there was a growing frustration: It became clear that Hull-House could not do it all. There were too many neighbors who needed help and not enough resources to do the job. The very idea of who was a "neighbor" was at stake. Nativist sentiments and the huge influx of immigrants made it hard to bound one's "community," and there was no systematic effort to keep track of who was doing what to help others in Chicago.

.   .   .

On New Year's Day 1892, there was little cause for celebration at Hull-House. There were mouths to feed, and the immigrant neighbors of the Nineteenth Ward were bracing themselves for what the papers were calling a "winter to remember." Addams was likely a bit unsettled as she prepared for what would prove to be a contentious meeting with the board members of the Chicago Relief and Aid Society. In the fall, Addams had agreed to join a group of concerned citizens who thought the city could do a better job of managing charitable activity. The group, which called themselves the Chicago Committee on Charity Organization (COCO), thought that ever since the Relief and Aid had absorbed the Chicago Charity Organization Society in the late 1880s, the lack of a charity organization was hurting the city.[27]

This was not just about challenging the Relief and Aid. Reading between the lines, there is a sense that times were getting tougher in Chicago, and Addams and other committee members thought charity organization might help. There was a tremendous strain on the existing system, as we can see from references by committee members to "the incompleteness of our present machinery for furnishing immediate and adequate relief in all cases of real need."[28] And the present machinery's main engine at the time was the Chicago Relief and Aid Society.

Recall that Addams did not choose to adopt the charity organization approach at Hull-House when it first opened. There was no statistical Christ at the settlement. But a few years into her work at Hull-

House, Addams was engaged in a concerted effort to bring formal charity organization back to Chicago. This is what ambivalence looks like on the ground. She was torn between two different ways of helping others, trying to revise her position in light of an ever-changing situation in Chicago. It was efficiency, tough love, and individualism on the one hand, and creativity, neighborly reciprocity, and experimentalism on the other. What is remarkable here is that Addams was advocating for the establishment of an organization that was, for all intents and purposes, quite different from Hull-House. She was not looking to expand Hull-House's efforts as a way to address perceived deficiencies of the Relief and Aid. She was revising and improvising, and this seemed like the best way to move forward.[29]

As part of this move forward, Addams went with thirteen fellow committee members to personally petition the Relief and Aid at its board meeting on January 2, 1892. The message from Addams and her fellow members was clear: The Relief and Aid must change its ways, "placing at the head of this work, some one who thoroughly understands the theory and practice of charity organization, who is fully in sympathy with the movement, and who has both the tact and determination to make it a success." If the Relief and Aid was not willing to change and become more organized and efficient, Addams and others suggested it consider supporting the formation of a new charity organization to fill the gap. The Relief and Aid board voted and determined that the idea of changing was "impracticable and not feasible." They then voted to think about supporting a new charity organization in Chicago.[30]

It was a moment that held potential for creativity. The current Relief and Aid practices were not effective, although the organization did not want to admit it. Addams's group saw room to create something new, but given the dominant position the Relief and Aid held in Chicago charity, it should come as no surprise that it resisted any attempts to *actually* create a new organization that could vie for control. A very public fight ensued, and Jane Addams was in the thick of it. Much of it took place in letters and press releases. Though often lengthy, the letters are entertaining and provide important color and depth to the back-and-forth between the two groups.

First, Relief and Aid board member Turlington Harvey, a prominent Chicagoan and lumber magnate, went to the press. He compared the Relief and Aid to various charitable organizations, including the one in New York, and tried to portray it as a dynamic organization that had adapted to the unique needs of Chicago. Then, in February 1892, the Relief and Aid board as a whole sent Addams's committee a strongly worded (if long-winded and defensive) letter that asserted the group was doing a fine job and did not need to change. But the challenge by the committee caused concern among Relief and Aid board members; immediately after approving the final version of the February letter, the Relief and Aid Board of Directors voted to create a "Committee on Visitors." This was an effort to keep up appearances and to defend the Relief and Aid's right to call itself a charity organization (most charity organizations had a visiting committee). Along those same lines, CRAS formed a committee on cooperation to "maintain and strengthen friendly relations" with other charity organizations and went on the offensive in the press, ordering 500 copies of the February letter to be printed and distributed in the city.[31] Addams and other committee members had clearly poked the hornet's nest.

The Relief and Aid soon received another letter signed by Jane Addams and thirty-two other members of the committee. It was read aloud at the March 7, 1892, Relief and Aid board of directors meeting. In the letter, the committee began by attacking the idea of the Relief and Aid as a charity organization:

> We grant that your Society has been organized to do charity work and thus is a charity organization though not the first, but that it is today or ever had been in any sense a Charity Organization Society

we must deny. In the name Charity Organization Society the second word is to be taken in the active not passive sense. It is a society whose business is to *organize* the various agencies that dispense charity into one *co-operating system*. This work the Relief and Aid Society has never accomplished. . . . So far as we can ascertain your idea of co-operation consists in a willingness to give any information you may have; and in the possession of certain privileges in other charitable institutions, derived originally through your having been the agency employed for the distribution of relief funds at the time of the fire. Co-operation implies mutual activity, a seeking or receiving as well as giving. There is nothing of the first in your work for the charities of Chicago are in no way coordinated or systematized. Does the present chaotic condition substantiate your claim—that you have been active for 31 years as an organizer?

So what? The committee was calling for more action and cooperation, in essence trying to get the Relief and Aid board members out of their club chairs and onto the city's streets. The Relief and Aid had been organizing major elements of social provision in Chicago for two decades, going back to the Great Fire. This exchange, then, was not so much about the need for charity organization in Chicago as the need to remove the Relief and Aid from its dominant position. The committee cast the current system as exclusive, with no room for innovation, and indicted the Relief and Aid for misuse of the remaining Great Fire relief funds:

We appealed to you to place your Society at the head of this movement because of your unique position in our City's history. Your building was the gift of the world to our City in the dark of a terrible calamity. That gift should be utilized to afford a great central office for Chicago's charities, a lasting memorial of the noble use to which we have put this applied love of the world. The same generosity enabled your Society to secure privileges in hospitals and other institutions.

Perhaps no city was ever more fortunately situated for carrying out the Charity Organization idea than is Chicago at this time. In fact the Relief and Aid Society belongs to the People of Chicago and as such should be brought into sympathy with the progressive spirit and character of our institutions. . . . If your Society will not accept the responsibility of joining in the inauguration of Charity Organization in Chicago, we hold ourselves ready to move in this direction fortified as we are by the earnest sympathy and co-operation of nearly two hundred churches and charitable agencies.

The framing of the argument by the committee shifts from gap-filling to public protection. In hoarding Great Fire relief funds, the committee believed the Relief and Aid Society had not fulfilled its responsibilities to the citizens of Chicago and the rest of the world.

The Relief and Aid ignored the accusations from the committee, illustrating the confidence gained through its years as the official, consecrated agency of social provision in Chicago. The group's confidence also likely derived from the powerful elites who made up its board and controlled the city. The Relief and Aid had no fear of the public domain; it had controlled public discourse around social provision since 1871.

The Relief and Aid's response was read at the same March 7, 1892, meeting. In the letter, they again refused to concede ground on their "first-in-the-city" status:

Incidentally it was said that the Society was the first actual Charity Organization Society. Previous to November 11th, 1867, the "Christian Union," the "Citizens Relief" and the "Y.M.C.A." were active in charitable work, with of course, more or less of duplication. At that date steps were taken to consolidate the work on the basis of harmonious co-operation of all parties in interest. The name of the new organization would appropriately have been "Associated Charities", but for the wish to use the then existing charter of the Chicago

Relief and Aid Society. We know of no earlier step in the direction of charity organization.

Again, this is a struggle over power to control charity in the city. The Relief and Aid was one of the first and best, at least in the minds of its board members, in helping others in Chicago. Why make room for change when no change was needed? In spite of this very pointed and public exchange, the Relief and Aid did almost nothing to change. Minutes of subsequent meetings in spring 1892 show that the organization's board devoted little time to addressing of the concerns and criticisms brought up during the exchange.[32]

Addams and her colleagues were stonewalled by the Relief and Aid. Addams was looking for a way to move forward creatively and address the challenges she saw in helping her neighbors. She did not have enough resources. No one was systematically keeping track of who was getting help. Her efforts as part of Chicago Committee on Charity Organization illuminate her failure to find a way forward by working with the Relief and Aid. Even other Hull-House residents complained of difficulties with the Relief and Aid. For example, while Addams was away from Hull-House during the summer of 1892 (probably exhausted by her failed efforts with the committee), Starr wrote that much of her relationship with the Chicago Relief and Aid Society involved "prodding the Relief & Aid (I've spent this morning, the 26th, in doing that)." Interestingly, Starr goes on to characterize her "prodding" as important "in the long run," as it helps "give one a hold on people to steer them through without a blow-up, or to use when the blow up comes."[33] In other words, the Relief and Aid was part of the problem, and helping Halsted Street neighbors manage their relations with the difficult organization was part of the job of Hull-House residents.

Addams had opened the door to charity organization with her ties to the Chicago Committee on Charity Organization. In March 1892, shortly after the committee began its dialogue with the Relief and Aid, Hull-House *itself* began to implement charity organization methods, such as friendly visiting and more rigorous tracking of relief recipients. A March 1892 weekly bulletin mentions "an effort is made in all the relief work of Hull-House to pursue Charity Organization methods."[34] Perhaps the timing is coincidental, but it seems reasonable to see some connection between Addams's activities on behalf of the committee and the insertion of new methods into Hull-House practice.

As part of Addams's summer away in 1892, she made a trip to Plymouth, Massachusetts, along with friend and fellow resident Julia Lathrop, to attend a conference at the School of Applied Ethics. Founded by Felix Adler in 1876, the school was designed to "foster ethics and morality." In Plymouth, Addams delivered a speech that would form the basis of her celebrated essay, "The Subjective Necessity of the Settlement," which details her vision of the need for Hull-House and other settlements. The speech also lays out the philosophy of the settlement house in more detail. It is fascinating that Addams's ideas on the settlement were crystallizing at the same time she was supporting the expansion of an alternative approach.[35]

Her curiosity and experimentation with charity organization may have also been encouraged by relationships she developed during her trip to the School of Applied Ethics. In particular, Bernard Bosanquet and Robert A. Woods, both proponents of charity organization, kept in touch with Addams after the conference. Bosanquet was a philosopher who taught at Oxford and the University of St. Andrews. As early as 1881 he also was active in the London Charity Organization Society. Bosanquet served the society in various official capacities, including as member of council, vice chairman, and chairman. He clearly made an impression on Addams, for they corresponded and socialized as late as 1896. Woods was also fairly supportive of charity organization. Just prior to the Plymouth conference, he wrote: "Charity organization . . . is making its framework available for those better forms of charity which have to do with prevention. It has given a clue to various associations for befriending children and young people." After the Plymouth trip, Woods, like Bosanquet, developed a relationship with Addams (both Woods and Addams were leaders of the so-called national settlement movement). Perhaps his correspondence influenced Addams's ideas on charity. In one letter in 1895, Woods wrote, "there are times when the greater love must even leave the starving to starve."[36]

The shift in Addams's work and her openness to the idea that we should leave anyone to starve (as Woods suggested) might have been an effort to combat the growing troubles in Chicago. In 1893, the economy of Chicago (and the rest of the nation) came under increasing strain; the ensuing depression would last until 1894. The city's notorious political corruption filled politicians' pockets with money and poor neighborhoods' streets with trash. Chicago was known widely as a sort of modern Gomorrah. A British journalist, William Stead, gave a November 1893 speech titled "If Christ Came to Chicago!" The gist, of course, was that Jesus would not be too happy with the Windy City.[37]

The depression of 1893–94 made the already tough job of helping neighbors even tougher. Times were as hard as they had ever been in Chicago. Across the nation, there were dramatic declines in the manufacture of everything from consumer durables to food, and "savage unemployment and demoralizing wage reductions" ensued. Old habits and practices were not adequate, and people (and organizations) changed. No citywide organization or institutionalized process was in place to help all those who fell victim to the brutal job cuts and were left without wages or shelter over the winter. The members of COCO were right to have been concerned: They had seen these economic troubles on the horizon and doubted the city's capacity to deal with increased need for help. As early as 1891, COCO had bemoaned "the incompleteness of our present machinery for furnishing immediate and adequate relief in all cases of real need."[38]

There was also concern about the strain the upcoming World's Fair would place upon the city. Chicago had successfully beat rival New York City in a highly publicized competition, culminating in a congressional vote for the Windy City. It had come down to money. Chicago's elites had raised millions, with Lyman Gage (president of the First National Bank of Chicago) securing enormous private support to bring Chicago's funding over the top in the eleventh hour. The exposition had been slated to open in 1892 as a commemoration of the 400th anniversary of Columbus's voyage to the New World, but Congress moved the opening to 1893. The fair site was in the southern part of the city and would host millions of visitors. Chicago worked to put its best foot forward, straining its resources to create a spectacle far from the poverty, joblessness, and corruption actually plaguing its residents.[39]

Chicagoans could see that existing efforts of the Relief and Aid Society and other organizations were not adequate, so they began to look around for alternatives. Hull-House ramped up its own efforts and began to provide relief to community members through its own Relief Bureau, a clearinghouse for organized aid. Those people who were not known to the settlement residents were put into the charity system and likely referred to the Relief and Aid or any one of the local eleemosynary (religious) organizations that provided outdoor relief. Those "with whom the house has summered and wintered" were helped directly by Hull-House when possible, most likely through use of a small relief fund designed to "help families in financial crisis." Hull-House residents were doing what they could, but this meant restricting these extra efforts to their own constituency of neighbors. The settlement's meeting minutes from October 1893 show that "a new male resident named Robert Waldo" administered this fund and the accompanying "bureau."[40]

The problems were so widespread that the leaders of the city came together for a series of meetings in the fall of 1893, eventually creating the Chicago Civic Federation. (This meeting was spurred, in part, by Stead's "If Christ Came to Chicago!" speech.) The fifteen trustees listed on the federation's corporate charter, as well as those involved as part of the larger committee of supporters, were a veritable "who's who" of Chicago elites, including Marshall Field, Cyrus McCormick (the inventor of the mechanical reaper), T. W. Harvey (from the Relief and Aid), Franklin MacVeagh (a director of the Commercial National Bank of Chicago who would serve as secretary of the Treasury Department in the Taft administration), and Lyman Gage. Jane Addams was also a trustee.[41]

Many of the Civic Federation's organizing meetings were held at the Palmer House, a symbol of the economy's triumph over the Great Fire and arguably the most luxurious hotel in the city (perhaps the nation). Potter Palmer, its founder, was one of the wealthiest men in Chicago and had given the original hotel to his wife, Bertha Honoré, as a wedding present. The hotel burned down in the Great Fire, thirteen days after opening. Potter Palmer immediately rebuilt it, with funds secured through one of the largest bank loans in American history. From the individuals involved to the location of the meetings, one can see and feel the influence of Chicago business elites over this "new" effort at helping. The Civic Federation, new in terms of its citywide civic effervescence, was really promoting more of the same business idea in charity: efficiency, the rooting out of fraud, and an emphasis on work testing.[42]

What was new was the Civic Federation's effort to systematize charity *across* the city. At a December 9, 1893, meeting at the Palmer House, a special committee (which included Addams) was charged with devising "ways and means to render more effective the various relief and aid organizations in the city." It is likely that the committee also considered how to make sure the federation worked hand-in-hand with the business community. Later that month, Addams received a letter from Albion Small, a leader of the Civic Federation and first chair of the Sociology Department at the University of Chicago.

Small emphasized that the Federation's connections to Chicago businesses were essential. He wrote, "it would discount failure from the start to permit anything which might create the impression that 'Civic Federation' is a piece of scholastic idealism. It must be a business man's plan and the other elements should keep in the background." Again, we see that Addams is being pulled away from settlement and toward the "business idea" underpinning charity organization. Her ambivalence was no doubt exacerbated by the obvious failure of the existing system. Why not try something new when what they were doing at the time, whether at Hull-House or the Chicago Relief and Aid Society, was not enough? Addams later recalled:

> The administration of charity in Chicago during the winter following the World's Fair had been of necessity most difficult, for, although large sums had been given to the temporary relief organization which endeavored to care for the thousands of destitute strangers stranded in the city, we all worked under a sense of desperate need and a paralyzing consciousness that our best efforts were most inadequate to the situation.[43]

The committee's most significant act was the formation of yet another organization, the Central Relief Association, that winter. In a meeting on December 14, 1893, the Association provided a statement of its overall purpose:

1. To ascertain in the most expeditious, practicable way, the nature and extent of want and distress existing among us at the present time, and to raise funds for its relief

2. To relieve this want and distress as far as may be through existing organizations, and where these are wanting in efficiency, to do it directly, or through other agencies to be created.

3. To bring about systematic co-operation among charitable societies, churches, individuals and agencies of every kind giving relief, so far as this can be done, thereby preventing waste, duplication

and imposition, and thus uniting economy with efficiency in the great work of relieving distress among the worthy poor. It is one of the leading purposes of the Association to help the needy by enabling them to help themselves through employment, wherever that is practicable, thus elevating instead of pauperizing the recipient.[44]

In this statement of purpose, one can see the hallmarks of the "business idea." Of course, these were just rules. But they were rules that were regularly followed by Chicago Relief Association volunteers. For example, the association continued what was referred to as "the work of transportation," that is, sending non-residents (like the Cherokees) out of town. It appears to have been more conscientious about making sure that these individuals would at least initially land on their feet, but it was not out of concern for the individuals. The association simply wanted to ensure that "no paupers should be sent to other places." It also blocked "tramps" from coming *into* the city by asking the city to station police at railroad depots and freight yards[45] to

> bring before a representative of this Association every man who enters the city from the outside who has no money to provide for his entertainment, or a letter form some responsible party offering him work. We will have such persons examined and returned at once to the place from which they came.

During the height of the depression, "upward of two thousand men were nightly accommodated in the police stations and in the corridors of the City Hall." The association was so worried about the numbers of unemployed coming to Chicago that they also made a deal with the city to "at once put a stop to the influx of tramps who are coming to the city by reason of the widely-advertised soup houses and free lodging places."[46]

All these rules mattered and take us back to the vignette in the opening of this book. That heart-rending scene took place when Addams volunteered for the Chicago Relief Association (remember, she helped create the organization). She described how, following "carefully received instructions [from the Association]," she denied relief to a shipping clerk whom she had known for quite some time:

> I told him one day of the opportunity for work on the drainage canal and intimated that if any employment were obtainable, he ought to exhaust that possibility before asking for help. The man replied that he had always worked indoors and that he could not endure outside work in winter. I am grateful to remember that I was too uncertain to be severe, although I held to my instructions. He did not come again for relief, but worked for two days digging on the canal, where he contracted pneumonia and died a week later.

Consider Addams as she looked at her desperate neighbor, unprepared for physical labor in the cold Chicago winter. Addams was torn between the values of helping another and promoting self-reliance and accountability. She was conflicted, and her decision was not made without pain and struggle. Moving forward from a dilemma and choosing one way of helping over another is not a theoretical exercise. It can be deadly.[47]

After the winter of 1893–94, the Chicago Relief Association closed down, apparently because the need for help was not as great as had been assumed, at least by Chicago's leaders. The superintendent of the Relief and Aid, during a presentation on the closing down of the association, pointed out that the latter "endeavored to gradually close their work without hardship or shock to anyone, and keep clear of criticism." But the Civic Federation decided to keep the Department of Registration in operation, thereby keeping the record-keeping system functional. Addams was a member of the committee appointed to oversee the remaining Chicago Relief Association registry work.[48]

So, the organizational space created by the establishment of the Chicago Relief Association was now vacant. It was a perfect opportunity for charity organization advocates (and members of the Chicago

Committee on Charity Organization) to reestablish a charity organization society. And here we come to another moment of ambivalence in Addams's life. She had seen firsthand the perils of applying the business idea to helping others. But she also could see that things were not getting better in Chicago. Her initial "scheme" at Hull-House, her participation in committee activities, her support of revisions in practice at Hull-House, and her support for additional relief through the Civic Federation all show that she was trying to create new lines of action that might be more effective at making a difference in the lives of her neighbors.

CHAPTER FOUR

A Clash of Ethical Standards

Let us take a neighborhood of poor people, and test their ethical
standards by those of the charity visitor, who comes with the
best desire in the world to help them out of their distress. A most
striking incongruity, at once apparent, is the difference between the
emotional kindness with which relief is given by one poor neighbor
to another poor neighbor, and the guarded care with which relief is
given by a charity visitor to a charity recipient. The neighborhood
mind is at once confronted not only by the difference of method,
but by an absolute clashing of two ethical standards.

Jane Addams[1]

IT WAS JUNE 1894, and Jane Addams had a lot on her plate. Hull-
House was busier than ever, and those needing help seemed to form
a never-ending line at her door. And she was running out of money. In
fact, nearly all the money she had inherited from her father was gone.
Describing her situation to a friend, she wrote, "I probably wont ever
be flush again." To make matters worse, times were tough all over and
those who had supported Hull-House in the past had also suffered
from the hard financial times and had nothing to offer.

Addams was also feeling a competitive spark due to the opening
of the University of Chicago Settlement under the direction of Mary
McDowell, a one-time resident of Hull-House. It was located in another struggling community in Chicago—the Stock Yards. The city

certainly needed more settlement houses doing good work, but it is interesting that Addams felt conflicted about the Stock Yards. She clearly knew she couldn't do it all herself, but a little friendly rivalry seemed to reenergize her. In spite of all of her efforts to increase the city's capacity to help, Addams had some mixed feelings, as evidenced by a letter to close friend Mary Rozet Smith: "Perhaps my ambition has been stirred by the undertaking of the settlement at the Stock Yards." Addams soon had a plan to scale up Hull-House's efforts with a new kindergarten and nursery space, securing a contribution of nearby land from Helen Culver and getting Smith to fund the building. Smith was a volunteer at Hull-House and Addams's closest friend, perhaps even her lover. She and her family members gave tens of thousands of dollars to Hull-House over a span of nearly thirty years.[2]

At a larger level, the city was torn in two at this time by the Pullman strike, which had begun the previous month and was now in full swing. On May 17, 1894, Pullman Palace Car Company workers walked out of its factory over a labor dispute on low wages. The American Railway Union, backing the striking workers, asked its members to boycott all Pullman-made cars on trains nationwide. The nation's rail system verged on a standstill. Pullman was able to break the strike with the government's help: Soldiers were deployed in Chicago to get the trains running again, and the union president, Eugene Debs, was jailed for ignoring the federal court's injunction against the strike. George Pullman was behind the scenes, pulling the strings in an effort to keep his profits flowing and his workers under his thumb.[3]

Addams had been involved with unions in Chicago for several years, largely due to the influence of Florence Kelley, a Hull-House resident and ardent labor activist. She knew about the plight of workers from the outset and was convinced that Pullman's workers were being wronged. As a member of the Chicago Civic Federation's Board of Conciliation, Addams went to the town of Pullman (created, depending on the standpoint, as either a workers' residential paradise or a paternalistic, village-style work camp) and visited the factory to investigate the potential for a settlement between management and workers. Pullman's vice-president told Addams that there was "nothing to arbitrate." Frustrated, Addams told the *Chicago Herald* that the events were emblematic of

> a struggle between one of the great monopolies on earth and the most powerful organization in railway labor. It is worthwhile for the Civic Federation to settle this question if it can. But Mr. Pullman . . . will not consent. And if the Civic Federation, representing all the best elements in the community, cannot effect so desirable a result, it cannot justify its existence.

No doubt, Addams's resolve about the Civic Federation representing the "best elements" was shaken when she learned that the president of the Civic Federation, Lyman Gage, had refused to contribute to the strike relief fund, stating for the papers that "people who voluntarily leave good work deserve to suffer." Addams went before the U.S. Strike Commission in August 1894, six weeks after the end of the strike, to plead on behalf of the workers for more equitable pay and benefits, but to no avail.[4]

Addams was furious. What a contrast—to be meeting with the heads of Chicago business while at the same time feeling her heartstrings pulled by the plight of the Pullman workers! Meanwhile, her sister Mary Linn was quite ill, and Addams was torn: "My sister is so pleased to have me with her, that I feel like a brute when I think of the days I haven't been here." She was being pulled in two directions—if not more—and her support for unions would not help her personal problems, nor would it solve the immediate and pressing needs of people in her neighborhood. In fact, her union ties cost her some support, and Hull-House saw a decline in donations:

> [W]hether Hull-House is in any wise identified with the strike or not, makes no difference. When "Labor" is in disgrace we are always

regarded as belonging to it and share the opprobrium. In the public excitement following the Pullman strike Hull-House lost many friends.[5]

Mary Linn Addams died in July 1894, leaving behind four children (two of them not yet adults) and a father unwilling to support them. Addams took all the children under her wing—the youngest boy, Stanley, moved into Hull-House as her ward. This incredible individual responsibility pulled at her attention just as she was growing increasingly frustrated with George Pullman and the rest of his capitalist cronies. In late 1894, she put pen to paper and began to write one of her most famous works, "A Modern Lear," drawing parallels between Pullman and Shakespeare's King Lear and describing the strike as a modern tragedy. The work was initially delivered in speeches in 1895 (and eventually published in 1912). Having taken ill with typhoid fever in 1895, however, Addams was forced to scale back and take care of herself, but her frustration with Pullman simmered.[6]

When she had recovered, she continued to refine her ideas. Her anger and confusion is plain:

> It is impossible to justify such a course of rage and riot in a civilized community to whom the methods of conciliation and control were open. Every public-spirited citizen in Chicago during that summer felt the stress and perplexity of the situation.

Addams saw clearly the contradictions of capital, wherein the profit-maximizing goals of Pullman were opposed to the social good:

> The shops are managed, however, not for the development of the workman thus socialized, but for the interests of the company owning the capital. The divergence between the social form and the individual aim becomes greater as the employees are more highly socialized and dependent.

She also saw connections between the plight of labor and the struggles of women to be free of the constraints of patriarchal society and find an independent voice:

> The relation of the British King to his family is very like the relation of the president of the Pullman company to his town; the denoue-ment of a daughter's break with her father suggests the break of the employees with their benefactor.

These ideas had their first full expression on March 4, 1896, in a speech Addams gave to the Chicago Women's Club that was reported by city newspapers.[7]

Beyond the Pullman strike, Addams was disgusted by the wide-spread corruption in politics. In particular, she felt Johnny Powers, alderman for the Nineteenth Ward, was no friend to Hull-House. Since 1892, Addams and other residents had been sparring with Powers. Concerned about the lack of adequate schooling for neigh-borhood children, Hull-House residents successfully lobbied for a new school, over Powers's objections. Addams also butted heads with the alderman over garbage in the streets. As part of her ef-forts with the Chicago Relief Association, she became concerned with "the question of the filthy streets and alleys of Chicago." Powers was in the thick of it (literally), as some of his most stalwart politi-cal supporters were the "scavengers" who made their money picking through the waste on the streets. These scavengers, who didn't want things cleaned up, took care of Powers on Election Day, and he kept them in garbage. But things were getting out of hand: Hull-House fielded over a thousand neighborhood complaints in the summer months of 1892 alone, all about the abysmal state of sanitation in the Nineteenth Ward.[8]

In an effort to make a change, the Civic Federation appointed Addams to its Sanitation Committee. She was to confer "with the Mayor and Council upon the necessity of reform in the methods of collecting and disposing of garbage and waste material." In other words, Addams began to develop direct relations with the city. She had a chance to clean things up. As a next step, she became the federation's Ward Nineteen sanitation inspector. The dirt and filth were so intolerable that Addams, backed by businessmen from the neighborhood, actually submitted a bid to the city for the removal of all garbage. Residents also lobbied the mayor, asking for new sanitation inspectors, but Powers was able to stymie these efforts on behalf of the scavengers. Still, in the early months of 1895, Addams pressured the state and took the issue public. A *Chicago Daily Tribune* editorial stated, "Miss Addams ought to be awarded the contract. . . . By all means let it be seen what she can do." The editorial went on to say, "Johnny Powers has reason to feel uneasy." Her bid was not accepted, but Addams received quite a bit of attention in Chicago. She had entered into the political fray she found so distasteful by, perhaps, the only appropriate means: garbage. It certainly was not what she might have envisioned as a way forward, but with creativity and her ties to elites, she was able to put herself in a position to make a difference.[9]

With the support of the federation's leaders, Addams began to strategize on how to unseat the alderman (and other corrupt politicians) in the upcoming April 2, 1895, elections. A member of the Hull-House Men's Club, Frank Lawler, ran as a candidate for the other Nineteenth Ward seat. Lawler won, along with a number of other "reform" candidates, upsetting the applecart of city politics and providing an opening for the federation to push for change. And push it did, immediately pressuring newly elected Mayor Swift to appoint Addams garbage inspector for the Nineteenth Ward. It was good-paying job, with a salary of $1,000 per year, and there is no doubt that many aldermen were upset that they had lost an opportunity to enjoy the patronage. Now Addams rolled up her sleeves. With the assistance of another Hull-House resident, she went to work, rising early each morning to survey the streets of the neighborhood.[10]

Her work made a difference, allowing her to minister to both her individual needs and her community engagement:

> Such daily living on the part of the office holder is of infinitely more value than many talks on civics for, after all, we credit most easily that which we see. The careful inspection combined with other causes, brought about a great improvement in the cleanliness and comfort of the neighborhood and one happy day, when the death rate of our ward was found to have dropped from third to seventh in the list of city wards and was so reported to our Woman's Club, the applause which followed recorded the genuine sense of participation in the result, and a public spirit which had "made good."[11]

In 1896, Addams backed another candidate who ran against Powers. She was "the mastermind behind the campaign," but it was a losing effort, as was the next campaign she and the other Hull-House residents supported. They were never able to unseat Powers, but he got his revenge for their attempts when, in 1898, he was able to eliminate the position of garbage inspector. Addams described:

> [T]he cleanliness of the ward was becoming much too popular to suit our all-powerful alderman and, although we felt fatuously secure under the regime of civil service, he found a way to circumvent us by eliminating the position altogether. He introduced an ordinance into the city council which combined the collection of refuse with the cleaning and repairing of the streets, the whole to be placed under a ward superintendent. The office of course was to be filled under civil service regulations but only men were eligible to the examination.[12]

Why didn't Addams ever run for any office beyond the realm of sanitation? She certainly had the name recognition and fame necessary to make a successful run for the city council. Candidate or no, Addams's embroiling of Hull-House in the politics of the city had consequences. What Addams and her colleagues had not realized was how much of Powers's success had to do with cronyism. He provided jobs for people, and they kept him in office. As Addams recalled: "We soon discovered that approximately one out of every five voters in the nineteenth ward at that time held a job dependent upon the good will of the alderman." Working against Powers threatened the livelihood of many in the Hull-House neighborhood, and it created a degree of animosity among community members. Addams had been naïve:

> . . . we did not yet comprehend the element of reality always brought into the political struggle in such a neighborhood where politics deal so directly with getting a job and earning a living.

Further, she found that politics was built on a more selfish type of reciprocity than she experienced at Hull-House:

> Another result of the campaign was an expectation on the part of our new political friends that Hull-House would perform like offices for them, and there resulted endless confusion and misunderstanding because in many cases we could not even attempt to do what the alderman constantly did with a right good will.

Adding insult to injury, Addams's political campaigning had cost money she could ill-afford to lose. Addams and a few others spent over a thousand dollars of their own money funding efforts against Powers in the 1898 campaign alone.[13]

The world of electoral politics offered Addams some ways forward, but clearly closed off others. Politics could not offer relief for the pressing day-to-day challenges faced by residents of the Nineteenth Ward. The dilemma of how to get things done and move forward in the face of innumerable obstacles remained. How to help those who literally knocked on the door of Hull-House every day?

The answer was to start a charity organization. Addams was not content to remain confined to Hull-House. Nor did she seem to think that the woes of Chicago could be met by scaling up Hull-House's efforts. The Relief and Aid had refused to form a charity organization several years earlier, so Addams and a small group of Chicagoans took the initiative. Turlington Harvey (of the Chicago Relief Association *and* the Relief and Aid) convinced Lucy Flower (a friend of Addams) to serve as chair of the proposed new organization and offered rent-free space at the Relief and Aid building to help defray expenses. To avoid confusion, the organization was named the Chicago Bureau of Charities (CBC). Using relief funds left over in Chicago Relief Association coffers, Harvey paid the salaries of the clerks who had previously worked for the association's Bureau of Registration and had them installed, along with all records and furniture, as employees of the Chicago Bureau of Charities.[14]

Addams was instrumental in the formal chartering of the Chicago Bureau of Charities. At the April 19, 1895, meeting of the bureau's Executive Committee, those present voted to:

> delegate all powers of the Association to Mesdames Flower, Stevenson and Addams, who are requested to act as Commissioners to procure a charter guaranteeing them power to organize a Corporation under the laws of the State of Illinois, to carry out the purposes of this Association and to this end the present Executive committee hereby transfer to said Commissioners all properties and moneys belonging to the Bureau for the purposes named.[15]

Sometime in April, the filing documents were notarized by Flower's husband, a prominent Chicago attorney, and they were delivered to the secretary of state's office in Springfield, Illinois, on May 7, 1895. Addams, along with John McLaren, signed the Chicago Bureau of Charities' formal charter at the Department of State.[16]

The creation of the Bureau of Charities took place only two months after Addams created a mission statement for Hull-House and incorporated it as the Hull-House Association. Addams was thus instrumental in incorporating two organizations with expressly different philosophies of helping others—as clear a demonstration of the American's Dilemma as we might find. The purpose of the Hull-House Association, Addams wrote in the mission statement, was:

> to provide a center for a higher civic and social life; to initiate and maintain education and philanthropic enterprises; and to investigate and improve the conditions in the industrial districts of Chicago.[17]

The Hull-House Association mission statement stands in sharp contrast to that of the Chicago Bureau of Charities:

> to register and co-ordinate the work of the public and private charities of Chicago; to rid its streets of tramps and beggars; to protect the public from imposters and to stimulate to orderly effort the philanthropic impulses of the citizens of Chicago and to discover and efficiently aid the worthy poor throughout said city.[18]

Addams not only founded the bureau, she was also deeply involved in its operations, attending a number of executive committee meetings in 1894 and 1895, many held in the opulent Egyptian Parlor of the Palmer House (where the Chicago Civic Federation met the year before). Here is a brief description of the parlor:

> This room is the gem of the parlor suite. It is furnished entirely in the style of the ancient Egyptians. The sacred stork, the Sphinx, the hieroglyphic emblazonry, the horoscopic clock, the candelabra are all carefully wrought. Yet we cannot believe that the ancients know how to upholster as well as the skilled workers who made these wonderful chairs and covered them with stains and laces.[19]

Addams must have seen the irony of talking about helping others in such a place. This great symbol of wealth and the triumph of capitalism was a far cry from the squalid neighborhoods where the bureau's clients lived.

In practice the CBC pushed the importance of working in harmony with business. For example, in a letter to contributors, read and approved at a November 20, 1894, meeting, the executive committee crowed "the general satisfaction expressed in business circles over the work accomplished by the Central Relief Association during last winter, furnishes abundant testimony to the efficiency of the work." We can also see economic principles—in this case relating to the division of labor—infusing their communication:

> It would help in the division of labor, to the end that each agency might be permitted to do things it can do best. The Bureau would serve as a center and rallying point for the charities of the city and a gatherer of every kind of information, to be drawn upon freely by any society or citizen.

It is as if the bureau were contributing to the development of a charitable version of Adam Smith's celebrated pin factory, in which each worker contributes a part of the product, but no one can craft the entirety on her own. Perhaps Addams bought in to this notion, but the idea of a division of labor within the community's efforts to help others does not fit with her work at Hull-House, nor does it match her writing.[20]

On November 20, 1894, Addams was elected one of seven members of the executive committee of the bureau. Those present (Addams included) drafted a fundraising letter that makes plain the organization's attitudes:

> This plan will make the care of the worthy poor more wise, more humane, more sustained, and more efficient than heretofore: 1st By securing promptness, 2nd By preventing duplication, 3rd By eliminating fraud, 4th By fixing the responsibility of Charitable Societies, 5th By directing individual effort to the care of the worthy poor.

Notice the language concerning the "worthy poor"; Addams was at this meeting and approved the wording.[21]

Addams served the Chicago Bureau of Charities in a number of capacities over the following decade. She was on the board of directors from 1898 to 1899, from 1901 to 1903, and from 1906 to 1907. She served on the West Side District Executive Committee from 1898 to 1899. Addams was also an occasional donor, giving $6 to the bureau at some point in 1900 and $12.80 to a bureau special fund. In the latter donation, Addams was listed alongside International Harvester and Franklin MacVeagh (a prominent banker and secretary of the Treasury under President Taft). Yes, the amounts were nominal, but what is important is the public use of her name as a supporter of the Chicago Bureau of Charities. Addams was taking an "all hands on deck" approach, embracing two different ways of helping others in order to move things forward.[22]

Rather than a reluctant participant, Addams was an ardent defender of the CBC against outside criticism. Along with her friends Sarah Hackett Stevenson and Lucy Flower, Addams penned a letter protesting the Relief and Aid's 1895 decision to "discontinue sending reports to the Bureau of Charities." The letter was read aloud at the Relief and Aid's March 4, 1895, meeting and addressed the organization's refusal to share information and their own inability to get a straight answer as to why:

> On January 15th just eight weeks after, without a word of explanation to any one of the committee, the Relief and Aid stopped sending any reports, and withdrew their visitor from the 19th Ward district. Mr. Gross was requested by the Executive Committee to see Mr. Harvey and ascertain the reason of this sudden change of policy. No satisfactory explanation was given. On Feby 15th *one month* later, Miss Lathrop then acting as Secretary of the Bureau of Charities, received a letter from Mr. Harvey stating that the Relief and Aid at their monthly meeting in Feby. had decided to have no further connection with the Bureau and that if the parties in interest

desired to know the reason for this action, they could obtain it by calling on Mr. Trusdell. In response to that letter, two of our number, Miss Flower and Miss Addams (Dr. Stevenson being out of town) called at the Relief and Aid office as requested by Mr. Harvey. We were informed that Mr. Trusdell would not be at the office that day, we went the next day and were absolutely refused any information by Mr. Trusdell, he saying the communications on which the Board had acted were *confidential*. We mentioned that we had come by request of Mr. Harvey. Mr. Trusdell then went to telephone Mr. Harvey and returned saying Mr. Harvey upheld his action and desired the whole matter referred to the Executive Committee. Now gentlemen, we feel we have a right to demand that these communications, affecting us to the extent of inducing you to vote to have no further communications with our Bureau, be submitted to us. As men of honor you cannot allow any person, much less any woman to be thus secretly attacked and given no opportunity either of defense or of knowing the assailant. If any clergyman has done what Mr. Trusdell says, sent in a communication he is unwilling to stand by openly, he is unworthy of credence and certainly honorable men cannot afford to countenance any such underhanded methods. We therefore ask that these reports be submitted to our inspection and we be allowed to judge of their truth or falsity.[23]

This letter is remarkable for its tone, for Addams was known as one who rarely became angry, particularly in a public fashion. In fact, she opposed personal antagonism of any sort. But whatever her initial ambivalence about using charity organization methods when she started Hull-House in 1889, she had revised her position in the ensuing six years.[24] She was not to be given the runaround.

Again and again, Addams allowed the bureau to use her name in its publications. From her battles against John Powers, Addams knew the importance of lending one's name to a cause. It appears as if Addams was convinced to do this by Professor Small, the University of Chicago sociologist. Writing about the Civic Federation, Small told Addams that "the business which the committee has in hand is so important that it must have the names which will carry the most weight with the men whose cooperation must make the movement a success." While Small referred to the importance of male names, Addams's name would serve as one of the most important ones on the letterhead of the Chicago Civic Federation and the Chicago Bureau of Charities.[25]

Addams even allowed her name to be used in at least two CBC marketing pamphlets published in 1899. One pamphlet lists her alongside J. Pierpont Morgan, Robert Treat Paine, and Rufus Choate as having "been active workers in the cause." Nothing like name-dropping to support a cause (even if two of the people had died long before charity organization became formalized in the United States). Addams also spoke publicly on behalf of the CBC, as part of "an active campaign intended to interest the public in the Bureau." She drew large crowds to her speeches: "The attendance upon the majority of these meetings ranged from 50 to 100 persons, although the Ravenswood meeting was attended by probably 300 and the South Central District meeting by 500 or more." Addams's name was clearly important as she drew nearly five times the crowds attracted by other speakers.[26]

Behind the scenes, Addams worked with other CBC leaders to try to garner symbolic and financial support from the mayor's office. The city had set up some sort of emergency relief fund, and in March 1897 Addams's friend Julia Lathrop reported to the executive committee of the CBC regarding a meeting she had between "Mr. H. S. Vail of the Mayor's Committee, and Miss Addams relative to the remaining amount in the Mayor's fund."[27] Reading between the lines, Addams and Lathrop met with Vail (the mayor's representative on the relief committee) and Franklin MacVeagh to determine whether there was any city money available for the CBC. The charity organization followed up by writing to the "Mayor's Relief Committee" on March 20, 1897:

> In a conversation with Mr. MacVeagh and Mr. H. S. Vail, chairman of the Mayor's Relief Committee it appeared:
>
> 1st. That the Mayor desires some permanent organization of the Relief Committee
>
> 2nd. That Mr. Vail is anxious to have one central collecting agency for the charities of Chicago.
>
> 3rd. That he wishes to bring this into co-operation with the Bureau of Associated Charities, as far as it can be arranged without destroying the autonomy of the Mayor's Committee. It is his thought that the re-organized and enlarged Mayor's Committee may raise the funds, not only for the Bureau of Charities, but, also for relief purposes in this city, possibly bringing the total sum to one hundred and fifty thousand dollars per annum.
>
> 4th. That the Executive Committee of the Bureau of Associated Charities in consultation especially with Miss Addams, Professor Graham Taylor, Professor Henderson and Mrs. Flower should send a request to the Mayor's Committee to take up the scheme of collection in the city.
>
> Mr. Vail has had the experience of 1893 and 1894 in raising money, beside this year's experience. The scheme which he proposed has been carried out successfully, for many years, in Liverpool. A list of the approved charities is sent out once a year to all of the business houses. They are requested to indicate to which societies they prefer their contribution to go. Any surplus is distributed at the discretion of the Committee.
>
> The same plan was tried in Denver, with partial success, being better adapted to a large place than a small one.
>
> It is Mr. Vail's hope that this committee may be the financial

arm of the general charities in Chicago, as the Associated Charities will be its administrative arm, and that eventually the two may coalesce, if desired. That here should be any organic at present, seems undesirable.

Mr. Vail desires that the statement of this suggestive plan should in no way become public.[28]

Notice the idea of an "approved" list of charities, as well as the importance placed on the support of "business houses" for funds and for deciding which charities were worthy. The letter shows that the CBC was looking to create stronger ties to the city, hoping to be provided economic capital (in the form of access to relief funds) and symbolic capital (in the form of control over which charities were on the "approved" list). It also shows that the mayor specifically requested Addams be included in any fundraising collaboration between the bureau and his relief committee. No doubt the mayor was keenly aware of the value of Addams's name. Two weeks later, the bureau received another letter from Mr. H. S. Vail,

indicating that the larger and permanent work of the Mayor's Committee was not likely to be carried out. Mr. Vail stated however, that he would endeavor to secure for the Bureau of Associated Charities the proceeds of the Athletic Carnival, shortly to be held, and the Military Carnival to take place next Fall.

What a disappointment it must have been for the Executive Committee to be refused. They had come so close to cementing a relationship with the city akin to that developed by the Relief and Aid after the Great Fire.[29]

Addams's heavy involvement with the CBC and her continued efforts at Hull-House left little time for individual pursuits, but she somehow carved out time for a foray into university teaching. She started as "a member of the university extension staff of the then new

University of Chicago." The extension program provided a personal space to test out ideas, and it resulted in perhaps one of the greatest series of lectures in nineteenth-century America, part of a course called "Democracy and Social Ethics," later to be published in 1902 as a book by the same name.[30]

Addams also found time to travel in 1896, with her friend Mary Rozet Smith footing the bill for a trip to Europe. The nearly five-month trip began in April, with stops in England, France, Germany, Switzerland, and Russia, where Addams hoped to meet her idol, Leo Tolstoy. Beyond the significant amount of time that Addams took away at the expense of her efforts in Chicago, the trip is noteworthy for her encounter with Tolstoy. His translator, Alymer Maude, offered to take Addams and Smith to Tolstoy's estate outside of Moscow. Addams was very much looking forward to the encounter: "The prospect of seeing Tolstoy filled me with the hope of finding a clue to the tangled affairs of city poverty."[31]

What Addams received was a dressing-down that shook her confidence to the core. Maude introduced the women and explained their work at Hull-House. Addams recounted the scene in detail:

> Tolstoy, standing by clad in his peasant garb, listened gravely but, glancing distrustfully at the sleeves of my traveling gown which unfortunately at that season were monstrous in size, he took hold of an edge and pulling out one sleeve to an interminable breadth, said quite simply that "there was enough stuff on one arm to make a frock for a little girl," and asked me directly if I did not find "such a dress" a "barrier to the people." I was too disconcerted to make a very clear explanation, although I tried to say that monstrous as my sleeves were they did not compare in size with those of the working girls in Chicago and that nothing would more effectively separate me from "the people" than a cotton blouse following the simple lines of the human form; even if I had wished to imitate him and "dress as

a peasant," it would have been hard to choose which peasant among the thirty-six nationalities we had recently counted in our ward. Fortunately the countess came to my rescue.

Addams was crushed, but Tolstoy was not finished. The conversation turned to her living arrangements:

> I was asked who "fed" me, and how did I obtain "shelter"? Upon my reply that a farm a hundred miles from Chicago supplied me with the necessities of life, I fairly anticipated the next scathing question: "So you are an absentee landlord? Do you think you will help the people more by adding yourself to the crowded city than you would by tilling your own soil?"

These challenges were very much on her mind as she dined with Tolstoy and other guests that evening. She left the encounter feeling perplexed and unsure.[32]

As her trip wound down and she prepared to return to Chicago, she resolved to try to act more in line with Tolstoy's ideas:

> I read everything of Tolstoy's that had been translated into English, German, or French, there grew up in my mind a conviction that what I ought to do upon my return to Hull-House was to spend at least two hours every morning in the little bakery which we had recently added to the equipment of our coffeehouse. Two hours' work would be but a wretched compromise, but it was hard to see how I could take more time out of each day.

We have all made resolutions like this one, to be "better" in some shape or form. Upon her return, Addams tried to follow through:

> . . . suddenly the whole scheme seemed to me as utterly preposterous as it doubtless was. The half dozen people invariably waiting to see me after breakfast, the piles of letters to be opened and answered, the demand of actual and pressing wants—were these all to be pushed

aside and asked to wait while I saved my soul by two hours' work at baking bread?

The incident with Tolstoy, and Addams's struggles to deal with the contradictory injunctions inherent in it, are emblematic of Addams's constant dilemmas.[33]

She was struggling to improve herself *and* maintain a voice as she moved forward, revising her efforts along the way. She became increasingly involved in politics, both backroom and electoral. And she supported other organizations in efforts that were at times antithetical to those she championed at Hull-House. But this is not just about what Addams did or did not do. Her actions, particularly her support of the CBC, had consequences. Beyond new mission statements, more board meetings, and pamphlets, her support helped the CBC do its own work to help others in Chicago. This work was *very* different from what was happening at Hull-House, at least in the early stages, and Addams was keenly aware of the difference, as evidenced in an 1894 publication: "Now, as I take it, a settlement differs radically from a charitable enterprise in that it enters the neighborhood for social reasons; in order that it may effect the life of a neighborhood, and give it, if possible, a higher civic, social and political ideal."[34]

The Chicago Bureau of Charities took a much harder line on who was "deserving" of help, and its workers were much more confident of their methods. For example, a document from an 1896 Bureau Central District Meeting contains a hand-written dialogue, presumably between the head of the district and a committee on visiting, on the matter of the "Hughes family." The committee asked, "What have we *given* the family in these 12 years? Could any special saloon be held responsible for the man's drinking habits? What is the rent at present & state of the alc [sic]?" Clearly, drinking was a problem, and the committee was not optimistic, as it questioned the "wisdom of spending so much on an apparently hopeless case," pointing out that it might be "better to deal with *more* of the opposite kind." The response from the district employee, written in pencil in the left margin, indicates that the family had received "considerable help . . . always with a purpose," but that it might be necessary to consider "correctional treatment for [the] man," specifically the "removal of [the] children from [the] family." The district employee had faith in the methods of charity organization, rhetorically asking the committee, "Is it not through our absolute knowledge of affairs by experience that we can today say further effort is useless?" One can certainly sympathize with the family that had to deal with alcoholism and abuse. But the idea of "absolute knowledge" touted by the bureau stands in stark contrast to the more experimental style of work at Hull-House.[35]

The CBC also published frequent cases of fraud in its reports, validating the need for a registry. A folder designed to hold charity referral cards (Chicago's elites were meant to keep the cards at the front door or in a coat pocket to give to anyone begging alms) exhorted Chicago citizens to contribute to "the work of stopping promiscuous begging." The problems of poverty and joblessness were even medicalized as the bureau began to call clients "typical cases cured." As the Chicago Bureau of Charities pointed out, "What a physician is to the sick the Bureau of Associated Charities is to the Poor." The bureau diagnosed a "disease which we politely call 'Lack of Energy'—commonly called laziness."[36]

The bureau made plain the economic dimensions of its role, reminiscent of today's welfare debates: "[S]ince every person or family which is not self-supporting must be maintained at the expense of some one else or of the public, the direct economic value of this portion of the Bureau's work is plain." In two workrooms, the bureau "offer[ed] a test of willingness to work where there was a suspicion of imposition of fraud and laziness." And, it was able to keep tabs on people with its friendly visitors. The following example was featured in a West Side District pamphlet:

> Mrs. S- was persuaded to befriend a family where the wife's mother was sick for lack of proper food and previous helpers had reported to our investigator that the man drank. Mrs. S. went to the despondent like a joint attack of electricity and sunshine. She interested her own friends in the matter, got the family's furniture out of storage, moved them into a good flat near her own home, secured a boarder for them to share their expenses, gathered furniture for the boarder's room, got the man of the family a new suit and then a fifty-dollar job, stopped the drinking. The family visited and the family of Mrs. S. herself have been mutually helpful and are very good friends.

In this instance, essentially a piece of marketing for the bureau, the organization's methods led to the desired ends. But this was not always the case, and there are a number of instances in which friendly visits by bureau personnel appear to have been extremely invasive without success.

At the same time this particular bureau pamphlet was published, Addams spoke about her frustrations with the friendly visit, particularly as part of her University of Chicago extension class:

> The charity visitor . . . is often embarrassed to find herself obliged to lay all the stress of her teaching and advice upon the industrial virtues, and to treat the members of the family almost exclusively as factors in the industrial system. She insists that they must work and be self-supporting, that the most dangerous of all situations is idleness, that seeking one's own pleasure, while ignoring claims and responsibilities, is the most ignoble of actions. The members of her assigned family may have other charms and virtues—they may possibly be kind and considerate of each other, generous to their

friends, but it is her business to stick to the industrial side. As she daily holds up these standards, it often occurs to the mind of the sensitive visitor, whose conscience has been made tender by much talk of brotherhood and equality, that she has no right to say these things; that her untrained hands are no more fitted to cope with actual conditions than those of her broken-down family.[37]

Jane Addams showed herself very skeptical of the friendly visitor:

The daintily clad visitor who steps into the little house made un-tidy by the vigorous efforts of her hostess, the washerwoman, is no longer sure of her superiority to the latter; she recognizes that her hostess after all represents social value and industrial use, as over against her own parasitic cleanliness and a social standing attained only through status.[38]

What right did the well-dressed Lady Bountiful, a friendly visi-tor by virtue of wealth and status, have to enter a working wom-an's home and lecture her on life? To the extent that the visitor in Addams's description recognized the inequality that underpinned her relationship with her "hostess," she was moving toward the awareness of her "social obligation." But while the friendly visitor might strive to achieve a dignified, reciprocal relationship, it wasn't common. For Addams, the friendly visitors of charity organization societies were by-and-large stuck on the "sequestered byway" of social provision. And yet part of her still felt it was important to support the bureau's friendly visiting activities.

Nativism remained, too. The CBC continued to police the bound-aries of who was a neighbor and who deserved the support of the com-munity. By 1900, it had developed a partnership with all the major railroads to administer a "transportation program," which was in actu-ality a deportation program similar to the one informally carried out by the Relief and Aid. "Chicago is a 'dumping ground' for paupers from many cities and states," said the bureau in a pamphlet published in 1897:

> Scarcely a day passes that the Bureau's agents do not discover some applicant for charity who has recently come from another locality, with no apparent reason except the hope of finding public support here. The Bureau has been active in sending such persons to the places where they belong. In 1897 about eight hundred and seventy-five persons were sent out of Chicago on transportation secured by the Bureau.

With Addams's leadership, the bureau took on the administration of the Chicago transportation program, with no apparent cost to the railroads. It indicated that it had done so "on the theory that . . . it was rendering a public service."[39]

Most of the major business leaders of Chicago contributed to the bureau; George Pullman, owner of the Pullman Palace Car Company and Addams's bête noire, was an early and prominent contributor to the bureau, giving $250 in 1896, less than two years after the infamous Pullman strike. He would give $1,000 to the CBC each year for the next five years, the equivalent of $28,000 per year today. It is not unreasonable to speculate that what seems to have been advanced were the interests of Chicago businessmen, rather than the interests of the public. And Addams had to have been aware of Pullman's contributions, which began at roughly the same time she delivered her "Modern Lear" speech. Funding sources, however, did not seem to bother her overly much. Writing of a former slaver's contribution to Hull-House, she was ambivalent: "[D]uring all the period of hot discussion concerning tainted money I never felt clear enough on the general principle involved, to accept the many invitations to write and speak upon the subject, although I received much instruction in the many letters of disapproval."[40]

Addams's ambivalence and uncertainty led to revisions of the work at Hull-House as well. There is evidence that Hull-House residents began to support and adopt charity organization methods, replacing some of the "settlement" methods in their work in the Nineteenth Ward.[41] But it took a few years; there were reservations about providing outdoor relief and engaging in charity organization practices. At a residents' meeting in September 1893,

> the matter of cooperating with [a local church] in giving outdoor relief was discussed. It was said that systematized charitable work was not the province of the house, and had been avoided heretofore, that if this were done it should be understood that it was in view of the emergency of the present season. Upon motion was voted to accept the assistance of [the] church.

Hull-House residents had previously done things differently from the charity organization approach, and seen results; they were ambivalent about shifting toward the "other" way of helping.[42]

Their reservations soon fell away in the face of the widespread needs of the neighborhood. At roughly the same time Addams was furious with the Relief and Aid for stonewalling her new organization, the Chicago Bureau of Charities, Hull-House residents tried to convince the Relief and Aid to do more work in the Nineteenth Ward. On January 7, 1895, the Relief and Aid board discussed a letter from "Miss Crain [a resident] of Hull House asking this Society to appoint an agent to occupy a part of their office, 228 W. Taylor St. free of expense to this Society." Two weeks later, the superintendent of the Relief and Aid reported that he had placed someone in the office. But it was a short-lived collaboration lasting just a week; the superintendent had the man removed, citing a lack of "business for us." This may be a reference to an event mentioned by Addams:

> In the midst of the [charity organization] district a young man who came to live at Hull-House from an eastern city where the charity organization society had already been successfully established, opened

an office with the backing of a group of trustees assembled by Julia Lathrop. It was a difficult performance and although long before spring the main office of the new undertaking had been moved down town with three branch offices of which the parent office was one, it was years before the more advanced method of administering charity was established in Chicago and developed into the present satisfactory United Charities.

Addams goes on to tell that the "young man" lost his mind and ran off to the West, living under another identity for thirty-five years. Perhaps his personal troubles were what caused the project at Hull-House to fail.[43] More likely, there was enough friction between the Relief and Aid and Hull-House to kill the effort, or perhaps there really was not much for the Relief and Aid employee to do.

In any event, Hull-House was exploring new practical options that involved charity organization and the business idea. The Hull-House residents' meeting dated January 7, 1895, mentions that "The 'Relief and Aid' sustainers made an unsuccessful attack upon the 'Charity organization' plans of Miss Crain—may the result be prophetic." The "attack" seems to predate the placement of the Relief and Aid man at Hull-House, but it is evident that there was some tension in the interactions between Hull-House and the Relief and Aid. Nonetheless, the residents were obviously still interested in the methods of charity organization. Resident Julia Lathrop gave a report on the Chicago Bureau of Charities, "comprising its history purpose etc." at a residents' meeting the following month.[44]

Practices at Hull-House were revised. The first *Hull-House Bulletin*, published in January 1896, lists one of its residents, Miss Gernon, as a "visitor" for the bureau. An information circular, published by the bureau in February 1896, mentions "in the Nineteenth ward at Hull House, one of the residents, Miss Gernon, in connection with the Bureau of Charities, gives especial care to the work for the families in distress." Remember, friendly visiting was not informed by a logic of helping for help's sake alone. In the same information circular, there is a discussion of the friendly visit:

> In almost every case of distress there is somewhere a defect or weakness that has made the sufferer in some degree handicapped in the fierce struggle of life. The friendly visitor seeks to discover this weakness and to remove it or to so direct it that it will not prove a defect. If the mother is shiftless and improvident, habits of thrift and skill in domestic economy should be inculcated. If the father is idle or given to evil habits of any kind, the visitor's energies are directed to the correction of this defect. . . . Through this plan each family is treated as a unit, with an effort to bring into the life of that family something of the culture and beauty that is so abundant among its more economically favored neighbors. It may be said to carry in some degree the Social Settlement idea into each home.

Culture and beauty are linked to economic success. The talk of defects leads to "correction" rather than unconditional help.[45] This is not the spirit of helping we saw Addams take up originally.

It is amazing that the same pamphlet evokes the social settlement. The circular clearly shows the business idea (and "blame the victim" sentiment) while also linking itself to the "settlement idea." The tension is apparent. Gernon ran the Relief Bureau for Hull-House. As part of her duties, she was "in constant communication with the Chicago Bureau of Charities. Information is given concerning the societies and charitable institutions of the city and every effort is made to put the applicants in communication with the proper sources for their relief." These ties must have been fairly strong, for when Hull-House decided to "discontinue" the Relief Bureau in October 1897, they began referring all relief applicants to the West District Office of the bureau.[46]

By the end of 1896, Hull-House was home to a "study class for Friendly Visitors," meeting every afternoon at 2 o'clock. The friendly visit was now an established part of Hull-House practice. Five years later, Hull-House was holding meetings for the hundred members of the People's Friendly Club twice a month. Hull-House also had financial ties to the bureau. In 1900, Hull-House made a small contribution to a special fund of the Chicago Bureau of Charities, with another in 1903. As in the case of Addams's personal contributions to the CBC, the point is not so much small dollar amounts as the willingness of Hull-House as an institution to lend its name as a supporting institution in bureau publications.[47]

The culmination of Addams's openness to methods grounded in the business idea can be seen in Hull-House's 1907 partnership with the Relief and Aid Society to run the Mary Crane Nursery. Apparently the family of Mary Crane wanted to give "the Crane building" as a memorial donation to the Relief and Aid, and then have it turned over to Hull-House for operation. The Relief and Aid's directors had been planning a day nursery since late 1905, but came around to the idea of the Crane Nursery. They decided "that the Executive Committee be authorized to enter into an arrangement with Hull-House on behalf of this Society, on terms to be mutually agreed upon, for the operation of the Mary Crane Nursery Building by this Society." The Relief and Aid and Hull-House were now full partners in social provision. The following week, the Relief and Aid's Board Executive Committee met with a "Mr. Pond" from Hull-House. They agreed that Hull-House would lease the Crane building for ten years for a "nominal rental, without any conditions as to operation, except that the building is to be used for education, benevolent and charitable purposes and no other."[48]

There was a gradual convergence of settlement and charity organization practices and logic in Chicago and across the country. In 1909, Addams became president of the National Conference of Charities and Corrections, the main professional association of charitable organizations. In this same year, the Chicago Relief and Aid Society and

the Chicago Bureau of Charities combined to form the United Charities of Chicago, with its first president chosen from Relief and Aid's
Board of Directors.[49] This convergence was grounded in Addams's re-
visionist actions:

> The man who insists upon consent, who moves with the people, is
> bound to consult the feasible right as well as the absolute right. He is
> often obliged to attain only Mr. Lincoln's "best possible," and often
> have the sickening sense of compromising with his best convictions.
> He has to move along with those whom he rules toward a goal that
> neither he nor they see very clearly till they come to it.

Addams clearly saw charity organization as one "best possible" way
to move forward in her difficult and ambivalent situation. It was the
story of her life; Addams found ways to move forward, but they did
not always conform to her highest ideals.[50]

The struggle between promoting individual responsibility and
helping others in the community was as pressing in Jane Addams's
time as it was for Barack Obama a hundred years later. Similar dilemmas, and a similar lasting legacy, are hallmarks of their stories. By the
age of forty, Jane Addams had altered the social landscape of Chicago
and the nation. Using her inheritance, her privilege, and her education
as social levers, she found her own unique voice and made a difference
in the world. It was a messy process, full of doubt and false starts. But
she constantly pushed herself out of her comfort zone, whether in the
East End of London, the Nineteenth Ward of Chicago, or Tolstoy's
backyard in Russia. And as she experimented, she tried to reconcile
the dilemmas presented to her by society. How to avoid the "selfish
reciprocity" of politicians and businessmen while securing their help
for her work at Hull-House? How to adjudicate the "clash of ethical
standards" between the "business idea" of the charity organization and
the more unconditional approach of the settlement house? How to
balance her own individual needs with those of her neighbors? She did

not always come up with definite answers, but the outcomes speak for themselves. She developed an immense community of friends in her neighborhood and made a significant impact on how we help others in the United States, leaving a legacy that endures to this day.

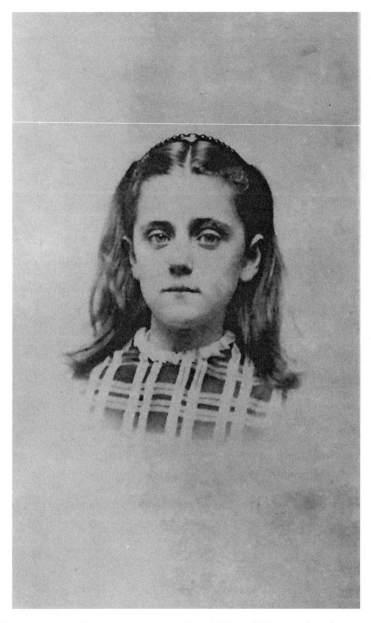

Figure 1. Jane Addams in 1868. Source: Jane Addams Collection, Swarthmore College Peace Collection. Reprinted with permission.

Figure 2. Hull-House, ca. 1890s. Source: Jane Addams Collection, Swarthmore College Peace Collection. Reprinted with permission.

Figure 3. At the front door of Hull-House. Source: Jane Addams Hull-House Photographic Collection, JAMC_0000_0125_0528, The University Library, University of Illinois at Chicago, Special Collections. Reprinted with permission.

Figure 4. Hull-House reception room. Source: Jane Addams Collection, Swarthmore College Peace Collection. Reprinted with permission.

Figure 5. Jane Addams reading to a young boy, ca. 1890s. Source: Jane Addams Collection, Swarthmore College Peace Collection. Reprinted with permission.

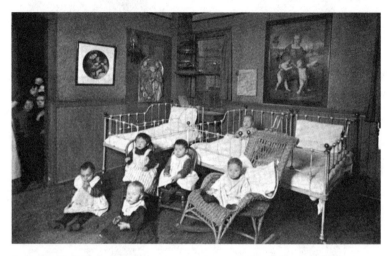

Figure 6. Hull-House nursery, ca. 1890s. Source: Jane Addams Collection, Swarthmore College Peace Collection. Reprinted with permission.

Figure 7. Obama in 1970 at age nine, with mother Ann, stepfather Lolo, and half-sister Maya. Courtesy of Obama for America.

Figure 8. Obama in New York in the early 1980s. Courtesy of Obama for America.

Figure 9. Obama at headquarters for Project Vote! in the fall of 1992. Courtesy of Obama for America.

Figure 10. Obama teaching at the University of Chicago in the 1990s. Courtesy of Obama for America.

CHAPTER FIVE

Wake Up! It's Morning in America

I had a hunger to shape the world in some way, to make the world
a better place.

Barack Obama[1]

THE YEAR WAS 1984, and Barack Obama felt torn in two. He
was unsettled, increasingly dissatisfied with his work at Business
International Corporation, even though he had only been there for
a few months. His job was a fairly mindless application of business
principles to client reports. How could they get ahead and make more
money? This question fit the times—business was booming as President Ronald Reagan oversaw the country's emergence from a major
recession. It was "morning in America," Reagan told the world in
his campaign for reelection. It was time to get to work and make the
country strong again.

Obama was the only black "professional" man at the firm; the others worked security or in the mailroom. But he had romantic notions
of becoming a community organizer, grounded in the influence of
his family and his knowledge of the civil rights movement. Working
within the white-dominated business world seemed unlikely to satisfy
his deeper yearnings. On the one hand, it was a well-worn track—now
open to blacks—that led college graduates to jobs with good pay that
helped them pay the bills and "get ahead" in the world. In his words,
he wouldn't be the first American man to have "given myself over to

stocks and bonds and the pull of respectability." On the other hand, he felt a drive to contribute to community growth, particularly for blacks in America. In Obama's mind, "communities had never been a given in this country, at least not for blacks. Communities had to be created, fought for, tended like gardens." Inherent in the American civil rights movement that had been so formative in Obama's thinking was the notion that "through shared sacrifice," people could create a more robust community that worked for everyone, regardless of color.[2]

Obama is clear in his memoirs that this was a moment of rupture in his life. He felt an almost physical tearing, pulled in different directions as he looked out his office window. He told the secretary at Business International that he was leaving for the day. He had no purpose, but, as he recalls, simply "wandered the streets of Manhattan" in an effort to collect his thoughts.

Much like Jane Addams roughly one hundred years earlier, Obama knew that there was more, that our communities had significant, unrealized potential. He, too, wondered how to move forward. He was well aware that "organizers didn't make any money," but at the same time "their poverty was proof of their integrity." Unlike Addams, Obama had no personal fortune he could draw upon to leverage a move to community organizing. He remained stuck for several months, musing about a way forward.[3]

Given Obama's rapid and spectacular rise to the American presidency, one might think that he was always an ideologue, driven by his ideas and education to make meaningful change in the world. As with Addams, Obama's early life shows sure signs of his upward social trajectory, but it does not necessarily point to where he would eventually end up. His childhood and young adult years were complicated. Out of these complications emerge some sociological and psychological clues that explain his dilemma in New York. But there is also something familiar about his struggle to reconcile seemingly contradictory demands.

The first part of Obama's story is well known. He spent much of his childhood in Hawaii, where he was born on August 4, 1961. It was a complicated period in which his father, Barack Obama, Sr.—a Kenyan exchange student at the University of Hawaii at Manoa—and his mother, Stanley Ann Dunham—anthropology student also at Manoa—separated shortly after Obama Junior's birth. Obama Senior went off to Harvard while Dunham, after a brief stint at the University of Washington, settled in Honolulu with her son and her parents. She filed for divorce in 1964 and took sole custody of her son. By all accounts, Obama's mother was the most formative influence on Obama. She was a scholar and humanitarian who infused Obama with an ethic of caring and helping.[4]

The next ten years of Obama's life found him living in Hawaii, then Indonesia, and then Hawaii again. Dunham had met an Indonesian man, Soetoro Martodihardjo (Lolo for short), who came to Hawaii in September 1962 on furlough from the Indonesian army and as part of a State Department immigration exchange program. Lolo received his master's degree in geography and married Dunham in 1965. They petitioned immigration officials to remain in the United States. It was a temporary strategy, and they were eventually forced to move to Indonesia so Lolo could apply for permanent, legal immigration status in the United States. Dunham finished her B.A. in August 1967, then she and Obama moved to Jakarta to be with Lolo.

Obama lived in Indonesia for four years, but his time there, as well as his mother's love for the country and its art, would leave a strong imprint. It was a tumultuous country (its leadership had just been overthrown in a coup), and living conditions were primitive—in fact, they were similar to those facing most immigrants in the Nineteenth Ward of Chicago in 1889. Poverty was widespread, and there was no real system of relief for the poor. The family lived in a working-class neighborhood with dirt roads and no sewers. Dunham taught English to locals as a way to bring in extra money.[5]

Obama's school in Jakarta was a mix of skin hues and religious faiths, but the fact that he only spoke English made him stand out in his first-grade class. He quickly learned Indonesian, and, by his second year of school, was able to converse freely. His ambition began to shine: Obama's third-grade teacher recounts a paper in which he declared he wanted to be president of Indonesia. Obama was also gaining an early education on living in a multiethnic, multifaith society. But his life in Indonesia was forcing on him a particular awareness, what W. E. B Du Bois famously called a "twoness" in his self-conception. He was, at the same time, an insider and an outsider. The boy had immersed himself in Indonesian culture and society. He ate, played, and spoke as if he was a local child. But, as biographer David Maraniss points out (based on interviews with those who knew Obama in Indonesia), Obama "was always apart and alone, trying to process what he saw, smelled, touched, and ate." Obama was acutely aware that his mother did not look like other mothers. And, he occasionally overheard his mother and stepfather fighting about events they had attended at a local club frequented by Americans. Lolo never wanted to go, pointing out the American businessmen were not *his* people.[6]

But perhaps more important for Obama's future was the instruction Lolo provided, particularly with regard to thinking about poverty. There were beggars "everywhere" in Jakarta, Obama said. His mother would routinely give money to those who came to the door or stopped them on the street (again, the scene is reminiscent of the interactions between rich and poor in nineteenth-century Chicago). Lolo thought this direct giving was foolish. He repeatedly told his stepson that it was impossible to stem the tide of poverty with their limited resources. "Better to save your money and make sure you don't end up on the street yourself," he told Obama. Lolo told the boy to be strong, teaching him to fight and repeatedly lecturing him on the pitfalls of being "soft" like his mother. Fine in a woman, Lolo believed, but a man needed to think differently. At a young and impressionable age, then, Obama was inculcated with the idea that helping others and showing compassion was the stuff of women, while men needed to be tough and to show practical "sense" in order to survive.[7]

Dunham and Lolo's tension grew. She brought Obama back to Hawaii at the age of ten. Ostensibly, the move was so that she could pursue a doctorate in anthropology at the University of Hawaii (under the supervision of Alice Dewey, granddaughter of pragmatist philosopher John Dewey). Her subsequent comings and goings are complicated and not of particular relevance to the line of this book. But Dunham's peripatetic life does matter in general for understanding Obama. It was, according to Maraniss, all part of a "cycle of leaving and being left. It taught him, inevitably, how to adjust to unsettled circumstances." In essence, Dunham was always willing to experiment and figure out how to move ahead—and Obama was along for the ride, watching her and living with the consequences. Learning how to keep going in unsettled moments is a skill that would stand Obama in good stead in the years to come, helping him figure out what to do during his time as a community organizer in Chicago.[8]

It is easy to read history backwards, to find the keys to a person's biography hidden away in middle school or the trials and tribulations of teenage years. It is also common for biographers to engage in armchair psychology, locating greatness or tragedy in choices made or events experienced in childhood. But we also know that the social world imprints on children from an early age. For understanding how Obama came to face particular moments of ambivalence and dilemma in his life, his time in Hawaii offers some traction. Obama lived with his maternal grandparents while in Hawaii, and his grandfather, thanks to connections at work (and despite his low income), was able to secure Obama a spot at the Punahou School. One of the most elite private schools in the United States, Punahou would give him seven years of education, both in and beyond books.

Obama began his studies at Punahou in the fall of 1971 as a fifth-grader. He was there until he enrolled at Occidental College in Los Angeles in 1980. At Punahou Obama received a world-class education. He also picked up nonacademic skills that would matter later in life. Elite private schools like Punahou are home to a hidden curriculum that emphasizes the cultivation of privilege. Students literally learn how to be at ease in the world of elites, in matters as mundane as confidently wearing a jacket and tie to conversing comfortably with the wealthiest individuals in society. Obama was in the thick of this world. Despite his family's relatively low income and his struggles to form an identity around his mixed race, he was cultivating privilege. A school friend from Punahou has said:

> There is a stigma attached to Punahou, and that's undeniable, and you hear that even when you're 8, 9, or 10 years old—oh, the rich kids or the snob kids or even all the rich haole kids, haole meaning foreigner, and in Hawaii more so: It means a foreigner from the mainland. So it was known to be a rich, haole school, and only the privileged got to go there. You had to be special.[9]

This education in privilege is another aspect Obama shares with Addams. Obama learned from an early age how to carry himself with grace and ease. In short, he too was socialized into privilege, and this cultivation would become invaluable when it came time to connect with Chicago's elites to assist in community organizing and helping the poor. Even though Obama (and even Addams, as a woman) saw himself as "apart" from this world, he *became* an elite, armed with social graces and connections. It emphasizes the twoness of his social identity.[10]

Hawaii provides another social key for understanding Obama's later ambivalence toward work and making sacrifices in the name of the daily grind to make money. This largely developed as Obama's grandparents took over primary responsibility for his upbringing. How did this come to pass? Dunham loved Indonesia and took a job there, but Obama was getting comfortable at Punahou and was reluctant to move again. So, she with Obama's half-sister in tow, she went back to Indonesia, leaving Obama with his grandparents. Though his grandfather was miserable as an insurance salesman in Hawaii, he and his wife were happy to raise Obama. They filled the breach admirably, and they exposed Obama to the daily realities of lower-middle-class working life. Not only did he see the slow wearing down of his grandfather, with so little to show for his life's work, but he saw the poverty endemic among native Hawaiians, many of whom did not (and still do not) consider themselves Americans but unwilling subjects.[11]

Obama believed his grandparents had paid too much through their participation in the daily grind of the work-spend cycle. We work to spend our money on the bountiful commodities available in America, maybe set a little aside for retirement. But, he came to think, this might come at the cost of something more precious.

Genevieve Cook, Obama's girlfriend in New York (who would become perhaps his closest confidant as he began choosing between business and community organizing), recalls "the only time he raised his voice and got really, really upset with me." In her words, Obama was upset about "the trade-offs he saw his grandparents make for some supposed safety net at the expense of something . . . he meant at the expense of their souls." Their sacrifice was a hot button issue for Obama years after he moved away from Hawaii, and it became part of his frame of reference as he decided how to move forward.[12]

Most biographers of Obama devote chapters to his childhood. But for understanding the particular American's Dilemma Obama faced in Manhattan, there are only a few analytically relevant experiences. His years in Indonesia exposed him to widespread, savage poverty (the likes of which did not typically exist in the developed world). He learned to see the social world as full of tensions. In his travels and at school, he was neither "in" the group nor totally outside it. In Hawaii, Obama attended one of the most elite private schools in the country, cultivating privilege while reading classics in literature and philosophy. At the same time, he watched his grandparents worn down in the working world. Obama experienced twoness, studying in the world of elites while also seeing the realities of the lower middle class.

Obama's time attending university is also held up as a formative period. There is no question his years at Occidental College and Columbia University were influential. However, it would be easy to overstate the importance of these institutions and understate the importance of the famous ideas on community and helping others, most notably those of Alexis de Tocqueville, Obama learned at those institutions. Tocqueville is perhaps best known for his ideas about reciprocal relations for building community and democracy. He saw these "habits of the heart" as essential and begun "on the ground," in everyday relations between neighbors. Obama was first exposed to Tocqueville's work in a large lecture class taught by Professor Roger Boesche at Occidental. By all accounts, Boesche emphasized the importance of community. He pleaded with his students "not only to have individual pursuits," recalled one of Obama's classmates, "but to have pursuits that would better humanity and better the common good for all."[13]

In accounts of the time, there is also a sense that Obama was beginning to be moved by his own majesty; he was striving to develop a larger "purpose" while feeling free to offer advice to others. There appears to have been some sort of interaction, in Obama's self-construction, between the idea of creating community and of fostering an ethic of compassion and humanism. His mother had preached empathy and compassion, and it clearly stuck. One of Obama's friends remembered "Barry" taking her to task for making a thoughtless and sarcastic comment to a mutual friend. Obama essentially told her to "Put yourself in the other person's shoes." That she remembers this advice years later speaks to its being unusual in coming from a fellow student.[14]

For most biographers, Obama's time in college also marks his first foray into the political realm. They draw on a speech he gave at a protest of the imprisonment of anti-apartheid activist Nelson Mandela in South Africa. Obama framed his speech in terms of choice and tension and seems to have given it in the "preacher's cadence" he'd be known for later in his career:

> There's a struggle going on. . . . I say there's a struggle going on. . . . It's happening an ocean away. But it's a struggle that touches each and every one of us, whether we know it or not. A struggle that demands we choose sides. . . . It's a choice between dignity and servitude, between fairness and injustice.

Other students recall that he was an excellent public speaker. But they also remember him being inattentive to the rest of the rally. One says Obama remarked later, "I don't believe we made any difference by what we did today." A blunt assessment, but, in some measure, true. In fact, this event seems less useful in showing Obama as increasingly politicized than in showing that he was rather unmoved by politics at the time (third-grade declarations of his presidential aspirations notwithstanding). It would be incorrect to think that Obama had always been a "political" person.[15]

By the end of his second year, Obama was done with Occidental. As his friend Phil Boerner recalls, "We felt like we were in a groove and we wanted life to be more difficult. It was a country-club atmosphere. We wanted to make things harder for ourselves." The two applied for transfer to Columbia University in New York City. Obama may not have been political, but he was able to make a change, to force a conscious break with his own social world. In this case, it was to seek out more diversity than he could find at Occidental, where the student body was, at the time, just over 4 percent non-white.[16]

Thanks to money from the Ford Foundation (his mother's new employer), Obama was able to take a major trip before his move to New York. He purchased a round-the-world ticket and spent the summer traveling to the far corners of the globe, including a three-week stop in Pakistan to visit friends from Occidental. His friend Wahid Hamid, whom he visited in Pakistan, recalled, "The trip gave him a grounding of sorts. . . . We went to this person's lands, where the feudal system is still strong. Barack could see how the owner lives and how the serfs and workers are so subservient."[17]

Much like Addams before him, Obama had traveled extensively by the time he was in his twenties. Traveling to poor and developing countries was not the typical path for young people of their times, though. Whether in Victorian London's East End or the streets of Jakarta or Karachi, Addams and Obama saw firsthand what struggle and suffering were like and that these problems were universal. This trip before moving to New York reacquainted Obama with some of the realities he'd seen in the developing world as a child. "When Obama came back," friend Margot Mifflin said, "he said he'd been shocked by many things, but especially the poverty. When they rode through the countryside, he was amazed at how the peasants bowed to the landowners in respect as they passed. It blew his mind." Travel also showed both Addams and Obama the common bonds of human-ity that might alleviate suffering. In this sense, Obama's education was unusual, perhaps even remarkable. Reflecting on his early adulthood in an interview from the White House, Obama pointed out that:

> The only way my life makes sense is if regardless of culture, race, re-ligion, tribe, there is this commonality, these essential human truths and passions and hopes and moral precepts that are universal. And that we can reach out beyond our differences. If that is not the case then it is pretty hard for me to make sense of my life. So that is at the core of who I am.[18]

With his trip over, Obama took his meager possessions and moved to New York. Obama would live in New York for approximately four years, from the summer of 1981 to the summer of 1985—roughly the first term of Ronald Reagan's presidency. Obama's junior and senior years at Columbia were spent in the company of a few close friends, and he was not significantly engaged in campus culture. Biographer David Maraniss goes so far as to say "at Columbia he [Obama] had been almost an apparition." For his own part, Obama remembers,

> Those two years were extremely important for me. I just stripped everything down and sort of built things back up. For about two years there, I was just painfully alone and really not focused on anything, except maybe thinking a lot.

In an interview with Columbia's alumni magazine, he said, "I spent a lot of time in the library. I didn't socialize that much. I was like a monk." His memoir says little of Columbia; we know more details from interviews with his friends and fellow students than from Obama's own recollection.[19]

Transfer students were not able to get campus housing, so Obama moved around a fair bit. He lived in cheap, run-down apartments (the first with his friend Boerner) in the poorer sections of the Upper West Side of Manhattan. Obama was a dedicated but unremarkable student, though he focused his studies primarily on political science. He did little in the public eye, save for publishing one piece in a student paper. This brief article is much written about in Obama biographies: It's said to illuminate his early thoughts on war and the nuclear freeze movement. But what is perhaps more noteworthy is one statement that highlights his ambivalence and frustration. In his mind, the university system did not equip students with tools to move forward: "The most pervasive malady of the collegiate system specifically, and the American experience generally, is that elaborate patterns of knowledge and theory have been disembodied from individual choices and government policy." He had a lot of education, but he, and others in his generation, felt stuck and voiceless.

Obama seems to have been bored; he wrote in a letter: "School is just making the same motions, long stretches of numbness punctuated with the occasional insight."[20] In this sense, Obama was no different from most undergraduates. We tend to emphasize difference in auto-biographies but what is striking is how much of Obama's life involves sameness. Many of us face the same struggles and ennui, regardless of our social position.

This stripped-down period of numbness was critical. Obama wres-tled with who he wanted to be and how that identity would manifest itself in his work. In a sense, he feared New York's "power to corrupt." The "Wall Street boom" was apparent in the conspicuous consumption of New Yorkers, and he wrote frankly that it all "dazzled my senses." He was left "uncertain of my ability to steer a course of moderation." Pulled by the wealth and prosperity of the big city and the bull market, Obama also felt a tug in the opposite direction, one that forced him to address what he called the "steady fracturing of the world" occurring at the intersection of race and class. Black Americans were being left behind, and Obama increasingly felt he could make a difference.[21]

As early as 1982, walking the city with his girlfriend Alex McNear, Obama talked about choices. Did he have any, or was his social trajec-tory locked in? Could he choose or was he chosen? Obama certainly felt what he called "the gravitational pull of graduate school, getting a degree in international relations and working in the State Department, in the Foreign Service, or working for an international foundation." But he resisted. And resisted. In the words of biographer Maraniss, "he was conducting an intense debate with himself over his past, present, and future."[22]

In their early twenties, both Obama and Addams struggled to find themselves. Their searches were confounded by the unexpected loss of their fathers. Addams was still a student at Rockford when her father died (she would turn twenty-one the next month). Obama's father died in November 1982. Obama recalls, "A few months after my twenty-first birthday a stranger called to give me the news. I was living in New York at the time, on Ninety-Fourth between Second and First." He received the news by telephone from a Kenyan aunt he did not know. For several weeks, he told no one. He kept it from his closest friends for years. His roommate, who had taken the call, did not even find out that the call was about the passing of Obama Senior until he read about it in Obama Junior's 1994 memoir.[23] Though Addams was close to her father and Obama was not close to his father, the loss was significant for both.

Both fathers were, at least in one sense, obstacles for their children. Recall that Addams's father denied her the opportunity to attend Smith College. And Obama is frank about the construct of his father:

> All my life, I had carried a single image of my father, one that I had sometimes rebelled against but had never questioned, one that I had later tried to take as my own. The brilliant scholar, the generous friend, the upstanding leader—my father had been all those things. All those things and more, because except for that one brief visit in Hawaii, he had never been present to foil the image.

The other significant men in his life had illustrated a messier reality, what Obama called "disappointments" and "compromise." These two fathers were also compasses for their children. As Obama wrote of the impact of his father's death, "the rabble of my head is free to run riot; I can do what I damn well please. . . . He could no longer tell me how to live."[24] At this critical juncture, Obama's father was still a significant force, a yardstick against which the young man measured his actions.

In his memoirs, Obama tends to present his newfound freedom from the expectations he imagined his father had as a bit of an epiphany. But in letters to Alex, who had moved to California, we see ambivalence. The detailed analysis of the letters by biographer Maraniss points to the fact that "Obama was the central character," but he was still unsure of who he was and what he was meant to do. He was a modern Hamlet. Obama wrote about how his friends were gravitating toward business or "the mainstream. I must admit large dollops of envy," he confessed. His path did not seem so clear, and he felt little control:

> Caught without a class, a structure, or tradition to support me, in a sense the choice to take a different path is made for me. . . . The only way to assuage my feelings of isolation are to absorb all the traditions [and all the] classes; make them mine, me theirs.

There are a number of ways to interpret this writing, but it is evident that Obama continued to feel an inexorable pull—to *what* was unclear. It was certainly *not* the presidency. Looking back from the Oval Office, he has said, "I don't think I could see a clear path [to the presidency]." He went on,

> At that age [at Columbia] I was much more interested in being a leader outside of politics. If you had asked me during that time what kind of career I'd love to have, more likely I would have said something like a Bob Moses [the civil rights leader], maybe with a slightly higher profile than that. . . . I would not have precluded politics, but during that period I was pretty skeptical of it. There weren't a lot of political figures at that time that I particularly admired. . . . Remember the political context of this time. This was a period where Ronald Reagan had been elected, a lot of excesses of the left, the student movements, the Democratic Party, had been rejected by a big chunk of the country. It wasn't like there was some natural place to land.[25]

Like Addams, Obama recalls that much of his forward motion was the result of "operating on impulse." There was no concrete plan; his motion was simply propelled by a strong aversion to the "traditional path," as his friend Wahid Hamid called it. There would be no law or investment banking for Obama.[26]

Obama graduated from Columbia in 1983 but did not attend the ceremony. He had his résumé ready and applied for a few jobs in community organizing. Harold Washington, the newly elected (and first black) mayor of Chicago, received one of those applications; as Obama bluntly recalls, "His office didn't write back." Whereas Addams avoided politics at first, Obama tried to enter into community engagement *through* politics, but was stymied. He went to visit his mother in Indonesia, writing to friends that he did not have firm plans for after the trip. He wrote to his friend Boerner, "My plans are uncertain; most probably I will go back after a month or two in Hawaii." But, in fact, he returned to New York, most likely disconsolate, definitely unemployed and without a place to stay. His gravitation toward and return to New York after Columbia appears to have just been the road most easily traveled. The job search letters he had sent out were still unanswered. In a letter to Alex in November 1983, Obama was clearly spinning his wheels. He didn't think he could make it as a community organizer—the pay was simply "too low to survive on." So his plan was to get a job

> in some conventional capacity for a year in order to store up enough nuts to pursue those interests the next. I've been slow getting the machinery of the job hunt in motion due to some cash flow problems (one week I can't pay postage to mail a résumé and writing sample, the next I have to bounce a check to rent a typewriter etc.).

He was flat broke.[27]

After a copy-editing test, Obama had his first interview with Business International. Cathy Lezere, head of "reference services," conducted the first interview, while Lou Celi, a company vice-president, ran the final interview, saying Obama "did not stand out in any material way. He seemed like a nice gentleman, smart." Obama got the job and quickly jumped on the very same "traditional path" he had so hoped to avoid.[28]

His studies in political science and international relations at Occidental College and Columbia University had not prepared Obama for work at what he calls a "consulting house to multinational corporations."

The job was not glamorous—the pay and responsibilities were quite low. (Lezere quipped, "I hired him, and let's just say the salary was nowhere near enough to pay off his college debts.") Unlike Addams, however, Obama had little choice but to take this job. He did not have resources to fall back on. His mother was comfortable but not wealthy, and his grandparents were lower-middle-class retirees. So he signed on at Business International, and his routine quickly solidified: "I arrived every day at my mid-Manhattan office and sat at my computer terminal, checking the Reuters machine that blinked bright emerald messages from across the globe." His mother wrote to Alice Dewey that, "He calls it 'working for the enemy' because some of the reports are written for commercial firms that want to invest in those countries."[29]

Divided as he felt, Obama fit right in at Business International. Colleagues recall him as easygoing, hardworking, and even conformist. Save one instance in which Obama brought up the notion of boycotting firms who did business in South Africa, he kept his head down, did his job. There was no railing against "The Man." One possible explanation is that, by the time Obama arrived at Business International, he had cultivated an aura of prestige and elitism. Lezere told an interviewer, "Most people assumed from his bearing that he was a wealthy preppy kid." While he may have felt some discomfort with the ideological ends of business and even a vacuity (there was no socially responsible element to his work), he was able to pass. He fit right in.[30]

At a 1983 Christmas party, Obama met Genevieve Cook. They would live together for a few months in the winter of 1984–85. Cook noted his ambivalence; on March 25, 1984, she wrote that Obama "feels all these people asking him to undo himself, be something he feels he's not, show things to appease other people's projections, regardless of whether they're in him or not." The following week she wrote, "He talked quite a lot about discontent in a quiet sort of way—balancing the tendency to be always the observer, how to effect change, wanting to get past his antipathy to working at B.I." There is a sense here that Obama was trying to find out what the "pioneering role" might be for a black man in the 1980s. In the 1960s it was clear: Get active and force change. But modest, though significant, changes in social structure meant that, in the mid-1980s, it was increasingly possible for an educated black man to pursue paths that had been closed only years before (similarly, Addams benefited from women's activists who opened many paths for her). Still, Obama was not satisfied with the options. As he recalled, "I was trying to raise myself to be a black man in America, and beyond the given of my appearance, no one around me seemed to know what that meant."[31] He was unhappy in his decent, respectable job. He looked around to see how he might move forward in a different way.

This takes us back to the opening of the chapter, when Obama was wandering the streets of Manhattan, facing his own American's Dilemma. Eventually, he just quit his job at Business International. It was December 1984, and he didn't have anything else lined up. "He just said he wanted to do something else," boss Lou Celi remembers:

I told him—like I told many young people then—it's important to have a plan. He just seemed not exactly clear of what he wanted to do. I told him he might be making a mistake, leaving a job when he did not have any plans except a vague notion that he maybe would do some public sector work.[32]

At the same time, Ronald Reagan had just been reelected and declared it was "morning in America." In one sense he was right: The economy *was* improving, but at the expense of some of the poorest Americans. Wall Street was booming, though largely because of a massive restructuring of American labor. In the eyes of many, the Great Society welfare programs of the previous fifteen years had failed. Now images of "welfare queens" and "big government" pervaded public discourse, and politicians like Reagan could insist that individualism and hard work, not public assistance, were what truly turned an economy around. He was, after all, the president who insisted gains at the top would "trickle down." But they didn't seem to be trickling. New York was struggling, with Mayor Ed Koch trying to bring the city back from financial insolvency and a deep racial divide marked by massive disparities in income, wealth, and rates of imprisonment.[33]

Given the widespread racial inequality in New York and across the nation, it should not be surprising that Obama turned to black civil rights organizations as an outlet for his ambivalence. In a 2007 interview, Obama again referenced idol Bob Moses:

> What really inspired me was the civil rights movement. And if you asked me who my role model was at that time, it would probably be Bob Moses, the famous SNCC [Student Nonviolent Coordinating Committee] organizer. . . . Those were the folks I was really inspired by—the John Lewises, the Bob Moseses, the Fannie Lou Hamers, the Ella Bakers.[34]

Obama was quickly offered a position at what he called a "prominent civil rights organization" in New York, but it didn't feel right. The director, a black man, had surrounded himself with the trappings of wealth, and the organization had clear ties to the business world. Obama was particularly cognizant of the board of directors' roster: After the black director's name came ten prominent white businessmen. Obama recalled the conversation as follows:

> "You see?" the director said. "Public-private partnerships. The key to the future. And that's where young people like yourself come in. Educated. Self-assured. Comfortable in boardrooms."

Since the whole point of Obama's search was that he was *not* comfortable in America's boardrooms, he left, unconvinced that community building required a partnership with the private sector. If it was morning in America, Obama was having a hard time waking up. He hadn't liked working in business, but the pressure to jump on the bandwagon of private sector success was ever-present. His ambivalent job search continued.[35]

Obama eventually took a job for the Public Interest Research Group (PIRG) in Harlem. This common move for idealistic college graduates often results with them knocking on neighborhood doors asking for donations. In Obama's case, his job, with an annual salary of less than $10,000, was to increase awareness about recycling among minority students. He volunteered, too, spending a week passing out flyers for an assembly race in Brooklyn. The candidate lost. Obama's first foray into community organizing and politics was a failure: Talking about recycling and handing out leaflets was hardly on par with his civil rights idols (ironically, recall that Addams's own first foray into politics found her picking up garbage in the streets).

To be sure, PIRG was a noble organization, founded by Ralph Nader to combat corporate excess and promote consumer protection, and Obama worked well and hard. Chris Myers, a board member of NYPIRG, gave an interview in which he called the young man "passionate about putting organizing theory into practice." And Eileen Hershenov, Obama's supervisor at NYPIRG, recalls him as "a star— who could make the case to students across the political spectrum." He successfully recruited volunteers and organized a recycling program for college students. But there was no connection to the work; his internal contradictions were unresolved, and he confided to Genevieve he did not find the work fulfilling. In an interview from the White House, Obama recalled that the job "had always felt sort of like a tryout of organizing as opposed to plunging into it in a serious way."[36]

Obama stayed at PIRG for only three months, barely enough time to make a difference or find his stride. In his efforts to resolve his American's Dilemma, the pendulum had clearly swung too far. Now he was "broke, unemployed, eating from a soup can," and considering a return to business, but knew it would not satisfy his yearning to make a difference. How could he reconcile the lure of a good, steady salary in the private sector with his ambitions to make change? Like many college graduates, Obama was again unsure. In his memoir, he writes, "even those with the best of intentions could end up further and further removed from the struggles of those they purported to serve."[37] Who did Obama purport to serve? The answer was unclear.

A way forward emerged from a trip to the New York Public Library. Obama was browsing the new edition of *Community Jobs* and found an interesting ad for a position with the Developing Communities Project (DCP) in Chicago. Obama applied and soon received a call from Gerald Kellman, a DCP organizer and leader of the Calumet Community Religious Conference. Kellman was looking to hire a black man and had profiled Obama based on his name. "Jerry had to hire a black organizer," says Yvonne Lloyd, a South Side resident who worked closely with Kellman. "Black people are very leery when you come into their community and they don't know you," she said. Clearly, South Side neighborhoods, primarily black, would be most receptive to a black organizer.[38]

Kellman had paid "a small fortune" just to place the ad. After he spoke with Obama on the phone, they arranged to meet in person (Kellman was coming to New York to visit family). The interview was aggressive and wide-ranging. Why community organizing? Why not politics? As Kellman recalled, "Obama said he wanted to make fundamental change . . . he wanted to make it from the grassroots and he wanted to learn." In Kellman's view, Obama was not interested in engaging in politics at that time:

> I think that when the question is asked to him, it is, "Why are you interested in doing this? You should be working for Harold [Washington]." And although he says, well, he sent a letter, they didn't respond, if he'd wanted to work in the Washington administration, he certainly could have. And he wasn't interested. He was interested in doing the grassroots kind of thing.

At the end of the interview, Kellman offered him the job, conditional on passing muster with the board of directors. Obama was not on his way to financial stability—he would receive a $10,000 annual salary, though with an additional $2,000 to buy a car.[39] But several weeks later, he was headed to Chicago. And for the first time in quite awhile, he was "awake" and fully engaged with his life.[40]

Obama and Addams arrived in Chicago in different ways. Addams had wealth, so she did not have to worry about room and board or a steady income. Obama, on the other hand, was broke. He had a beat-up old Honda and the promise of about $700 per month in take-home pay. But both were pulled to the city, even "chosen" by it because of their at once unique and similar American's Dilemmas. Chicago offered a social space in which each could work things out, move forward, and experiment. From the White House, Obama summarized:

> I think I had a hunger to shape the world in some way, to make the world a better place that was triggered around the time that I transferred from Occidental to Columbia. So there's a phase, which I wrote about in my first book, where, for whatever reason, a whole bunch of stuff that had been inside me—questions of identity, questions of purpose, questions of, not just race, but also the international nature of my upbringing—all those things started converging in some way. And so there's this period of time when I move to New York and go to Columbia, where I pull in and wrestle with that stuff, and do a lot of writing and a lot of reading and a lot of thinking and a lot of walking through Central Park. And somehow I emerge on the other side of that ready and eager to take a chance in what is a pretty unlikely venture: moving to Chicago and becoming an organizer . . . you know, it's hard to say what exactly prompted that.[41]

CHAPTER SIX

A Big City with Big Problems

When I arrived in Chicago at the age of twenty-four, I didn't know
a single person.

Barack Obama[1]

DRIVING WEST ON INTERSTATE 80, he had to be a bit nervous.
Obama had only been to Chicago once, when he was ten years
old. Much like Jane Addams before him, he moved to Chicago without a clear sense of what he was going to do, let alone how he might
do it. In June 1985 he settled in Hyde Park in the South Side, describing his apartment as "near the University of Chicago, which maintains
a nice mix thanks to the heavy-handed influence of the University.
But generally the dictum holds fast—separate and unequal." It was
a shabby, cheap place on East Fifty-Fourth Street. His neighborhood
was primarily black and poor, with the "nice mix" perhaps referring to
the various neighborhood academics of one sort or another. The apartment also put him close to the West Pullman and Roseland neighborhoods he'd been assigned by Gerald Kellman.[2]

But, in another sense, where he lived was very, very far away from
places like the Altgeld Gardens Public Housing Project where he did
much of his work. Today, the Chicago Housing Authority describes
Altgeld as

> on the border of Chicago and Riverdale, bounded by 130th and 133rd
> Streets and St. Lawrence and Doty Avenues. Expansive green space

and open common areas are just two of the amenities featured in this development, which was built in 1945 for Black war-industry workers during the Second World War.

Obama described it as "a dump—and a place to house poor blacks." It was a series of two-story brick buildings with army-green doors and grimy mock shutters: "Everyone in the area referred to Altgeld as 'the Gardens,' although it wasn't until later that I considered the irony of the name, its evocation of something fresh and well tended—a sanctified earth."[3]

While Addams had settled right into the neighborhood she hoped to help, Obama chose the bohemian and intellectual confines of a University of Chicago neighborhood. No plunking down in public housing for him. This created a distance between the organizer and the community in which he worked. It would be problematic at some points and empowering at others.

Obama was clearly cognizant of the vast divisions between neighborhoods, writing in a 1985 letter that "Chicago's also a town of neighborhoods, and to a much greater degree than NY, the various tribes remain discrete, within their own turf, carving out the various neighborhoods and replicating the feel of their native lands."[4] Obama did not consider these discrete neighborhood divisions to be a good thing; he noticed early on that Kellman's own choice to live apart was unhelpful in his efforts:

> As I listened to him lay out his plans, it occurred to me that he'd made no particular attachments to people or place during his three years in the area, that whatever human warmth or connection he might require came from elsewhere.

By 1988, Obama seemed to regret his own choice to live in Hyde Park:

> People shop in one neighborhood, work in another, send their child to a school across town and go to church someplace other than the

place where they live. Such geographical dispersion creates real problems in building a sense of investment and common purpose in any particular neighborhood.

Still, when not in Washington, Obama continues to live in a much-gentrified Hyde Park to this day.[5]

Upon his arrival in Chicago, Obama also had to be vetted by the principal figures of the Calumet Community Religious Conference (CCRC). Kellman describes the conference's origins:

> We organized it because the Calumet region, which is a bi-state region of Indiana and Illinois, was the largest producer of steel in the world. And those steel mills began to shut, one by one, or go down to skeleton crews, and with them, all the related factories and jobs. So this is an area that had faced enormous economic devastation.

Economic decline drove the erosion of the neighborhoods of the South Side. The city could not afford to invest in them, and the result was social and physical deterioration. Unions, too, were at a low point, fighting both the recession and Reagan. Kellman and others hoped coordination and organization could help fill the gap in institutional capacity.[6]

Notice that nearly one hundred years later, the people of Chicago and its environs were still wrestling with the need to help one another. Despite its particular ideology, nineteenth-century charity organization had been an attempt to avoid overlap and send resources where they were needed. The prevailing sense, in the words of Kellman, was that in 1985 Chicago, "the churches were the only . . . institution that had a big stake in the neighborhood and had any kind of hope of doing something. So it [the Calumet Community Religious Conference] was to organize an organization of churches." Just as in Addams's day, religious organizations were doing most of the on-the-ground helping. Obama said plainly, Chicago was "a big city with big problems."[7]

None of the churches in the area where Obama was to work had the means to contribute to anything resembling a working budget. And there was tension between the needs of the urban and suburban parishes; they were, in Kellman's words, "unequally yoked." He decided to split the urban parishes into a separate group, which he named the Developing Communities Project (DCP): "[T]he CCRC applied for a grant from the National Conference of Catholic Bishops to fund work in this specific area by a separate smaller organization. . . . The DCP hired Obama."[8]

Obama's office was in the Holy Rosary Church, a Catholic Roseland neighborhood parish originally created for Chicago's "nineteenth-century blacks"—the Irish. One of the first events Obama attended in Chicago was a celebration of a $500,000 grant from the Catholic Church to fund a CCRC jobs program. Cardinal Bernadin was the keynote speaker, and nearly a thousand people attended. Where Addams had funded her efforts from personal wealth and gifts from a few wealthy individuals, Obama's efforts were supported, in large part, by funds from a religious institution. It appears resources for creative efforts—and connections to community—can come from a variety of sources.[9]

Neither Kellman nor Obama looked to business for funding. Obama had soured on corporations after leaving Business International, and the CCRC was charged with helping laid-off workers. Obama recalled a conversation with Kellman (whom he calls "Marty" in his biography) on their way to the jobs program event:

> "It's going to take a while to rebuild manufacturing out here," he said. "Ten years, minimum. But once we get the unions involved, we'll have a base to negotiate from. In the meantime, we just need to stop the hemorrhage and give people some short-term victories. Something to show people how much power they have once they stop fighting each other and start going after the real enemy." "And

who's that?" Marty shrugged. "The investment bankers. The politicians. The fat cat lobbyists."[10]

The very people Obama had walked away from in New York. He had
found a home.

At a jobs program event, Obama began to make connections
and develop resources of his own. Though he was unaware that each
had been part of approving his hire, Obama met Loretta Augustine
and Yvonne Lloyd of the CCRC and the DCP board. They were
both struck with how young Obama looked, and he was quick to
admit he had little idea how to begin his work. As it turned out,
this casual conversation was still part of Obama's interview: Lloyd
and Augustine asked a number of pointed questions and came away
quite pleased with the new black organizer.[11] He had earned their
seal of approval.

In the days following, the women took him on a tour of the Gardens' derelict housing and visited Our Lady of the Gardens, at the
time Chicago's poorest Catholic Church. The archdiocese could not
even get a priest to take a post there in the 1970s and 80s. At the
church, Lloyd and Augustine were struck by a seemingly small event:
Obama was offered a piece of pie by a nun who was infamous for terrible cooking. He ate it with gusto. Maybe it wasn't that bad? More
likely, Obama already had an intuitive feel for respect and connection
with others.[12]

Obama had never really had a mentor before this time. He had
kept to himself. But things changed in Chicago. Much like Addams,
who was nurtured and challenged by the advice and model of Julia
Lathrop and Florence Kelley, Obama surrounded himself with excellent teachers. Kellman's early guidance is notable. Biographer David
Remnick goes so far as to say "in the formation of Obama's ideas
about community, effective political change, storytelling, and form-
ing relationships, Kellman may well have played the most influential

role in Obama's life outside of his family." In addition, Lloyd and Augustine taught him of the importance of black women in bringing about change:

> Traditionally, community organizing has drawn support from women, who due to tradition and social discrimination had the time and the inclination to participate in what remains an essentially voluntary activity. Today the majority of women in the black community work full time, many are the sole parent, and all have to split themselves between work, raising children, running a household and maintaining some semblance of a personal life.[13]

These guides, in particular, pushed Obama to network and connect. Kellman urged him to make learning what the community was all about his top priority in the first few months. "And he did that," Kellman recalled,

> through a massive number of interviews, what we would call one-on-one interviews, listening to people and trying to make sense of it. This was the point of the individual meetings with community members. When that was all finished, he was ready, you know, with some advice from myself and others who had done this work a long time, to try to invite those people to come together to do something.[14]

Chicago was known to be suspicious of outsiders (it wasn't that long since charity workers had been sending non-residents away with one-way train tickets). Writers on Chicago organizing and politics often invoke the famous line, "We don't want nobody nobody sent" to convey the Chicago attitude. Pastors of Protestant churches in the South Side were particularly wary of Obama, seen to represent the Catholics. He was too young to know anything, wasn't from Chicago, and didn't even belong to a church in the city.

This distrust was a problem. The DCP and Obama needed to bring more community leaders into the group, especially Protestant leaders. In Kellman's words, Obama had

> to take people who did not necessarily agree on things, who might even dislike each other, and get them to work together and take people who had given up hope of anything changing and get them to the point that they were willing to, one more time, try it again to have enough hope and confidence in him to get involved one more time.[15]

As a Chicago outsider and, by employment, a religious outsider, Obama had quite a task ahead of him. Recall that Addams was also challenged for her obvious outsider status. She lived in a fancy house, wore nice clothes, and was clearly well-to-do. "Why would she want to live here?" the neighbors wondered. "What's her game?" She had to work through children to make connections to adults. Obama, on the other hand, had long-since cultivated his "twoness"—a dual persona that put him as much at ease in the poor neighborhoods of Chicago as in the elite halls of Columbia. As he had learned in Indonesia and perfected in Hawaii, California, and New York, Obama could be at once inside and outside the group. He did not stand out like Addams had. Instead, he carefully maintained some distances and, when needed, changed to fit in. For example, Obama began his DCP work by wearing a uniform of khakis, a shirt, and tie. Linda Randle, a community member who worked closely with Obama on public housing issues, chided him: "Wear jeans. No one's going to open the door if you look like a public aid caseworker."[16]

No problem. As Kellman put it, "He had so much learning to do about how people live their lives, but he learned almost effortlessly. He had gifts. He was comfortable with people and talked easily with people." This ease was an advantage. Obama was soon meeting in what Kellman called "one-on-ones" with people who lived in the neighborhood and priests who might convince their parishes to join the DCP. This was textbook Saul Alinsky organizing.[17]

In fact, Alinsky had appeared on the Chicago scene just as Jane Addams left (she died in 1935). Along with Joseph Meeghan, Alinsky created the Back of the Yards Council to organize the Union Stock Yards made infamous in Upton Sinclair's *The Jungle.* He brought people together and empowered them to make significant change in their neighborhood. With this effort, Alinsky became an organizing star and began a successful career that spanned three decades. He created the Industrial Areas Foundation as a vehicle for his methods, which he put to work across the country. The CCRC's main organizers—Kellman, Gregory Galuzzo, and Mike Kruglik—all learned their craft through the Industrial Areas Foundation and passed their knowledge on to Obama. Alinsky's method—summarized in his book *Rules for Radicals,* which Obama had read—boils down to developing power relations with the goal of creating a kind of "power to" in each community. But each community has unique problems, so organization starts with investigation. What are the community's needs? What is its capacity? Who might be able to lead? Alinsky put it in radical, violent terms:

> The organizer dedicated to changing the life of a particular community must first rub raw the resentments of the people of the community; fan the latent hostilities of many of the people to the point of overt expression. He must search out controversy and issues, rather than avoid them, for unless there is controversy people are not concerned enough to act.[18]

The links between Tolstoy, Addams, Alinsky, and Obama create a sort of biblical lineage. But at the end of the day, Obama appears to have been more Addams than Alinsky. Like Addams, he spent a lot of time listening.

According to Kellman, they would meet with six or seven people each day, talking about their views of the community. They would ask the residents to define their challenges, rather than make a clumsy attempt at an outsider's diagnosis, much like Addams one hundred years earlier. Kellman calls Obama a "naturally good listener" who embraced his ignorance in these one-on-ones. Dan Lee, a church deacon and DCP leader, recalled Obama saying early on, "I know you all think I'm a young whippersnapper. Let me set your fears to rest. We're going to learn together." Obama was soon out on his own, spending his time "talking to people, day after day." Obama said the sit-downs "taught me a lot about listening to people as opposed to coming in with a predetermined agenda."[19]

His openness led to connections. Reverend Alvin Love recalled when Obama came to his office at the Lilydale First Baptist Church in 1985. Strangers came to see Love all the time, but this man was different. Obama did not have an apparent agenda; he just wanted to listen. Love recalled: "He asked what I wanted to see get done and what was important in this neighborhood." Love was hooked. He joined the DCP, eventually becoming its president.[20]

Obama was gaining insight with every meeting. At the close of each day, he would take his notes, usually written on note cards, and compile them, looking for the connections, the shared barriers. "He was linking narrative to community, to power." In Kellman's view, this work naturally led to Obama turning the gaze inward. Who was Barack Obama? "It was a very significant period of growth, I think, for him, his two years in Chicago." Obama kept a record of his experiences in a journal and confided to Kellman that eventually he might want to become a novelist. His ascetic lifestyle did nothing to disabuse others of this notion. He was like a cliché of the American writer, reading and writing constantly, living alone, barely scraping by, all the while looking for inspiration in stories. Kellman summed it up well:

You spend time as an organizer going from one person to another doing interviews. You're listening for story, because story communicates more about a person than simply facts. When people share their story, they get a different sense of themselves, and you get a different sense of them. Barack did that very well. One of the remarkable things is how well he listens to people who are opposed to him.[21]

The short stories Obama wrote at night were an extension of his field notes, a creative site for him to work through his experiences. Occasionally he shared his stories with friends and coworkers. Mike Kruglik, a fellow CCRC member and seasoned trainer in community organizing, remembered years later:

> They were about the streets of the South Side of Chicago, what they looked and felt like to him, the dreariness of the landscape in winter. One was about a pastor who is overwhelmed by his problems but he still wants to build a strong congregation and take care of himself, too. Something shines through the pastor's spirit that allows him to do that. The stories were very descriptive. At first, I wondered, how does he have the energy to do all this? I figured he must have copied it somehow from someone. But they were about people I knew.[22]

The summation of all of these intensive experiences did not come easily, though:

> I tossed my third-week report onto [Kellman's] desk and took a seat as he read it through. "Not bad," he said when he was finished. "Not bad?" "Yeah, not bad. You're starting to listen. But it's still too abstract . . . like you're taking a survey or something. If you want to organize people, you need to steer away from the peripheral stuff and go towards people's centers. The stuff that makes them tick. Otherwise, you'll never form the relationships you need to get them involved.[23]

Obama accused Kellman of being too cold and calculating, but Kellman retorted, essentially, "I'm not a poet, Barack. I'm an organizer." Upon reflection, Obama grudgingly conceded Kellman's point: "Later,

I had to admit that [Kellman] was right. I still had no idea how I might translate what I was hearing into action."[24]

The fact that Obama was considering what difference his writing might make for people's lives is vintage Addams. As with other pragmatists of her time, Addams was focused on the "cash-value" of her efforts. What's the point of putting words on a page if it doesn't lead to something? The people he worked with knew what the issues were but did not know how to fix things. Through writing, Obama's sense of the community emerged. He didn't yet have solutions.

So he tried to improve. Obama was asking questions, listening to the answers, and writing up his conclusions, very much in the "Chicago School" tradition of chronicling social problems. As Yvonne Lloyd put it, "We knew what was wrong in the community but we didn't know how to get something done about it." Addams and her fellow residents of Hull-House had engaged in one of the first mappings of social problems in the city, while Obama was mirroring ethnographers like Robert Park or even Alinsky.[25]

Obama was very, very good at drawing out people's stories. Perhaps it was the influence of his mother, the anthropologist, or simply his life experience as a cultural omnivore. In any event, he had a knack. He began training others at workshops sponsored by the Gamaliel Foundation. Participants would practice one-on-ones in front of a room full of people. One observer noted that Obama "was great at it because he actually cared about people and he was unafraid to share about himself. It's creating a safe environment for somebody else to share. . . . There were a handful of people who had that ability, but he was by far the youngest who could do it."[26]

Still, at times there was a bit of the Alinsky doggedness in how Obama engaged with others. Kruglik remembers having coffee with Obama when a beggar approached. Obama was stern, asking, "Now young man, is that really what you want to be about? I mean, come on, don't you want to be better than that? Let's get yourself together." This is reminiscent the college days when Obama admonished his friend at Occidental to be more empathetic, to put herself in the other's shoes. Before Obama had ever read Alinsky, he was agitating others. Addams had a lighter touch, using meetings with neighbors to develop relationships that would lead to trust and sharing of confidences. Obama would move right to the heart of things, asking probing and personal questions. But in his own way, he positioned himself, like Addams, as part of a potential solution. In Kruglik's view, Obama was one of the best organizers he had ever worked with.[27]

Obama visited a number of union halls, and listened to story after story of frustration and desperation. He spoke with steelworkers who had lost their jobs and their way. The CCRC had formed, in large part, to address such challenges, but it was easier said than done. Obama acted as a connector, putting them in touch with the Mayor's Office of Employment and Training (MET), where they could receive new training. A few found work as computer programmers, but many wound up working low-wage jobs making paint at the Sherwin Williams plant or candy at the Brach's factory.[28] It wasn't enough.

Obama's training had taught him to listen, listen some more, then reflect. But what about taking action? The CCRC's $500,000 jobs grant had been used to create the Regional Employment Network. But the benefits went mostly to suburban workers with skills that lent themselves to retraining. The blacks on the South Side got next to nothing; MET was no help to Obama's community. Those things it *could* do—counseling and training—were out of reach, anyway: Its closest office was in a white neighborhood, a two-change, one-hour bus trip from the South Side. With his constituents bemoaning the absence of even basic literacy, the hopelessness was palpable.[29]

This was Obama's first real creative moment on the job. His ideas emerged, like Addams, out of relations with the people he was trying to help. They needed jobs, particularly those requiring little in the way of specialized skills or education. Bringing the MET into the South Side made sense. Obama contacted Maria Cerda, the director of the MET, and invited her to the Our Lady of the Gardens church. It was packed for Cerda's visit, a rowdy affair (in part because of Obama's influence). Cerda tried to give a canned speech until Loretta Augustine, prepped by Obama, steered the conversation toward jobs training in the neighborhood. Things became contentious. Obama shouted, "Let Loretta speak!" and the entire audience echoed his call. Cerda was convinced to come for another meeting. Six months later, MET put a jobs center in Roseland, in an empty department store building. This center was much, much closer to Altgeld's needy. Obama had gotten creative, and it paid off: He succeeded in guiding the community to modify a barrier.[30]

What's more, Mayor Washington attended the official ribbon-cutting ceremony at the Roseland MET center. Augustine was tasked with cornering the mayor to let him know more about the DCP and invite him to an event later in the year. Not only was she successful, but the MET center got off to a fine start. It began a program for children—much like Hull-House—at Our Lady of the Gardens. It also helped connect some locals with the training they would need to get good jobs. And it was symbolically important: It was concrete evidence that Obama and the DCP could get things done and connect with the powers that be.[31]

Though they held a party for the jobs grant and a ribbon cutting for the new MET center, Obama and the DCP were careful not to stick with splashy events. In one instance, DCP members held their meeting on a street corner, so that people in the neighborhood would come out to see what was going on. It worked, and the DCP had a chance to talk to people about what could be done to make the neighborhood better. They even managed to catch the eye of Emil Jones, the local state senator, who, like the others, came out of his nearby home to see what was going on in the street.[32]

Obama was emboldened and set his sights on a bigger target—the Chicago Housing Authority (CHA). A few stories about asbestos in public housing in the South Side had made it back to the DCP. One particular story, recalled Kellman, enraged people:

> There was a housing project where he had found out that asbestos was being removed from the manager's office. Now the manager's office was just another apartment. So if there was asbestos in the manager's office, then it was everywhere in the housing project. And the Chicago Housing Authority was just going to leave it there.

Obama saw this story as a possible fulcrum to leverage action. In spreading the word about the problem, he found it hard to gain traction; community members were more focused on the day-to-day struggles of finding jobs and paying bills. They didn't have time to care about the environment. But Obama framed the issue as one of justice—nobody cares about whether or not blacks on the South Side are going to get cancer and die, but if this happened in the Loop, you can be sure it would be taken care of right away. It resonated, and Obama was able to galvanize support to bring pressure to bear on the Chicago Housing Authority.[33]

Obama taught community members the skills they needed to effect change, from event planning to strategies for talking to politicians and the media. As Kellman remembers,

> From that point on, he was their coach. It's hard for people to conceive that his job was not to be on camera, not to have his picture in the newspaper, when he's probably the most photographed person in the world right now. But in those days, it was his job to help *them* get on camera. You know, it was their community, and he was their coach. He was in the background. He was taking people who, because of income, because of education, had no experience working with large corporations and challenging them or government, and didn't have the basic public skills that some other people might have. So from scratch, he needed to work with them on how to organize a

meeting, how to talk to a powerful person, how to negotiate, how to talk to the news media, how to get the news media to cover you, how to do research to find out the nature of the problem.[34]

Even with Obama's coaching, it was a hard slog. Obama recalled the day when they planned to bring a group to the CHA offices to make their demands in person:

> I counted only eight heads in the yellow bus parked in front of the school. Bernadette and I stood in the parking lot trying to recruit other parents as they came to pick up their children. They said they had doctors' appointments or couldn't find baby-sitters. Some didn't bother with excuses, walking past us as if we were panhandlers. When Angela, Mona, and Shirley arrived to see how things were shaping up, I insisted they ride with us to lend moral support. Everyone looked depressed, everyone except Tyrone and Jewel, who were busy making faces at Mr. Lucas, the only father in the group. Dr. Collier came up beside me. "I guess this is it," I said. "Better than I expected," she said. "Obama's Army." "Right." "Good luck," she said, and clapped me on the back.[35]

Despite Obama's lackluster recollection, the trip was fairly successful. Obama and his team, along with several reporters, laid siege to the Chicago Housing Authority director's office for several hours. The director never appeared, but his staff indicated he would come down to Altgeld. When he eventually made the visit, it was a disaster. He was almost two hours late, and then bobbed and weaved, avoiding direct answers to questions about what the Housing Authority was going to do. "The CHA was going to wait until test results were in, then decide what to do," the director said. The meeting dissolved into chaos, and angry community members mobbed the director's car as he drove away. But the pressure made a difference in real terms. The Chicago Housing Authority asked for $8.9 million from the federal government and began a larger asbestos abatement program in the buildings. Soon, there were workers taking care of the worst problem areas.[36]

Obama became a dynamo, organizing multiple issues at the same time, all the while coaching community leaders on how to take the initiative. It was a time of "constant action," Kellman says. Obama was feeding off the energy that came from helping others:

> I've learned to care for them very much and want to do every-
> thing I can for them. It's tough, though. . . . But about 5% of the
> time, you see something happen—a shy housewife standing up to
> a bumbling official, or the sudden sound of hope in the voice of a
> grizzled old man—that gives a hint of the possibilities, of people
> taking hold of their lives, working together to bring about a small
> justice. And it's that possibility that keeps you going through all
> the trenchwork.[37]

In addition to environment and jobs, Obama also pushed the issue of school reform. In the Illinois capital city of Springfield, there was a move to distribute power to the local level by establishing parental school councils. Chicago Democrats opposed this move—it wasn't under their control and might encourage political organizing out of step with their goals. Obama was not cowed by the Chicago politicians; his community wanted the change. He bused a group of South Side parents to Springfield, with each having been assigned a legislator to personally lobby. It is hard to tell if these efforts made the difference, but the bill passed. No less important was the jubilation and empowerment the parents felt on the ride home. One remembered that the group felt "energized, like we could do anything."[38]

This energy helped fuel a related program, initiated by Obama, to keep South Side kids from becoming high school dropouts. It was called the Career Education Network and aimed to find tutors to spend time with kids after school working on classroom skills as well as work and life skills. They would start in four South Side schools. Rather than work over and against city officials, this time Obama tried to gain the support of Mayor Washington's office. He set up a meeting with the mayor's education advisor. This was a pivotal moment. Obama had long had Harold Washington on his mind, and he knew that there was value in having the mayor's support (just as Addams and the Chicago Bureau of Charities worked to get the mayor's office to provide financial support to their efforts).[39]

The meeting was a practical success for the DCP, but a political (and perhaps personal) failure for Obama. Perhaps the mayor's office was still smarting from the loss of control over its schools following the recent Springfield vote, but the advisor and Obama did not see eye-to-eye. The two argued, and the advisor reportedly told a colleague "[Obama] doesn't know shit about Roseland or Chicago."

Undeterred, Obama contacted the state senator, Emil Jones, who had once found the DCP meeting on his block. That earlier connection facilitated Obama's request for help, and Jones was able to shepherd a DCP proposal through the legislature. The DCP was awarded just $150,000 of the $500,000 it requested, but it was a success. Career Education Network now had funding, and the DCP was able to pay for the salaries of a director, four tutors, and rental space in a local church. The money made a difference in the everyday lives of kids in the DCP's core community, but there was not enough funding to build the network portion of the project.[40]

As always, money was often needed to make change. All this work envisioned by Obama required funding, and he was beginning to believe community leaders could convince the elite established organizations of Chicago philanthropy—the Joyce Foundation, the Woods Charitable Fund, and the Wiebolt Foundation, to name a few—to give to the DCP. Though it was a turning point, Obama did not seem to have any struggles with the idea of asking for help from what he called the mainstream. Perhaps he saw it as a sort of alchemy that turned bad money into good deeds. He coached DCP representatives going into meetings, even driving them there, and the appeals worked. The DCP remained financially solvent.[41]

It is easy to overstate the impact and success of what Obama did in Chicago. Obama was hardly the only Chicago organizer, and he was working on just a few of the many issues affecting South Siders. Many of the programs and partnerships were short-lived. But close analysis does not support the argument some have made that Obama's heart wasn't really in it, that he was always looking toward bigger and better things. In an era of welfare state retrenchment under Ronald Reagan, rhetoric was particularly targeted at poor urban blacks. That Obama worked to find help for people who were being derided in the national media as "welfare queens" and "the problem" with America is absolutely significant.

Most of Obama's failures came down to a lack of funds or structural shifts in employment beyond his control. The MET job-training program shut down after three years. "I do know that we got some training done," Alvin Love said. "But I don't know how many people really got new jobs." There simply weren't jobs. The asbestos abatement program also ran out of funds. Over twenty years later, some residents of Altgeld and the other housing projects still had asbestos problems.[42]

There was also a meeting Obama tried to organize between police and community members that, in retrospect, reminds one of the Hull-House's Diet Kitchen. Obama had been learning in his one-on-ones about gang violence and how it directly affected people. As he put it later: "My ears perked up; this sounded like self-interest." A woman—Obama calls her Ruby Styles in his memoir—brought a particularly poignant tale to Obama's attention. Her son's close friend had been shot and seriously injured. Now Ruby was worried about her son's safety, and she introduced Obama to other parents with similar concerns. Obama thought the community and the police needed to start working together, but before he contacted the local district commander, one enthusiastic parent suggested first connecting with the pastor of the Baptist church near to where the most recent shooting had occurred. Obama contacted the pastor, Reverend Reynolds, and Obama was invited to an upcoming meeting of a group of local ministers. What an opportunity! He could galvanize community support through the churches, get some traction, and really push for some meaningful change.[43]

It did not go as planned. Obama showed up at the church's conference room and made his presentation to a group of black ministers. Gang violence was increasing, community members wanted to start a dialogue with the police, and it would be helpful if the ministers would spread the word. Cooperation could develop into a partnership on a host of other issues, including job creation and school improvement. Rather than his usual approach—listen first, ask questions, listen some more—Obama was telling them how it was. They already knew. As Obama was wrapping up, a latecomer—"Reverend Smalls"—arrived. Reverend Reynolds quickly brought Smalls up to speed, and everything went sideways.[44]

Smalls began to interrogate Obama, asking if he was working with the Catholics, and making clear that he had already told Kellman he was not interested in a partnership. Smalls pulled no punches:

> . . . the last thing we need is to join up with a bunch of white money and Catholic churches and Jewish organizers to solve our problems. They're not interested in us. Shoot, the archdiocese in this city is run by stone-cold racists. Always has been. White folks come in here thinking they know what's best for us, hiring a buncha high-talking college-educated brothers like yourself who don't know no better, and all they want to do is take over. It's all a political thing, and that's not what this group here is about.[45]

Obama tried to press on, touting the benefits of multifaith community partnerships, but Smalls was undeterred:

> "You don't understand," [Smalls] said. "Things have changed with
> the new mayor. I've known the district police commander since he
> was a beat cop. The aldermen in this area are all committed to black
> empowerment. Why we need to be protesting and carrying on at our
> own people? Anybody sitting around this table got a direct line to
> City Hall. Fred, didn't you just talk to the alderman about getting
> that permit for your parking lot?" The rest of the room had grown
> quiet. Reverend Reynolds cleared his throat. "The man's new around
> here, Charles. He's just trying to help." Reverend Smalls smiled and
> patted me on the shoulder. "Don't misunderstand me now. Like I
> said, I know you mean well. We need some young blood to help out
> with the cause. All I'm saying is that right now you're on the wrong
> side of the battle."[46]

The Chicago Machine still channeled politics, and the message was
clear: Even with Mayor Washington in power, you did *not* go outside
the lines.

To Obama's credit, he left with his resolve intact. He organized the
community–police meeting:

> We went forward with our police meeting, which proved a small di-
> saster. Only thirteen people showed up, scattered across rows of empty
> chairs. The district commander canceled on us, sending a community
> relations officer instead. Every few minutes an older couple walked in
> looking for the Bingo game. I spent most of the evening directing this
> wayward traffic upstairs, while Ruby sat glumly onstage, listening to
> the policeman lecture about the need for parental discipline.[47]

Obama's experimental efforts to gain traction on the issue of gang violence had merely resulted in a dressing-down by a local minister and a
classroom-style lecture by a public relations functionary.

Perhaps these particular failures are made more obvious by the fact that Obama was trying to directly change large-scale, structural issues rather than everyday concerns like laundry, showers, and childcare. As a student of Alinsky, he knew that a radical response that overturned existing structures was the way to make real change. He was unwilling to mess around at the margins.

As a result of Obama's choice not to live in the neighborhood in which he worked, it can also be argued that he did not know much about day-to-day ups and downs in his constituents' lives. Alinsky's method asked Obama to be a coach, but it did not preclude him from being a neighbor. His choice to remain distant kept him from bolstering his failures with a multitude of smaller, local victories, in which the life of perhaps just one person might be slightly altered. It was at times an all-or-nothing approach. Obama later recalled a growing feeling that the problems he was working on were not local, but of a much larger scale: "People were still poor, kids were out on the corner selling drugs, schools weren't working." He just couldn't seem to make a lasting difference, and it was frustrating.[48]

His frustration resulted in a conscious effort to move away from the Alinsky approach, as evidenced in remarks he made at a later event sponsored by the Woods Charitable Fund in 1989:

> I think Alinsky to some extent may not have emphasized this, but I think the unions that Alinsky saw—I think [Civil Rights leader] John L. Lewis understood that he was building a culture. When you look at what's happened to union organizing, one of the losses has been that sense of building a culture, of building up stories and getting people to reflect on what their lives mean and how people in the neighborhood can be heroes, and how they are part of a larger force. That got shoved to the side. . . . [Young blacks] are not necessarily going to town hall meetings, and they are not going to pick

up Reveille for Radicals. They are going to see the Spike Lee film, or they are going to listen to the rap group.[49]

The ideas he had picked up on the ground endured. He went on, summarizing what his past five years had been all about:

> In theory, community organizing provides a way to merge various strategies for neighborhood empowerment. Organizing begins with the premise that (1) the problems facing inner-city communities do not result from a lack of effective solutions, but from a lack of power to implement these solutions; (2) that the only way for communities to build long-term power is by organizing people and money around a common vision; and (3) that a viable organization can only be achieved if a broadly based indigenous leadership and not one or two charismatic leaders can knit together the diverse interests of their local institutions.[50]

Above all, Obama believed in the kind of social growth that Addams had generated in Chicago so many years before:

> Organizing teaches as nothing else does the beauty and strength of everyday people. Through the songs of the church and the talk on the stoops, through the hundreds of individual stories of coming up from the South and finding any job that would pay, of raising families on threadbare budgets, of losing some children to drugs and watching others earn degrees and land jobs their parents could never aspire to it is through these stories and songs of dashed hopes and powers of endurance, of ugliness and strife, subtlety and laughter, that organizers can shape a sense of community not only for others, but for themselves.[51]

The idea of a building up a community and creating a larger force, what Alinsky and Addams would call the "power to" in a neighbor-

hood, was elusive. But the gradual unraveling of Obama's work with
the DCP was not just about methods. In fact, Obama had not completely given up on Alinsky's' method, as evidenced by his attendance
at a two-week training program in Los Angeles, sponsored by the
Industrial Areas Foundation, which had been founded by Alinsky.
The unraveling and disconnecting was partly a function of Obama's
ambivalence. The question of how Obama fit in, what path he should
follow, was still not completely clear to him, at least in the eyes of
Kellman, who observed:

> And certainly he's figuring out how he proceeds with this life with all
> his diversity. I mean, Barack not only is racially diverse, but he's able
> to hold different ideas together. He's a person who does very well
> with difference in holding it together. But the world doesn't always
> do as well as he does. And so where does he fit in?[52]

The bloom was also off the political rose for Obama. In November
1987, Mayor Washington died from a heart attack. It was a devastating
blow for Chicago blacks: "Everywhere black people appeared dazed,
stricken, uncertain of direction, frightened of the future."[53] An old
friend and schoolmate from Punahou visited for a few days in Chicago, shortly after Washington's death. Obama seemed discouraged
as he returned from one of his community listening sessions, telling
the friend: "I just can't get things done here without a law degree. . . .
I've got to get a law degree to do anything against these guys because
they've got their little loopholes and this and that. A law degree—
that's the only way to work against these guys." But the plan, such as
it was, did not yet involve becoming a politician himself: "I was somewhat disdainful of politics. I was much more interested in mobilizing
people to hold politicians accountable."[54]

Obama would work as an organizer at DCP from June 1985 to
May 1988. Why he left is a complicated question, but the simple an-

swer is that he was stuck again. A chance to be creative through community organizing had brought him from New York to the South Side of Chicago, but as is often the case, another dilemma appeared. The challenges faced by the communities served by the DCP were too big to tackle. Obama was discouraged. As to his own future, it seemed graduate education was the key to unlocking doors. Maybe he could be more effective with more training, particularly in the law. As Kellman described it:

> The only option left to him is the option that he has gifts for, which is he's just stronger in a larger arena. He's weaker in that small arena. He's not weak one on one, but the more self-interested and narrow things become, the more he has to turn himself inside out in order to make that appeal. And he simply wasn't good at it.[55]

These thoughts were reinforced by people like Al Raby, a close political advisor to Harold Washington and director of Chicago's Human Rights Department. Raby saw potential in Obama and took him under his wing. He introduced Obama to elite liberals of Chicago, people like Jacky Grimshaw, who then ran Chicago's Office of Intergovernmental Affairs; Stephen Perkins, of the Center for Neighborhood Technology; and John McKnight, a professor at Northwestern University.[56] Obama talked with them about his future plans, getting their perspectives on how to move forward. His growing connections became an impetus for change—and he knew he needed more of these connections to be more effective. Kellman says: "[Obama] didn't have the experience of connectedness to the levels of public policy and academia and government that other people might have had. And to do that, he needed to connect with one of the major universities."[57] Addams had much the same experience, but her ties had grounded her in Chicago. Obama could not see a way to scale up his efforts while continuing at the DCP.

Obama was frank: Big changes would not come from working at the community level. Kellman recalled one particular conversation in which they discussed, in his words, that

> community organizing changes small issues in people's lives, and we transform people's lives in terms of teaching them skills and giving them hope they didn't have before. But it structurally was not going to change racial discrimination. It was not going to change poverty in the United States. There simply would not be enough power there. That would only come through electoral politics. And that's what he said to me when he said he was going to leave. That was one of the reasons for leaving organizing. But I did not see that he'd go in that direction until he told me.[58]

Obama applied for admission to Harvard Law for the 1988 fall semester. Raby wrote one of his recommendation letters. However, to frame Obama's decision to leave Chicago as purely driven by a desire to make a larger difference would be to ignore his internal dilemmas:

> I was a little troubled about the notion of going off to Harvard. I thought that maybe I was betraying my ideals and not living up to my values. I was feeling guilty. And this pastor friend of mine, who was an older gentleman, he had been in the Civil Rights struggles for a long time. I went to talk to him. And he said, "Go. Go to Harvard. It'll be good for you. You'll learn a lot." He said, "But one thing, don't let Harvard change you. Don't let Harvard change you." And I didn't know exactly what he meant, "Don't let Harvard change you." Because he knew that I didn't come from the streets of Chicago. He didn't mean, "Don't let Harvard educate you." He didn't mean that, "You're not going to meet new people and get new ideas." I think what he meant was, "Don't forget the larger story that you're a part of." He also meant, "Don't misplace your dreams."[59]

Obama still heard the siren song of the corporate world, but the lure of Harvard, his father's alma mater, was similarly strong. Kellman remembers a conference the two attended at the Harvard Divinity School in 1988. Obama had just found out he was accepted into the law school's fall class, and he broke the news to Kellman:

> He was just getting to know his father's biography in a more detailed way. I mean, his mom really wasn't in touch with his father; there was nobody giving that information. But his half-brother and half-sibs were beginning to come over to the States and to Europe to go to—and then to the States to visit—to go to graduate school from Kenya, and so he's getting the story. And the story as he understood it was that his dad had been overly idealistic and not practical. They had fallen on the outside of the government in Kenya. And not only had he been ineffective at dealing with his own ideals, but he ended up impractical and destitute financially. And although Barack didn't have much interest in wealth, he had a strong interest in having a secure income to marry and raise a family. He did not want to follow in his father's footsteps. He wanted to be more practical in his choices and more practical in terms of how he might bring change to the country. And so his perception of who his father was figured in that.[60]

It would take a very serious effort to pull off the balancing act required to make *enough* money to satisfy his needs, while avoiding the trap of the corporate sellout. It was a bittersweet moment when Obama received his Harvard Law acceptance:

> The letter came with a thick packet of information. It reminded me of the packet I'd received from Punahou that summer fourteen years earlier. I remembered how Gramps had stayed up the whole night reading from the catalog about music lessons and advanced placement courses, glee clubs and baccalaureates; how he had waved that catalog and told me it would be my meal ticket, that the contacts

I made at a school like Punahou would last me a lifetime, that I would move in charmed circles and have all the opportunities that he'd never had. I remembered how, at the end of the evening, he had smiled and tousled my hair. . . . And I had smiled back at him, pretending to understand but actually wishing I was still in Indonesia running barefoot along a paddy field, with my feet sinking into the cool, wet mud, part of a chain of other brown boys chasing after a tattered kite. I felt something like that now.[61]

Several months later, Obama packed his bags and was off to Boston.

CHAPTER SEVEN

Balancing a Hard Head
with a Big Heart

I always thought that the compromises involved in politics
probably didn't suit me, and that I'd rather just go out there on my
own, helping poor people and helping folks in need.

Barack Obama[1]

A S OBAMA WALKED through Harvard Yard for the first time as a
student, he must have felt a sense of satisfaction. Who wouldn't
have? It was the best university in the world. His father had studied
there. In fact, the legacy of his father was very much on his mind as
he began classes in the fall of 1988. That summer, after concluding his
work for the DCP, Obama had taken a trip to Kenya to visit his family.[2]

Making the rounds, Obama found that his family members did not
quite understand his descriptions of his work in Chicago as a "community organizer." He would explain that he was to attend Harvard
in the fall. This they understood. Obama recalled one relative's comment: "Your father studied at this school, Harvard. You will make us
all proud, just like him." In another visit, he recounts: "The house was
sparsely furnished—a few wooden chairs, a coffee table, a worn couch.
On the walls were various family artifacts: the Old Man's Harvard di-
ploma; photographs of him and of Omar, the uncle who had left for
America twenty-five years ago and had never come back." Harvard
loomed large in Kenya. Obama was now the standard bearer of success
in his African family's eyes.

He was so moved by the tangible connections to his father and family that when visiting his grandmother, he stepped outside the house, overcome:

> I sat between the two graves and wept. When my tears were finally spent, I felt a calmness wash over me. I felt the circle finally close. I realized that who I was, what I cared about, was no longer just a matter of intellect or obligation, no longer a construct of words. I saw that my life in America—the black life, the white life, the sense of abandonment I'd felt as a boy, the frustration and hope I'd witnessed in Chicago—all of it was connected with this small plot of earth an ocean away, connected by more than the accident of a name or the color of my skin. The pain I felt was my father's pain.[3]

If this was a moment of freedom, the familiar pull of contradictions returned as he traveled, particularly when he was confronted with vast inequality. On a visit to see Ruth, his father's third wife, Obama became uncomfortable with the obvious economic disparities between neighborhoods in Kenya, describing Ruth's neighborhood, the Westlands, as "an enclave of expensive homes set off by wide lawns and well-tended hedges, each one with a sentry post manned by brown-uniformed guards." It stood in stark contrast to the poorer neighborhoods where other family members lived. He was also pressured into giving money to his Aunt Sarah. She made a direct appeal: "I reached for my wallet and felt the eyes of both aunts as I counted out the money I had on me—perhaps thirty dollars' worth of shillings. I pressed them into Sarah's dry, chapped hands, and she quickly slipped the money down the front of her blouse before clutching my hand again." It was a complicated visit, to be sure. His own relative material success was apparent, but his responsibilities were not. His privilege was likely an uncomfortable mantle. His twoness was again a burden.[4]

If Obama had any kind of home, it was in Chicago. He even made a quick visit there before heading to Harvard. The DCP put together a

party for him: "I made these enormous attachments, much deeper attachments than I would have expected. I knew that I would come back.
. . . I had relationships there, people who cared deeply about me and
that I cared deeply about." These connections were grounded in shared
experiences trying to help others. They were strong ties that pulled him
in ways that his family ties did not. But how could he explain all this
to the younger and more privileged students in his cohort at Harvard
Law?[5] How could they understand any part of his wayward journey?

Adding to the swirl of thoughts and emotions, Obama was trying
to process his last three years with the DCP. At the very same time
he began classes at Harvard, *Illinois Issues* published Obama's article
"Why Organize? Problems and Promise in the Inner City" as part of
a series sponsored by the Woods Charitable Fund. A reflection on his
experiences as an organizer, the piece shows that Obama saw neither
economic development nor electoral politics as a panacea for what
ailed Chicago. He wrote, "Neither approach offers lasting hope of real
change for the inner city unless undergirded by a systematic approach
to community organization. This is because the issues of the inner
city are more complex and deeply rooted than ever before." In spite of
his misgivings, Obama was still convinced, at least on one level, that
organizing mattered. Community work was what was most needed in
Chicago, and Obama envisioned young people as the vanguard: "As
long as our best and brightest youth see more opportunity in climbing
the corporate ladder than in building the communities from which
they came, organizing will remain decidedly handicapped."[6] Yet he
had left the DCP for Harvard, one of the most elite proving grounds
in the world. He needed to make more money, to have a sense of security. He was still torn.

At Harvard, as in New York, Obama largely kept to himself. Surprisingly, the 1988 presidential election is not mentioned in his memoir,
and there is no evidence that he did much more than vote. At the time,
had he been as politically charged and committed to electoral politics

as some biographers say, he certainly would have been on the campaign trail. He had knocked on doors before, after all, and this presidential election was particularly acrimonious and racialized. It was a referendum on Reaganism and the neoliberal policies that had made it increasingly difficult for organizers like Obama to get federal support.

The election featured George Herbert Walker Bush, the sitting vice-president, against Michael Dukakis, the governor of Massachusetts. Perhaps the most infamous symbol of the campaign was the digitally darkened mug shot of Willie Horton, a black man who had been furloughed from prison under Dukakis and had gone on to commit rape and murder. Many believe the ad, with its chilling voiceover, showed Dukakis was not only soft on crime, but a dangerous doofus (the other key image of the contest was Dukakis posing in a tank, dwarfed by his helmet and looking wholly out of place) who could not make good decisions or protect Americans. How could Obama *not* be galvanized? He was focused on himself and making the most of his time at Harvard.[7]

He lived in a basement apartment in Somerville, a working-class neighborhood with better rents than ritzier Cambridge. His landlord recalled that he lived a rather ascetic lifestyle, keeping his apartment clean and tidy: "He was a model tenant." He stayed in the same apartment for all of his three years at Harvard.[8]

The classes he took clearly influenced his intellectual development, but they did not diminish his strong, albeit fairly recent, connections to Chicago. Biographers and journalists make much of this time at Harvard, citing it as the place where he took up his destiny. This seems a bit overdone, given the evidence. But there is no question that the embodied privilege and ease he had begun to cultivate at Punahou, Occidental, and Columbia had provided a good foundation for his social life at Harvard, a small pond full of big fish.

Obama stood out: In 1990, he was chosen by his peers at the *Harvard Law Review* to be its leader—its first black president ever. He caught the eye of Professor Laurence Tribe, famed liberal and noted constitutional law scholar. Tribe called Obama the "best he had ever had" and made him his top research assistant. In spite of his apparent isolation, Obama developed close friendships with people—from students to professors—who would become members of his team after he was elected president of the United States.[9]

Still, he did not attend many of the requisite first-year parties and seemed to make most of his connections around ideas. His education was progressing by leaps and bounds, and classmates, who asked him to give a speech on their behalf and present an end-of-term gift to a particularly cantankerous professor, saw him as a leader. As one classmate recalled, "It was a moment of diffused tension and levity. . . . He pulled it off."[10]

Obama's community orientation and social activism had been completely subsumed by his efforts to make the most of his personal experience at Harvard. Obama circumvented his personal dilemmas by turning inward. In fact, the clear path at Harvard Law left little room for meandering. But his heart was still in Chicago. During the first year, law students typically arrange internships at law firms for the coming summer. Obama found a position at Sidley Austin, one of Chicago's top firms, where he met Michelle Robinson, a new associate at the firm. A 1988 Harvard Law School graduate, she was tasked with his orientation. They soon began dating seriously.[11]

Obama was still very much the passionate organizer from the DCP in Chicago. When they first met, he quoted Alinsky to Michelle. But at a Robinson family event, Michelle's brother Craig asked Obama about his future plans. Craig recalled, "He said, 'I think I'd like to teach at some point in time, and maybe . . . at some point he'd like to run for the U.S. Senate. And then he said, 'Possibly even run for president at some point.'" He was already aiming high.[12]

Michelle Robinson cemented Obama's connections to Chicago. He traveled back to Chicago every chance he got. Kellman recalled,

"When he's back, he's worried about the DCP. You know, he's got this, for a young man, an overdeveloped sense of responsibility. And he's running in to see if the budget's there, if the organizers are screwing up, you know, trying to induce us to help out since he's not on the scene anymore. He doesn't lose sight of that." Harvard, as it often does, had kindled the loftiest aspirations in Obama, but the DCP kept him grounded. And so did Michelle; she provided Obama with a center he had never had. Their courtship was intense, and they were married in Chicago just two years after they met. Friends report that Obama had a new confidence after the marriage. Kellman recalled, "He married a woman who just doesn't buy into everything he says, who will challenge him in a variety of ways." Marrying Michelle also opened up a whole new network of wealthy and successful black Chicagoans.[13]

In this big year—when he met Michelle and was elected president of the *Harvard Law Review*—Obama briefly gained some celebrity, with features in the *New York Times* and *Ebony*, among other publications. The results of the campaign for *Harvard Law Review* president must have been a bit intoxicating. The seed had been planted. Because of the publicity, a book agent, Jane Dystel, contacted Obama. She managed to negotiate quite a deal for Obama—Simon & Schuster gave him a $125,000 book contract to write about his experiences. As Obama recalled:

> In the wake of some modest publicity, I received an advance from a publisher and went to work with the belief that the story of my family, and my efforts to understand that story, might speak in some way to the fissures of race that have characterized the American experience, as well as the fluid state of identity—the leaps through time, the collision of cultures—that mark our modern life.[14]

His individual focus—running for office and writing a memoir are nothing if not selfish acts—was reinforced by the realities of a serious relationship. If he and Michelle were to have children, Obama really needed more financial security. Kellman sums things up: "Barack didn't have much interest in wealth, [but] he had a strong interest in having a secure income to marry and raise a family." This had always been in the back of Obama's mind as he lived hand-to-mouth in New York and Chicago.[15]

At the same time, Obama was still passionate about the importance of making a difference in the social world. At an address to the Black Law Students Association in 1991, Obama gave a rousing speech. One Harvard professor recalled it as "a clarion call. . . . We've gotten this education, we've gotten this great halo, this great career-enhancing benefit. Let's not just feather our nests. Let's go forward and address the many ills that confront our society."[16]

Upon finishing at Harvard, the world was his oyster. He had the time to turn his attention to writing his book, and he had a host of job interviews and offers. He knew he wanted to go back to Chicago; he and Michelle were planning to marry in the fall of 1991. But returning to Chicago was not just a matter of marital convenience. A professor of Obama's recalled: "He said that he wanted to write a book about his life and his father, go back to Chicago, get back into the community, and run for office there. He knew exactly what he wanted and went about getting it done."[17]

While many thought he might run for city office, Chicago politics was relentlessly hostile to upstarts and outsiders. Mayor Richard M. Daley, son of the legendary Mayor Richard J. Daley, had established himself and would likely remain in power for some time. There was no end-run in Chicago city politics. You had to work your way up.[18]

So the traditional path open to Obama was to take a job at a law firm, embed himself in a network, and make some money. But again, he was in a situation where the traditional path for those in his social position did not suit him. And he rejected this way forward. He found a more innovative path—Project Vote!—created by Sandy Newman, an attorney in Washington, DC. Newman was active in civil rights and believed that the registration of minority voters was one of the biggest civil rights challenges facing the United States. Black voters lead to black elected officials, so voter turnout was one way to alter the racial disparities in government.

Newman's organization had not done much work in Chicago as of 1991, save putting a bit of energy into a registration drive during Harold Washington's election.[19] But black politics was stagnant in the early 1990s, thanks in part to the fact that Mayor Daley—in the wake of Washington's death—had defeated black candidates in the past two elections. Black voter turnout was at a historic low in Chicago, and Newman thought his organization could make a difference. In making calls, Obama's name kept coming up. Newman tracked him down and got Obama to agree to direct the newly formed Cook County Project Vote! Reflecting years later on Obama's willingness to take the job, Newman remained puzzled: "I'm still not quite sure why. . . . This was not glamorous, high-paying work. But I am certainly grateful. He did one hell of a job." People who knew Obama from his time at the DCP were not as shocked. Take Mike Kruglik, for example: "It wasn't really a surprise when he came back to head up Project Vote! I think it was kind of an extension of his own thinking about creating a synthesis between community organizing and electoral politics."[20]

The position was temporary, with Obama working through the 1992 fall election. In a lucky turn of events, just after Obama took the position, Carol Moseley Braun, the Cook County recorder of deeds, declared as a Democratic candidate for the U.S. Senate. There would be a primary election, but the prospect of a black woman candidate was just what Project Vote! needed to galvanize a disconsolate black electorate. The incumbent, Alan Dixon, had voted to confirm Clarence Thomas, a black man accused of sexual harassment, to the U.S. Supreme Court. Braun was angry that Thomas had made it through the confirmation process. The mathematics of the March primary were on Braun's side, with Dixon and a third candidate splitting the white vote, while Braun won with the near unanimous support of black Chicagoans and white liberals.[21]

The table was set—a black woman was standing for the U.S. Senate. However, this was only one piece of the puzzle. Like all projects, this one needed money. The difference now was that Obama had connections through Michelle. Like Jane Addams in 1892, Obama saw a new way to make a difference on a larger scale in Chicago, but he would need Chicago elites to get it done. One hundred years later and the basic dynamics of power were the same.

The Obamas had already situated themselves in a dense set of network ties. During the summer of 1991, Abner Mikva—a Court of Appeals judge in Washington, DC, and a professor at the University of Chicago—began developing a friendship with Obama, taking him to the Quadrangle Club in Hyde Park for meals. Obama had turned down an offer of a clerkship with Mikva, but the two became close. Recent law school graduates do not usually befriend judges, but Obama never had a typical trajectory. Mikva recalled Obama mentioning that, at some point in the near future, he wanted to run for office himself. Meanwhile, he needed to get Project Vote! up and running in Illinois.[22]

The Obamas also developed a lasting friendship with Valerie Jarrett about this time. Michelle was looking to change jobs, and Jarrett had received Michelle's résumé from a City Hall coworker. Michelle's reputation preceded her, recalled Jarrett: "They said she was a terrific young woman, disenchanted with the practice of law," Jarrett recalled. "And I thought, I know that type, because that's exactly what I was. I thought that sounds like somebody I would get along with." Jarrett offered a job, but, in a surprising move, Michelle said she would not accept until Jarrett met her fiancé. The three of them went out to dinner, and Michelle quickly accepted. It is unlikely, given Michelle's reputation for being a strong woman, that the request was a paternalistic attempt by Obama to vet his wife's future job. More likely, the dinner was an effort to see whether the position fit the Obamas' social trajectory in Chicago.[23]

Like others, Jarrett got to work connecting the Obamas to Chicago elites. She invited them to dinner parties with businesspeople, lawyers, and elected officials. They attended charity events and sat on the boards of foundations. Jarrett even invited the couple to Martha's Vineyard for vacation. The informal, unspoken curriculum of America's elite schools had prepared Obama well; in spite of his time in the trenches of Chicago, Obama fit right in. A prime example of the dividends of privilege can be seen in the Obamas' membership at the East Bank Club in downtown Chicago. A social epicenter, the club saw politicians, powerbrokers, artists, and even stars like Oprah Winfrey exercising, sharing meals, and hobnobbing. One member described the club as a gathering place that "reinforces a center to this provincial town and provides a nexus of relationships for people obsessed with being buff." Social clubs remained an important piece of the puzzle for getting things done in Chicago politics.[24]

These connections paid immediate dividends for Obama. He crisscrossed the city raising funds to add to the $200,000 in startup money provided by Newman for Project Vote! New lines of action had opened. He was able to recruit a staff and gather a veritable army of volunteers. He partnered with Brainstorm Communications, a black-owned media firm, and launched a media blitz. He met and became friends with prominent Chicago blacks like Gary Gardner (the brother of Terri Gardner, president of Brainstorm), who had made millions through his company Soft Sheen Products, and John Rogers, head of Ariel Capital Management in Chicago. These men gave thousands of dollars to the Project Vote! effort and would become key figures in Obama's fundraising efforts when he ran for political office. Obama also connected with the political establishment in Chicago, asking John Schmidt, Harvard Law alumnus and former chief of staff for Mayor Daley, to chair Cook County Project Vote! Obama's choice to take a different path than his peers was inspiring to Chicago's elites. Schmidt recalled when Obama approached him in late 1991 and asked if he would help:

> He came to see me and asked if I would help raise money for Project Vote! . . . I was, frankly, kind of taken aback at the idea that someone coming out of the Harvard Law School, someone who could obviously have been clerking for a distinguished federal judge or working at a big law firm was instead saying that he was going to spend the next six months of his life registering voters in the minority community of Chicago.

Obama had shifted from working within one community to something much larger. He required the help and support of elites to move forward, and he was not worried about any potentially corrupting influence of those elites. One of Obama's colleagues recalled that, during the DCP days, he would say of elites: "They're not enemies. They're both working for their constituents, and they have to do this. Whoever can help you reach your goal, that's who you work with. . . . There are no permanent friends, no permanent enemies."[25]

While his new efforts clearly required that he breathe the rarefied air of elite Chicago society, Obama did more than just raise money and connections. Thinking back on his work at Project Vote!, Obama recalled that he put his community organizing skills to work:

> The most important thing I learned as an organizer is don't do all the talking. Spend a little time listening and finding out what is on the minds of people, what they are concerned about. Because the more you do that, the more you connect with them and the more you can tie the act of voting or politics to their day-to-day lives.[26]

And it worked. As Brian Banks, South Side coordinator for Project Vote!, remembers, "I probably remember mostly the ease of which it was to work with Senator Obama. . . . I remember there just seemed to be the right amount of management touch." Obama had returned to his comfort zone, speaking at churches in black communities across Chicago. In contrast to his time with the DCP, though, Obama was now the face of the project. No longer was he the guide on the side, urging community members to step forward and agitate for power. Obama spoke at rallies, he was interviewed on the radio, and he began to develop citywide name recognition.[27]

Obama also needed the support of black politicians in Chicago. He sought advice from Sam Burrell, a West Side alderman with experience with voter registration drives, most notably during Washington's mayoral campaign. Burrell lent his support, tasking his office manager, Carol Harwell, to help. But Obama wasn't about to let the machine take over. Staffer Mike Jordan recalled, "The traditional way with the party [in Chicago] was start with the committee men, start with the aldermen, start top down and spread it out. There he reversed it, and instead the thinking is let's go to the grassroots folks." Obama began the grassroots push in his old stomping grounds, enlisting the help of his friend Reverend Wright and members of his church.[28]

But the South Side did not have enough votes to win Cook County. Project Vote! needed to register voters *across* the city. That effort would require a sense of the social geography of Chicago that Obama just did not possess, particularly in terms of West Side Chicago, a black community even more destitute than the South Side. Obama had spent little time there, so Harwell gave him a crash course:

> He didn't know anything. He was so naïve. I gave him the address
> of a meeting on the West Side. We didn't have cell phones or pagers.
> Barack is very punctual. He was a couple of minutes late. He has this
> Kansas City twang. He said, "Y'all didn't think I was ever gonna get
> there. I had no idea Chicago is that big."[29]

He had connections to elites, he had new knowledge and skills, but in one sense Obama was still on the ground floor.

Much as he had done in the past, Obama listened and learned. Some volunteers advocated for registering and organizing first-time voters in Chicago's housing projects. Rita Whitfield suggested trying to register all the inhabitants of the Robert Taylor Homes (a city public housing project): "We started from the 16th floor, all the way to the first floor. We knocked on every door in that building. And it was amazing to hear young women, young mothers, say that no one had ever asked them to register to vote." It was a creative approach that emerged out of Obama's willingness to listen to his staff and volunteers.[30]

Creativity alone would not get Obama the votes he needed. So he compromised. Alderman Burrell had created the United Voter Registration League for Washington's mayoral race, and Obama asked for access to its staff and volunteer resources. Obama covered volunteer registrars' expenses for travel and meals so that they still got money in their pocket, but without the old-fashioned money-for-votes approach. Obama had come a long way from the day when he waited in the parking lot hoping for volunteers to show up for the bus ride to the state capital. He had developed an understanding that politics required pragmatism, and he did whatever it took to get results.[31]

It worked. Obama's unusual cocktail of grassroots organizing, elite support, and practical politics resulted in the registration of over 150,000 new voters. These voters made the difference in the November election, with Braun winning the U.S. Senate race with 53 percent of the vote. "It was the most efficient campaign I have seen in my 20 years in politics," recalled Alderman Burrell. Obama was now front and center in Chicago politics, and the media began to press him as to whether he might run for office himself. Just after the 1992 election, his response was still ambivalent:

> Who knows? But probably not immediately. . . . My sincere answer
> is, I'll run if I feel I can accomplish more that way than agitating
> from the outside. I don't know if that's true right now. Let's wait and

see what happens in 1993. If the politicians in place now at city and state levels respond to African-American voters' needs, we'll gladly work with and support them. If they don't, we'll work to replace them. That's the message I want Project Vote! to have sent.[32]

Obama didn't really have room to contemplate a run for office if he was ever going to finish his book. He told *Chicago Magazine* in January 1993 that he planned to finish it that month, but he would need nearly an entire year to complete the manuscript. Meanwhile, he also needed to make money. He had laid the groundwork for his next career steps before taking the voter registration job, receiving an offer of a fellowship from the University of Chicago. And he had multiple offers from Chicago law firms. Obama also found time for his own personal growth, as he and Michelle married in October 1992. It was a banner year.[33]

Obama's decision to join the faculty at the University of Chicago offers a striking parallel to Jane Addams, who had taught there approximately a hundred years earlier. Obama had a connection to the university through his great-uncle Charles Payne, who worked there as a librarian. When Obama became president of the *Harvard Law Review*, Payne naturally shared the news with colleagues, and word of Obama made it to Douglas Baird, in charge of the faculty hiring committee for the law school. Obama's reputation preceded him, with several of Payne's colleagues, most notably Michael McConnell, singing his praises based on his editing work at Harvard. In 1991, while Obama was still at Harvard, Baird offered a fellowship to support his book project. Baird recalled the conversation: "I don't remember his exact words, but it was something to the effect that, 'Well, in fact, I want to write this book.' What he really wanted was the Virginia Woolf equivalent of a clean, well lighted room." Obama got what he wanted: an office with a computer, access to the library, and a token salary. Perhaps most important, Obama would acquire status and build cultural capital with this prestigious new affiliation. For its part, the University of Chicago Law School, which at the time had virtually no black faculty, was able to improve its diversity profile.[34]

Baird had initially been under the impression that Obama was writing a book on race relations. But as Obama continued to write, he realized, and informed Baird, that the book was turning into an autobiography. Obama took the material he had put together for his initial contract with Simon & Schuster (he had missed the deadline and returned the advance) and gave it to his agent, Jane Dystel, who secured him a contract with Times Books, along with a $40,000 advance. Audacity. Just the self-confidence to write an autobiography at age thirty is unimaginable to most—Addams would not write any biographic treatment of her life's work until she was past fifty.[35]

In fall 1992, Baird offered Obama a position as a lecturer (essentially an adjunct or temporary faculty member) and convinced him to teach "Current Issues in Racism and the Law." Obama would continue in this position from 1992 until 1996. Personally and professionally, even he admitted he was trying to do too much:

> There are times when I want to do everything and be everything. . . .
> And that can sometimes get me into trouble. That's historically been
> one of my bigger faults. I mean, I was trying to organize Project
> Vote! at the same time as I was writing a book, and there are only so
> many hours in a day.[36]

At the same time, having finished Project Vote! and become a University of Chicago lecturer, Obama took a position at a firm then called Davis, Miner, Barnhill, & Galland. Judson Miner had been part of Harold Washington's administration and remained well connected, and Carol Moseley Braun had even worked there. The firm was known for its work in civil rights law:

> Law school and practicing law put the framework around how this
> country works, but it also drove home that social change through

the court system is a very difficult thing. There are very few moments in our history, *Brown v. Board of Education* being a singular
exception, where substantial change was initiated through the court
system. . . . So it was at this point that I started thinking more seriously about political office.

The negotiations with the firm had started in 1991, though Obama
secured a year deferral in order to work for Project Vote! and finish
his book.[37]

The book was still unfinished when, in 1993, Obama started as a
legal associate with an annual salary of roughly $50,000. He was still
teaching, too. Allison Davis recalled that "Obama spent a lot of time
working on his book. . . . Some of my partners weren't happy with
that, Barack sitting there with his keyboard on his lap and his feet up
on the desk writing the book." The next two years were spent writing, teaching, and working at the firm. Obama (and his biographers)
tend to characterize his casework as involving social justice, but he also
worked on a number of rather mundane and trivial cases defending
nonprofits in lawsuits. In one, a woman sought a payment for $336 in
babysitting, in another a man slipped on a sidewalk due inadequate
maintenance, and in a third, South Side tenants did not have suffi-
cient heat in their apartment building in the winter of 1994. These are
a far cry from the "substantial change" Obama had envisioned cham-
pioning. Kellman saw this as a time in which Obama was "still growing and exploring. He gets this book contract, and the major thing
is that it's a big advance. And he owes a ton of money for law school
and law school debts. But he's so busy he can't get himself to write the
book." It was a tremendous amount of pressure.[38]

Somehow, in spite of the demands of the book, the job, the teaching, and his marriage, Obama still found time to work with foundations. It helped him to balance his individual pursuits by making a
difference at a much larger scale than when he was with the DCP,

and it let him network with the city's powerbrokers. He was asked
to serve on the Joyce Foundation Board, the very organization that
had supported Obama's earlier work with the DCP. In late 1994, the
Annenberg Foundation announced plans to give nearly $50 million
to support school reform in Chicago, on the condition that the newly
created local chapter, the Chicago Annenberg Challenge, would raise
$50 million from private funds and obtain another $50 million in
public money from the city. Deborah Leff, the president of Joyce,
recommended Obama for the board, alongside powerbrokers like the
president of the University of Illinois. Meetings were held at the Spen-
cer Foundation's luxurious offices in downtown Chicago, the modern
equivalent of the Egyptian Room at the Palmer House, where Addams
had gathered with other Chicago Bureau of Charities board members. Surprisingly, this young, relatively insignificant board member
was elected president of the board at their first meeting. Not only was
Obama making ties, he was also laying foundations.[39]

It must be noted, Obama wasn't solely involved with these boards
for the money and prestige, as Chicago lawyer Newton Minow
recalled:

> [Obama] called me one day, and he said he wanted to have lunch with
> me, wanted some advice. He told me he'd been offered a job, paid a
> good income, as head of a foundation, and what did I think? I told
> him to take it. And he said, "Yeah, but if I do that, I'll have to give up
> any political activity." And I said: "Well, it's worth it. Do that for a
> while. Get some financial security, and then you can go into politics.
> And he thought about it and thought about it. He rejected that."[40]

Obama had moved from outsider to insider with his efforts to
help others in Chicago. While he still used the Alinsky-style organizing techniques of listening and engaging, Obama had moved far away
from Alinsky's emphasis on upsetting the balance of power. Obama
was now part of the establishment. With this shift in position came

access to significant resources. With the Chicago Challenge's millions, it was nothing to secure $100,000 in support for DCP efforts to increase parent engagement with South Side schools (the same type of program that Obama had created ten years earlier, but that had faded away due to lack of funds). The biggest difference was that he was no longer engaged with the community where the money was going. He was just too busy.[41]

The book needed to be finished; it was getting in the way. Obama made a major push, spending a few months in Bali with Michelle so he might, in the words of his half-sister Maya, "find a peaceful sanctuary where there were no phones." The timing is important, as Obama needed to turn his gaze inward. This self-reflection occurred just as he was starting to think about what he might do next. Kellman described this time as a moment of significant change and rupture in Obama's life:

> And he goes off on the beach to write the book. But everything tends to happen for a reason. And Barack used the book as an opportunity to explore, you know, who he was and his own story and to write it down in a disciplined fashion, something he wouldn't have done probably at that stage if he hadn't been forced to.[42]

Dreams from My Father was published in 1995. Several major national media outlets reviewed it, including the *New York Times* ("persuasively describes the phenomenon of belonging to two different worlds, and thus belonging to neither"), and received significant attention from Chicago media.[43]

At roughly the same time that Obama finished the book and was full of self-actualized intent, a structural opportunity appeared. A chain of events, starting with the indictment of Congressman Mel Reynolds, resulted in State Senator Alice Palmer, who represented Obama's District Thirteen in Chicago, launching an effort to claim Reynolds's seat. That left Palmer's seat open. Obama made the rounds, taking the pulse of local politicians and potential donors. He needed to be sure he could win the ground game with volunteers, and he needed to raise money.[44]

Ivory Mitchell, a seasoned political operative and chair of the Democratic Committee for Chicago's Fourth Ward, recalled the first time Obama approached him about running for Palmer's seat. Like most campaign operatives, Mitchell's first question was about money. Did Obama have any? "I don't have any money," Obama told him. Mitchell's response was, "Well, if you don't have any money, we're going to have to finance the campaign for you." What was left unsaid was that with this money would come obligations, a different and more venal type of reciprocal relations that took Obama far away from community-based democratic growth. It was the kind of selfish reciprocity that Addams had found so distasteful. As it turned out, money would not be a problem. In addition to Mitchell, Obama had cultivated a vast network of rich and powerful people used to funding political campaigns. Alan Dobry marvels:

> Everything seemed to be falling into place that autumn. . . . Obama had friends who would put up the money for him: people from Judd Miner's law firm, Harvard people, colleagues at the University of Chicago. He knew people in the habit of funding independent political campaigns.

Obama was set, but he was not autonomous. Obama was completely dependent on his network. He moved forward, declaring his intentions to Palmer and securing her support.[45]

Obama was focused, but it would be a mistake to assume he was single-minded. Once again, there was some struggle and contradiction, some dilemma, as he wrestled with the choice to run for office. Besides the obvious (that he would need to rely on the support of the business establishment, the very group he had avoided and even worked against less than ten years earlier), there was a more personal pull. Michelle was not convinced that politics was the way to make a real difference in real people's lives. She recalled their discussions: "I wasn't a proponent of politics as a way you could make change. . . . I also thought, was politics really a place for good, decent people?" In essence, Obama's wife was asking him to consider why he wanted to enter the political fray. Was running for office a way for Obama to move forward with his communitarian vision? Or was it an expression of narcissism? More the former than the latter it seems, but these were still important questions. Not to mention the idea of starting a family.[46]

Obama truly believed that he could take money from elites while staying true to his communitarian roots. In an interview conducted in 1995, while the campaign was in full swing, Obama expressed his view on the seemingly irreconcilable position:

> I want to do this as much as I can from the grass-roots level, raising as much money for the campaign as possible at coffees, connecting directly with voters. But to organize this district I must get known. And this costs money. I admit that in this transitional period, before I'm known in the district, I'm going to have to rely on some contributions from wealthy people—people who like my ideas but who won't attach strings. This is not ideal, but it is a problem encountered by everyone in their first campaign. Once elected, once I'm known, I won't need that kind of money, just as Harold Washington, once he was elected and known, did not need to raise and spend money to get the black vote.

He was confident he could manage this balancing act.[47]

Others were not so sure. Soon after Obama declared his candidacy, the political winds shifted. Alice Palmer lost her primary bid for the Second Congressional District. Her supporters immediately launched a "Draft Palmer" committee, pushing for Obama to drop out of the race. Palmer supporters were particularly concerned about Obama's commitment to secure funding for community projects. They weren't sure he could or would bring in money for them. Linda Randle, who worked closely at the DCP with Obama in the 1980s, recalled:

> They could see with Barack that wasn't getting ready to happen. . . . They worried about losing their funding, because Barack was less sympathetic to them—much less. Barack is cheap. If he puts money out there, he wants to see how you use it. Alice less so, because those were her friends.

This doubt was not just about finding reasons to support Palmer over Obama. Some people just thought Obama was too good to be true.[48]

The outcome of this election is a commonplace. Obama won and took his Senate seat in the Illinois state capitol in January 1997. But *how* he did it is less widely known. He used dirty tricks in the age-old Chicago way. Obama's campaign team knew that many of the signatures Palmer obtained in her effort to get her name on the ballot were fake. This was usually the case in last-minute efforts. So, Obama supporters, with his reluctant consent, officially challenged the signatures, filing a complaint with the Chicago Board of Election Commissioners. Seeing names like "Superman" and "Pooky" on the registration lists helped Obama justify the approach, but it was still unusual to try to unseat an incumbent in such a fashion. The city upheld the challenge, and Palmer was removed from the ballot. It was an inauspicious way for a self-styled "new breed" of communitarian politician to get elected. Obama had regrets: "That part of it I wish had played out entirely differently."[49]

In the wake of Obama's election, Adolph Reed, Jr., a political science professor at Northwestern, wrote in the *Village Voice*:

> In Chicago, for instance, we've gotten a foretaste of the new breed of foundation-hatched black communitarian voices: one of them, a smooth Harvard lawyer with impeccable do-good credentials and vacuous to repressive neoliberal politics, has won a state senate seat on

a base mainly in the liberal foundation and development worlds. His fundamentally bootstrap line was softened by a patina of the rhetoric of authentic community, talk about meeting in kitchens, small-scale solutions to social problems, and the predictable elevation of process over program—the point where identity politics converges with old-fashioned middle-class reform in favoring form over substance.[50]

Was Reed right? Was Obama's community-talk just a "patina" that covered more of the same? Perhaps, but the evidence shows that Obama, up until he ran for office, had made a concerted and fairly consistent effort to take nontraditional paths, with at least one eye pointed toward making a difference in people's lives. Like most Americans, he was pushed and pulled by the competing demands of society. At times, these demands pulled him toward family, education, and his profession. But sooner or later he would innovate, zig instead of zag, and do real things. Politics can be a very selfish enterprise. But Obama truly wanted to be the exception. He had gained a remarkable understanding for a man of his age, and he was prepared to move forward on another nontraditional road:

> What if a politician were to see his job as that of an organizer as part teacher and part advocate, one who does not sell voters short but who educates them about the real choices before them? As an elected public official, for instance, I could bring church and community leaders together easier than I could as a community organizer or lawyer. We would come together to form concrete economic development strategies, take advantage of existing laws and structures, and create bridges and bonds within all sectors of the community. We must form grass-root structures that would hold me and other elected officials more accountable for their actions.[51]

In Obama's mind, he had never stopped being a community organizer. When Obama saw Kellman years later during a presidential campaign stop in Chicago, he told his old friend: "I'm still organizing." At a loss for words, Kellman replied, "I know you are." The exchange seems absurd.[52] But upon reflection, Kellman, who had always seen the tension in Obama, thought the soon-to-be president was sincere:

> Nobody runs for president of the United States unless they're ambitious. Anybody who thinks otherwise is silly. And Barack does want to be the best. He wants to achieve personally. But he's also got this strong, strong sense of service to others. And so they coexist.[53]

The struggle and effort required to adjudicate between individual and collective responsibilities was as challenging for Obama as it was for Jane Addams a hundred years before him. And Obama, like Addams, made his mark on society in a very short time. Drawing on the twoness of his identity and his education and privilege, he envisioned and then constructed a unique path forward as a community organizer in Chicago. And he never got comfortable. He was constantly shaking things up while at the same time striving to connect with others, whether in Kenya, the South Side of Chicago, or at Harvard Law School. Obama's life thus far has been one of adjustment and coexistence, of finding a balance in the face of his dilemmas. How to make a decent living while at the same time doing socially meaningful work? How to pursue individual creativity through writing when there are not enough hours in the day? How to stay grounded in his community while accepting support from elite politicians and business leaders?

It is a never-ending struggle, as Obama himself points out: "What I am constantly trying to do is balance a hard head with a big heart."[54]

CHAPTER EIGHT

Mixing on the Thronged
and Common Road

We are learning that a standard of social ethics is not attained by
travelling a sequestered byway, but by mixing on the thronged
and common road where all must turn out for one another, and at
least see the size of one another's burdens.

Jane Addams[1]

MOST BIOGRAPHIES would tell the reader what happens next.
How did Addams help Hull-House adapt as the United States
moved into the twentieth century? What was it like for Obama as he
joined the Illinois State Senate, and how did he parlay that experience
into a run for higher office? The answers to these questions and more
can (and do) fill the pages of several books. Below, I offer a précis.

Addams became a leader in the women's suffrage movement and
the anti-imperialist movement. Her stance against World War I eventually earned her a Nobel Peace Prize. Her work at Hull-House and
beyond catapulted her onto the international stage and gave her a
voice of authority in shaping the profession of social work—she is
often referred to as the discipline's founder or "mother." British MP
John Burns went so far as to call her "America's only saint." Beyond
her legacy of deeds, she left behind ten books and more than one hundred articles. Addams's autobiography is still required reading at any
school of social work today.[2]

Obama's successes are already the stuff of legend. His stratospheric rise to the presidency occurred after he barely warmed a seat in the U.S. Senate. He wrote another bestselling book in 2006, and like Addams, was awarded the Nobel Peace Prize (only the third sitting U.S. president to receive the award, and having just taken office, Obama was described by the Nobel Committee as demonstrating "extraordinary efforts to strengthen international diplomacy and cooperation between peoples"). All this with decades of his life ahead of him.

Providing the rest of the story is the job of biographers, not sociologists. My focus on these two Americans is in the service of illuminating the American's Dilemma. How are their lives illustrative of dilemmas and contradictions in society, and how did they move forward? The social world is messy. Our stories, particularly concerning great Americans, oversimplify how they deal with their dilemmas. Decisions are not always simple means–ends things. We are often ambivalent, we muddle through, we are hesitant and unsure. Despite our efforts to tell a story of ascendance in biography—"She was destined for greatness"—our great Americans feel many of the same pressures and pulls of the most mundane. What may be different is how they move forward, following lines of action they have inherited and created.

Addams chafed against the bindings placed on women of her time. Her socialization, largely through her father, led her to value democracy and helping in the spirit of the Social Gospel. But the same source that gave her social inspiration also kept her in her social place. Women were told "Stay at home, go to church, do not overtax yourself." These sentiments presented a formidable obstacle. Addams had a different vision of her own potential and wanted to realize it. The removal of her father, both literally and figuratively, opened the door for her to take action, and that led to Hull-House. But the gender dimensions of her struggles are only a part of the picture. Addams felt the pull of inherited money and its responsibilities. She also had real health concerns and a love of travel, particularly in the company of good friends. All these individual needs tugged at Addams; at times they succeeded in pulling her out of her orbit.

Obama's peripatetic life did not lend itself to any kind of grounding, save in his relationship with his mother. She was his guiding star, and her efforts to help others through development work had a lasting impact on Obama. Through his travels, Obama became aware at an early age of the twoness of his racial identity—he was neither fully black nor fully white in Indonesia or Hawaii. There was no clear path for him to follow as a young black man: The victories of the civil rights movement had opened up some doors to traditionally white careers, but these would not satisfy Obama's desire to make a difference. And the vanguard of the black community, at least in Obama's eyes, appeared to have comfortably ensconced itself in corporate-style offices in the skyscrapers of New York.

Obama blazed his own trail, which led him to the South Side of Chicago. He, too, felt the pull of more individual needs. He wanted to make enough money so that he did not have to sleep on couches at friends' houses. He valued travel and wanted to see more of the world that had been opened up to him by his mother and his friends. He wanted to nurture his creative side and write. He valued solitude and felt the pull of ambition. He wanted to be a leader on issues of substance, maybe even mayor of Chicago, like Harold Washington before him. These individual callings were in his ears as he worked his way from Hawaii to Los Angeles to New York to Chicago to Cambridge and to the White House. At times, they subsumed him.

Race and gender loom large in the early ambivalence of both Addams and Obama.[3] There were only certain lines of action open to white women of the 1880s and non-white men of the 1980s. They both hungered to answer the call of a purpose greater than themselves, but they had trouble seeing the way forward. Ironically, privilege helped them both. Addams, thanks to her inherited wealth and cultivated ease, was able to make connections at Toynbee Hall and in Chicago. These provided the social network, ideas, and additional funds required to begin her experiment at Hull-House. While Obama was not wealthy, the privilege he learned to wear at Punahou let him cross class borders comfortably. At Punahou, Occidental, Columbia, and Harvard, Obama was cultivating the same kind of privileged ease as Addams. They both knew how to be confident in the world of wealth and power.[4]

The argument here is not that Obama and Addams were upper-crust snobs who were most comfortable with the elite. Far from it—at an early age they both possessed a remarkable humility and were keenly aware of their social position. And they both willingly made significant material sacrifices by moving to the poorest neighborhoods of Chicago. Rather, the point is that they knew the worlds of both the dominant and dominated—at least in terms of gender for Addams and race for Obama—and as such, they were able to comfortably exist in both. The "charmed circle" that Obama recognized was more like a road opening up new territory.[5] The privilege each possessed and culti-vated allowed them to have multiple effective voices: They could speak with authority among those who needed help and those who had the resources to fund such help.

Travel also links the experiences of Addams and Obama. It was a way for each of them to generate new energy. It took each of them out of their comfort zone. From bullfights to East End London pov-erty, from Indonesian agriculture to the slums of Pakistan, these two individuals experienced worlds outside their own. They grew as indi-viduals and, more importantly, developed a stronger sense of the larger world and the importance of contributing to it.

On their travels, Obama and Addams had guides. Mentors are crit-ical to understanding how these two moved forward from their dilem-mas.[6] Addams's earliest guide was her father. As she grew older, Addams had a number of female mentors—including her friends Ellen Gates Starr, Mary Rozet Smith, and Julia Lathrop—who exposed her to new possibilities and new ways of thinking them through. The Barnetts at

Toynbee Hall, Leo Tolstoy (who inspired and challenged her in equal measure), and even her neighbors in the Nineteenth Ward showed Addams how to forge ahead and put her ideas into action.

Obama had his mother to start, with Lolo and his grandparents also offering guidance. The almost mythical idea of his father was a pull on Obama as well, but with his father's death, Obama was, like Addams, able to find his own voice, his own *auethoritas* as a non-white in the United States. Kellman and the women at the DCP in Chicago provided Obama with the social tools and vision required to channel his voice and bring his values to the ground in the service of helping others, while Michelle and her legal and society networks taught him additional ways of working. All along, this constellation of people surrounding, supporting, and even blocking Addams and Obama's efforts were creating and reinforcing habits of the heart—that is, social norms of helping others.[7]

But putting ideas into practice—through Hull-House, the Chicago Bureau of Charities, and the Developing Communities Project—cost money. Addams had plenty at the start, and it was liberating. She could do what she wanted. There are pockets of this kind of work in other parts of society today. The artist who produces art "for its own sake," for example, or the nonprofit worker who makes less money than she could in the private sector because "it is the right thing to do." The less encumbered one is by preconceived ideas, particularly those tied to the logic of the market ("the business idea"), the more room there is to experiment and grow. While Obama was constrained at times by his financial needs, he too chose a path relatively free of obligations to the logic of the market. His first efforts were funded by the Catholic Church, governmental agencies, and foundations, but there is little evidence that religious or any other ideology lurked behind the funds at Obama's disposal. Congregations were simply the primary social nodes of the South Side community network. Like Addams, Obama was able to do what he wanted, to a certain point.

Eventually, the money at Obama's disposal was just not adequate to address the needs as he saw them. The same was true for Addams. She looked to the powerful elites of Chicago for help, and got it. But this money did come with strings. They could no longer forge ahead alone, but needed to cooperate with business leaders in Chicago. As a result, their work changed. Obama left the DCP and shifted his focus to a larger playing field of politics and foundations. He had, by his own admission, developed a "hard head." Addams founded an organization with principles seemingly at odds with those of Hull-House. This organization would be funded in part by George Pullman, who personified the uncaring and tyrannical nature of the labor market. She opened up Hull-House to friendly visiting, a practice about which she had serious concerns.[8]

How tempting it is to judge those who have come before. Or even to project our own dilemmas onto people like Addams and Obama, intensifying their struggles and then holding them responsible when they fall short. They hold up the weight for the rest of us, so to speak.[9]

The standard narrative of ascendance that surrounds Addams and Obama makes it easy to spot times when they went off-course. Such judgment, though, is an overly simplistic and unfair approach. As Obama himself once pointed out, "that kind of hindsight is pretty shaky. And I think it's just as shaky for me to engage in that kind of speculation as it is for anybody."[10] People want a certain Addams or Obama and forget the rest. But what was it like in reality? Considering their lives and work in light of the commonplace American's Dilemma, let's not see Addams and Obama as rocket ships, blazing a trail across the sky, traveling ever higher and higher, but as individuals searching for equilibrium in a messy world. Their social biographies are full of contradictions and false starts. Our estimations must allow for their seemingly endless revisions.

Both Addams and Obama struggled with identities that were contradictory or anachronistic. As people of action, they tried to confront their ambiguous situations by moving forward and making choices, rather than wringing their hands (or washing them of the world's troubles). Action opens up the potential to push through dead ends and even change social structure. At times they retreated and tried again. And at times their vision of how to proceed was shaped by the vocabularies available to them. Obama and Addams learned these vocabularies of potential action from those they encountered—from poor, struggling neighbors to the richest and most powerful leaders in Chicago. It was a constant process of creation, perplexity, and blockage, leading to the need for ever more creation and experimentation. Dilemmas drive action, as we struggle and seek balance.

The way forward might be seen as a quest for understanding. The books and lessons of Rockford, Columbia, and Harvard only took Addams and Obama so far, providing a certain type of scholarly knowledge. The trips to places like Europe, Russia, and Pakistan only opened their eyes to some facets of the world. At a certain point they both realized that knowledge can only do so much. *Understanding* comes from doing.

Hull-House, the Developing Communities Project, Project Vote!, and the Chicago Bureau of Charities were examples of crucibles of action, of Addams and Obama trying to do *something*. From these sets of social relations emerged new ways forward, new habits. Not all of them worked. Not all of them were consistent. This is what creation looks like on the ground. It is messy. There is no absolute truth, but a shifting and constantly developing social morality that takes us closer and closer to democracy.

·   ·   ·

Gunnar Myrdal, sociologist and Nobel Prize winner, famously wrote of the "American Dilemma" in race relations. Americans talk a good game, said Myrdal, but in practice, blacks were then (and are now) excluded from society and politics in many important respects. So there are unseen divisions, but there are also imposed divisions. We are constantly being *told* that we are divided—red states and blue states, black and white, 99 percent and 1 percent. The list goes on and on. But Americans are not all that divided on whether to help others. Most Americans think helping is good and desirable; they just aren't always sure how to do it. They worry about compromising their principles and their personal desires. They are torn.[11]

As we saw in the stories of Addams and Obama, we are asked by American culture to do contradictory things simultaneously. We are stuck with (and because of) these things—it is part of what makes America so interesting, and at times so frustrating. These kinds of dilemmas are not unique to America. The American's Dilemma is emblematic of global challenges about how to balance the self and the social. These challenges take on particular nuances within different national, political, and social cultures, and they vary across context and history.[12]

We are not always in a state of dilemma. Much of our day-to-day activity is governed by unreflexive action in which we follow routine. We do not always think about what we do. Brewing the morning coffee, taking a jog, scanning the daily headlines—these are all actions requiring little or no reflection once they have been ingrained (or embodied) as habit. But when routines and habits break down, one must then consider the situation, examine what courses of action are possible, and experiment. One must try something and see what happens. It is a messy social dynamic. Some things work and others do not. In this sense, we grow as individuals, and as a society, by getting stuck and then moving forward through creative experimentalism—a sort of personal scientific method.

The American's Dilemma can be a fulcrum for action, pushing us to create and try out different ways to satisfy our needs. Once we figure out something that works, we build it up into something that endures. Call it what you will—I like William Graham Sumner's idea of a "folkway"—a sort of avenue for social action.[13] These new folk-ways can eventually become rather durable, like America's ubiquitous highways. Sure, not all roads are "good" roads in terms of quality. Some stay that way or become impassable, but we repair or improve others. The work has costs (time and money), but makes our trips easier. And since not all roads take you where you want to go, some-times you build new ones, bringing status to the towns and cities that are now connected.

This is also the case with people. Like Addams and Obama, as we connect to each other by folkways, we are put on the social map. Whether each person is seen as marginalized or valued, worthy of re-spect or contempt, is very much a function of a society's folkways. Sumner, who developed his ideas in the early twentieth century, did not think the state or even organizations had much potential to carry out our folkways. We part ways there: This book advocates for think-ing and constructing folkways in communities and neighborhoods, for creating paths for social action in local contexts and often through the organization of a handful of people.

At bottom, there is a sameness to our struggles and those of Obama and Addams. In asking "How does someone like Addams or Obama come to do such creative things?" and "What type of person sees a new option and moves ahead?" we are essentially asking "Who am I?" and "What might I do?" These are critical questions as each person confronts his or her own American's Dilemma.

The good news is that there aren't clear answers. There are many ways to do it. Addams and Obama had advantages in the form of money, education, and an exposure to a broad range of ideas. In other words, they had plenty of social, economic, and cultural capital. They were also subject to limitations or disadvantages: Their times relegated women and people of color to the sidelines, diminished their voices, asked that they remove themselves from helping (even when help was required). Women of her time just didn't *do* what she did at Hull-

House, but Addams would not allow others to be in control of the construction of her social self. And black men in the 1980s suddenly had access to high-paying jobs in the economic boom of the Reagan years, but Obama chose a different path. Neither Obama nor Addams could completely throw away the mantle of the social world (none of us can), and neither would denigrate the work done by their forebears who opened so many avenues of opportunity to them both. They simply worked to modify or move around barriers. They each created a "third way." Where they ultimately ended up does not take away from the very common contradictions they faced on their journeys.

.   .   .

As Tolstoy asked, "What is to be done?" Or put another way, "What is the moral of this story?" It is one thing to show that two individuals have been able to find ways to address their own American's Dilemma, helping others while finding their own success and happiness. It is quite another to ask that we do the same ourselves. One does not have to run for president or found a new approach to community helping. It is enough to act in small ways, contributing in some measure to the growth of our communities as we move beyond our own contradictions. These actions are to be celebrated. Through an engagement with the early community work of Addams and Obama, I hope to convince the reader of the merits of three things:

Don't get comfortable.   As we go about our daily lives, it is easy to follow the same well-worn paths. But if the stories of Addams and Obama show anything, it is that shaking things up and crossing boundaries leads to interesting outcomes. Be a person of action. Be a boundary crosser. This is easier said than done in the face of serious resistance, but the hardest things are usually those worth doing. And it is not always clear, at least at first, what might have changed as a result of your efforts. An obvious way to go about doing this is to travel. But travel can take place in your own backyard. Go to the "other" side of town, a place you aren't familiar with, and look for those common bonds of humanity that Addams wrote about.

Look for deeper connections, rather than flitting through life without engagement. In the words of Zygmunt Bauman, be a "pilgrim" not a "tourist."[14] This is not just about how we actually travel, whether in our own town or across the globe. It is about how we live, how we travel through life itself. Deeper attachments are more sustaining and offer the potential to give you something in return.

And as you move through new situations, take a page from Obama and listen. Don't try to "tell it like it is" before hearing what people have to say. As we see the size of others' burdens, we come to understand our own burden in a different way. But moving out of your comfort zone doesn't mean you have to be completely selfless. Addams and Obama did not stop living their own lives. It is critical to leave space for yourself while helping others.

Connect with your neighbors.   One solution to the American's Dilemma is to try to become grounded in one's own community and cultivate the "habits of the heart" that were so effective for Addams and Obama. But not just any connection will do—writing a check to a local charity, donating to Good Will, or joining a bowling league (as sociologist Robert Putnam famously described) isn't enough. Nor is simply engaging in a joint attack of electricity and sunshine in the spirit of a nineteenth-century friendly visitor—that is, pure enthusiasm is not enough. Addams and Obama show us that if the goal is to do good in the world and help others, one needs to step outside and start connecting to people in the neighborhood. One might start by volunteering at a local community center, shelter, or church. This kind of local, small-scale action creates connections to others, and through these connections, as we see in the cases of Obama and Addams, the actor gets back as much as, if not more than, she gives. Learning what neighbors truly need will put one in a better position to do more—and to do it in a way that will make real change for the neighborhood.

Both Obama and Addams show us that communities are something we create, not something given to us. Their efforts to create community show the merits of the idea that "if at first you don't succeed, try, try again." Community creation is messy and requires constant work as each individual links herself to something bigger. Save for the very wealthy, it would be difficult to follow in the initial footsteps of Jane Addams, who funded her early work at Hull-House out of her own pocket. So, as a society, we might cultivate a research and development space in the American welfare system, one that supports and rewards creative, community-based efforts. Imagine a system in which a future Jane Addams or Barack Obama might receive government funding to start an innovative, community-based program to connect with and to help others. Such funding might be part of an effort to improve the existing welfare system by finding and encouraging local community engagement and fostering norms of reciprocity.

It doesn't have to be an either/or situation. (This is not a call for another thousand points of light.) We can and should provide basic supports that allow all members in society to live in dignity, and at the same time encourage efforts that build and nurture community growth. Some communities actively turn to their neighbors out of necessity. But in a society with rising inequality and childhood poverty, the overall system is flawed. One way we might improve things would be to look to the best of both Obama and Addams—a system that will incentivize and enable a return to the creative potential of Addams's time *without* taking away (or gradually defunding) the safety net and devaluing the social citizenship we have today.[15]

Watch out for selfish reciprocity.   As we can see with Addams and Obama, they both chose to become active in politics, but only after building on-the-ground relations with real people in their own communities. Addams and Obama also received support from business leaders, whose money and names made a difference at times. As one begins to make neighborhood connections around helping in the community, it will likely become apparent that many of the problems facing neighbors are structural and require policy changes. This in part is what happened with Addams and Obama. But bringing about these kinds of changes often requires one to step out of the neighborhood and into politics and the halls of power. Money and influence are required.

This is where it is necessary to be careful, because often the world of business and politics is about cronyism and self-interest, rather than a concern for the community. The selfish reciprocity Addams warned us about is a matter of "you scratch my back and I'll scratch yours." Nothing comes for free in business and politics. This is not an injunction to avoid electoral politics or turn down a check from a well-heeled businesswoman. Just be cautious.

The point is that once you relinquish your independence from elites, you will probably have to compromise your efforts at community-based helping. Pressures come to bear, and the ability to be creative and experimental is diminished. As we saw with Addams and Obama, at times these elites blocked creativity and experimentation. It is worth remembering that the business of business is first and foremost making a profit, not helping other people. The same is true with electoral politics, which is as much about fundraising and campaigning as governance and policy creation. This is perhaps as it should be, but we should not confuse the goals (and methods) of business or politics with those of building a community.

·   ·   ·

Let's return to the opening scene of the book. What would *you* do if you held someone's life in your hands? Imagine a neighbor, someone you know fairly well, coming to you and asking for help. What would *you* want to happen? Would you want a rigid set of rules and procedures that you could point to? Or would you want more flexibility and room to problem solve?

Put another way, how will *you* balance your hard head and big heart as you face your own future social dilemmas? My sincere hope is that my presentation and analysis of the early efforts of Jane Addams and Barack Obama as community organizers might offer you creative inspiration.

On Methods and Theory

There is a significant amount of secondary source material on Addams that informs this project. The first substantive biography of Addams was published in 1935 (the year she died) by Addams's nephew, James Weber Linn. This work, while a treasure trove of information on Addams and Hull-House, was not particularly analytical. It stood as the main work on Addams until 1960—the centennial of Addams's birth—when a series of scholarly lectures and publications emerged. The rekindling of interest in Addams in the 1960s led to closer scrutiny of her work, particularly using lenses of gender, class, and culture. The advent of Addams's 150th birthday in 2011 precipitated another round of publications delving more deeply into Addams's pragmatist methods and how they contribute to the (re)construction of citizenship, democracy, and peace. Several recent biographies of Addams provide a comprehensive overview and analysis of her life, while focusing on Addams's contributions to democratic theory and practice. Other recent work has picked up or paralleled the investigation of the nexus of Addams's practice and democratic (and social) growth with the goal of reinterpretation or recovery.[1]

But this most recent phase is an incomplete project. For example, there is still a lack of understanding regarding Addams's complicated relationship with relief and charity organization in Chicago, let alone how this relationship influenced her work. The narrative that has been mapped onto her life at times feels too tidy for the messy social world we inhabit. To these authors, Addams was a cooperator, a vanguard feminist, a spearhead, a visionary, and even a saint. I argue that she was at times all of these things and at times none. Like most social actors, she was muddling through, full of ambivalence and uncertainty. This book tries to capture both her vision and her struggle, making her life more accessible and less magical.

Many of the hard choices Addams made are not clear in her autobiographical writing. I suspect that this comes, in part, from the fact that she did not write her autobiography *Twenty Years at Hull-House* until much later in her life. Our recollections change as we grow older, and we often repackage events, tidying them up to make them fit a narrative and make more sense. We forget things, avoid certain topics, and occasionally tread lightly lest we offend others. Given this, I have tried as much as possible to find data that corroborate or fill in the blanks of Addams's own recollections.[2]

Along with the secondary sources, I also spent months and months gathering new data in the archives on Addams and the organizations she worked with in Chicago. Particularly, I used the special collections libraries at the Chicago Historical Society and the University of Illinois–Chicago. By focusing on the struggles Addams had with other organizations, I was led to the Chicago Relief and Aid Society's meeting minutes from the late 1880s and early 1890s. The CRAS was the main player in Chicago, so I suspected there must have been significant interaction between her and the organization, though there was scant mention of it in her memoirs. The investigation was fruitful, and the data inform some key points in my discussion of Addams's dilemmas. Finally, there are Addams's letters, a treasure trove of data that I deeply examined. These are available on microfilm and as part of the *Selected Papers of Jane Addams* project located at Duke University.

The data on Obama is surprisingly scant. There is a significant amount of noise, but little substance. Few of his letters to family and friends survive (or are public). He published several articles and was interviewed at a few points in his early adulthood as his accomplishments garnered municipal and national attention. Once rumors of his candidacy for president surfaced in 2006, his life was subjected to a scrutiny unlike any other in history. This is good news for the researcher, as nearly all of his family, friends, and acquaintances were interviewed at one point or another, and all of this information is available online. Scores of newspaper and magazine profiles, as well as a number of serious biographies (as distinguished from the half-crazed rants of those with an axe to grind), all draw on the same few letters, interviews, and journalistic profiles from major news outlets. A recent spate of interviews, conducted by *Frontline* as part of the PBS effort to provide biographic material as candidate background for the 2012 presidential elections, has offered some new terrain. These interviews, refreshingly raw and with little analysis by PBS, informed some key parts of the book.[3]

The challenge in looking at information on Obama is pushing past the journalistic framing to see the data. Nearly all of the analyses of Obama's biography were written after he started running for politics. They are typically one or two-dimensional views of Obama that reverse engineer a trajectory or narrative arc—either a struggle with racial identity or a burning desire to lead—instead of considering him as a person facing a number of competing social pressures. Some analytical treatments have begun to appear, but they tend to focus on particular aspects of Obama's political life either as a candidate or as president.[4]

While the data may have been scant at times, there was more than enough material on both Addams and Obama to consider their difficulties in balancing the American's Dilemma: How to pursue self-interest and individualism while connecting with and helping community? This book is neither a biography nor a comprehensive history of Obama and Addams as they worked to help others. I focus on illustrative moments in their early lives—points where they seemed stuck and then moved forward with experimentation and revision.

. . .

One of the main jobs of sociologists is, following Pierre Bourdieu, to "focus on the struggle" and learn how people deal with life when it doesn't go as planned (or hoped).[5] I rely heavily on Bourdieu to make sense of the struggles Addams and Obama faced in their work. From Bourdieu, I go a bit further back into French intellectualism to help figure out what it means to be a torn American. Jean-Paul Sartre understood the difficulties of making choices on matters of consequence. In each choice is a sort of vision of "what we ought to be." We are creatively building an image not just of ourselves, but also of mankind, with every decision we make:

> Of all the actions a man may take in order to create himself as he wills to be, there is not one which is not creative, at the same time, of an image of man such as he believes he ought to be. To choose between this or that is at the same time to affirm the value of that which is chosen.

Sartre gives the example of one of his former students, a young man living in France during World War II. His brother had died fighting the Germans in 1940, while his father was a German collaborator. The young man wanted to join the Resistance to avenge his brother and counterbalance his father's collaboration, but understood that now his mother lived for him, her only surviving child; his possible death would "plunge her into despair." The student, Sartre wrote,

> found himself confronted by two very different modes of action; the one concrete, immediate, but directed towards only one individual; and the other an action addressed to an end infinitely greater, a national collectivity, but for that very reason ambiguous—and it might be frustrated on the way.

Ambiguity is extremely difficult because there are values at stake—we construct our morals through our actions and our choices. "There is no reality except in action," Sartre asserts. But choosing *how* to act can be anguishing, and, in choosing, we are making morals—valuing one course over another with our very actions.[6]

Not acting is also a choice. Sartre labels inaction "quietism," or the "attitude of people who say 'let others do what I cannot do.'" It is a common way of thinking: "If only it hadn't been for X, I would have done better." Quietism evokes the idea of Marlon Brando's character Terry Malloy in *On the Waterfront*, who famously says "I coulda been a contender. I coulda been somebody." A stance of quietude allows for the sense that possibilities exist, but our potential cannot be understood by looking at what we have actually done. Sartre rejects quietude, preferring to see the moment of choice as the wellspring of action, a moment when we generate values and construct a humanist morality: "You are free, therefore choose, that is to say, invent."[7]

One of America's foremost sociologists of the twentieth century, Robert K. Merton, talked about the torn person as "ambivalent." Merton looks to social structure for explanation, asking, "How is it that these opposed pressures exist?" He tells us that these pressures can also be thought of as "normative expectations," which are part of social structure. Each position in social structure has an accompanying role, and taking on that role leads to particular dilemmas. As such, Merton writes that "sociological ambivalence refers to incompatible normative expectations of attitudes, beliefs, and behavior assigned to status (i.e., a social position)."[8] For example, a person may believe that helping her neighbors is a good thing, and she may want very much to volunteer at a local food bank. But her status as a working mother demands that she work long hours and be an intensive parent. She cannot do it all. What happens when we are ambivalent? Merton tells us that we oscillate. First we are helpful, and then we are selfish and turn away. Later, perhaps, we turn back. It is too much to be everything all at once.

Robert Lynd, another American sociologist, helps Merton develop the idea of ambivalence by pointing to contradictions inherent in our social structure. We are expected to live according to certain assumptions or ideas, even if they are diametrically opposed. "[T]he culture may carry along side by side both assertions: the one reflecting deep needs close to the heart's desire and the other heavily authorized by class or other authority." Lynd blames history and our lack of critical thinking for this bind: Ideas that were developed at one time are carried to the next, without much questioning. There is also a sense in which this legacy of contradiction is emblematic of power differentials. Lynd summarizes the tensions of the American's Dilemma (without naming it as such) as follows:

1. The United States is the best and greatest nation on earth and will always remain so.

2. Individualism, "the survival of the fittest," is the law of nature and the secret of America's greatness; and restrictions on individual freedom are un-American and kill initiative.

   But: No man should live for himself alone; for people ought to be loyal and stand together and work for common purposes.[9]

The potential for ambivalence is clear. Perhaps what is most helpful in the work of Merton and Lynd is that they help us see that the American's Dilemma is not, at least in the first instance, a question of individual moral failure.

Much of sociology is aimed at peering inside the commonsense notions, like ambivalence, that shape our lives. But understanding one social process usually leads to more questions. In this instance, one naturally wonders how to become *sure*, how to shed ambivalence. American pragmatism, which emerged along with the industrial revolution as we "searched for order" in a sea of chaos, can perhaps be helpful.[10] The late-nineteenth century was a topsy-turvy time, with massive immigration feeding a growing industrial juggernaut. John Dewey, William James, Charles S. Peirce, and even Jane Addams (to name just a few) were dissatisfied with the ability of European philosophy to make sense of the world around them. So the pragmatists developed their own strand of thinking and a new set of theoretical lenses to view the world in a different way.

Addams, prefiguring Merton and Lynd, talked about "perplexity" in daily life, particularly when habits break down. For her, moments of "rupture" left people unsure of know how to move forward—perplexed. Dewey characterizes this rupture as a moment when "'there is something the matter,' when there is some 'trouble' in an existing situation." Mary Parker Follett, one of the first women on the faculty at Harvard Business School, called it a "mystery moment." Whatever the name, these are moments, big and small, when we pause, without a clear roadmap. We move forward in intermediate stages, tentatively, and with uncertainty. We might even think of it, following Charles Lindblom, as "muddling" through. While frustrating, this time is a creative and experimental moment in social action, what Follett called a "dynamo station." Out of this creativity comes new ways we might accept or reject based on whether they work (in Dewey's words, "define and clarify the problem at hand").[11]

When Addams and Obama faced "contradictory cultural values," they broke through their ambivalence in unique ways. Addams started a new type of organization in Chicago and made up the rules as she went along, taking cues from her neighbors. Obama did something similar, listening closely to South Side Chicago community members, then empowering them to go get what they needed. At times along the way, both had troubles and faced confusion. But they always created a way forward in due time.[12]

. . .

Creating new ways of acting—as opposed to doing something once or twice in order to maintain social distance—is something that William Graham Sumner, the second president of the American Sociological Association (1908–1909) wrote about at length in his book *Folkways*. Sumner opens his book with a quote from Castiglione, a sixteenth-century author who wrote a book on courtiers:

> Thus it is clearly seen that use, rather than reason, has power to introduce new
> things amongst us, and to do
> away with old things.[13]

Action (use) is the driving force behind social creation. Through action, Sumner explained, we develop "folkways," which can be understood as a metaphor for the lines of social action we follow. When a number of people all choose a similar way to satisfy a given need, they are traveling the same "way," and a custom is developed. Habits of individuals become collective customs (we might hope for a sort of culture that would make helping each other and asking for help normal). Alexis de Tocqueville, who wrote of his observations on America during his travels in the 1830s, identified reciprocal relations or norms of reciprocity as being a major element of our society. What he called our "habits of the heart" and what Sumner called "folkways" are what keep things working.[14]

When a custom has some relation to social welfare in our neighborhood (as opposed to something like fashion or entertainment), folkways are converted into mores. We need to travel existing folkways or create new ones in order to satisfy our impulse to help others, to live up to our values. We travel the road together, find new roads, and create values. Addams herself evoked this metaphor of the road:

> We are learning that a standard of social ethics is not attained by travelling a sequestered byway, but by mixing on the thronged and common road where all must turn out for one another, and at least see the size of one another's burdens.[15]

The emphasis on the importance of satisfying needs in order to create new habits is important for understanding this book. Following Sumner, the dilemma should be considered an "impelling force" that pushes us to creativity, trying out different ways to satisfy our needs. Once we figure out something that works, we "unconsciously cooperate to build up associations, organization, customs, and institutions which, after a time, appear full grown and actual, although no one intended, or planned, or understood them in advance."[16] For Sumner, the process of building folkways is simple. People simply try over and over until their actions feel "true" and "right," then they make a habit of those particular actions.

In fact, based on the thought of those men and women considered so far, the community emerges as the creative center for helping in society. Follett's thinking about democracy might be understood as having emerged out of the "dynamo station" of the Roxbury Children's House, the Roxbury debating club, and numerous other groups centered on the civic engagement of new immigrants in her Boston suburb. In Follett's terms, coming to help in these spaces was a relational process, with each "experience as an interplay of forces, as the activity of relating leading through fresh relatings to a new activity."[17] She helped her neighbors, and they helped her see things with fresh eyes and take up new actions. This vision of democracy empowers every social actor through "power-with," a "co-active" rather than "coercive" power. Follett's ideal, one that Obama and Addams enacted in Chicago, is reciprocal community interaction that creates energy and gives us the capacity to bring about change through new, shared habits.[18]

Tocqueville went so far as to say that the habits we develop in our communities are crucial to American democracy. Dewey agreed, arguing that, through our relations with one another, Americans gain social intelligence and move toward a more robust democracy. It is a continual process that Dewey calls "perfecting, maturing, [and] refining" as we develop habits and grow.[19]

Hannah Arendt suggests a way to think of such a continual process as one of "understanding" as opposed to gaining knowledge. Perhaps one only needs to know so much before heading out on a new venture. Academics, in particular, are leery of new ventures unless they are backed by adequate preparation and knowledge. Having "correct information and scientific knowledge" is one way we might know the social world. But the approach has its limits. It is "unequivocal" in its content. At a certain point, we know what there is and what we ought to know about something, and then we act accordingly. The search for understanding, informed by a more activist knowledge, is different. It involves looking for meaning and includes a dose of imagination. Social life is messy, strange, and full of "vicious circles," says Arendt. Using our imagination, which is not mere "fancy," allows us to

> see things in their proper perspective, to be strong enough to put that which is too close at a certain distance so that we can see and understand it without bias and prejudice, to be generous enough to bridge abysses of remoteness until we can see and understand everything that is too far away from us as though it were our own affair. This distancing of some things and bridging the abysses to others is part of the dialogue of understanding, for whose purposes direct experience establishes too close a contact and mere knowledge erects artificial barriers. Without this kind of imagination, which actually is understanding, we would never be able to take our bearings in the world. It is the only inner compass we have.[20]

The idea of using imagination to transcend scholarly knowledge in search of understanding is slippery. Simply put, Arendt is suggesting that understanding, as a concept, helps us see action differently. If we are searching for meaning, we do not gather up information and then act on it. We engage in a never-ending process of dialogue with the world and ourselves, and at times we are rewarded, "catch[ing] at least a glimpse of the always frightening light of truth."[21] At certain points, there was only so much for Addams and Obama to know before they intuited that it was time to act. We cannot read our way out of our dilemmas. Dewey, the pragmatists, and Arendt all held that we experiment until we see that glimpse of truth.

.   .   .

Armed with the ideas presented above, I looked for particular instances in the lives of Addams and Obama. Seeking out when they showed ambivalence, when they took action or engaged in quietude, when they came up against roadblocks or moved forward creating new folkways—all these questions and more guided my examination of the data from both cases. Their individual biographies are sites for exploring common social dilemmas and thinking through the dialectical relationship between biography and history.

What I left behind was the assumption of a unitary society. Locating dilemmas in individuals, but given by social structures, shifts the analytical frame. It allows one to consider the context and situate an individual in a *particular* society and particular context, then ask how that structure might have pushed and pulled in a contradictory way. What emerged, as shaped by the theoretical underpinnings of my study, was a certain rhythm of social action: Incommensurable choices force us eventually to experiment, revise, and create new habits. These habits guide us, but at times they break down in the face of new contradictions, and we have to begin the creative process anew. Or we stay stuck. But when we continue to create together, eventually we develop our social ethics and contribute to democracy.

Acknowledgments

Push and shove, first is best. I want to thank my wife, Mary-Priscilla Stevens, who deserves more than a dedication for her endless suffering as she read and reread everything I wrote for this book. I would never have started, let alone finished, this project without her help.

The book has changed quite a bit since I first sat down with Kate Wahl in the Denver convention center in 2012. What has not changed is her support and her editorial professionalism. Kate, you are the best.

Thanks to the two anonymous reviewers who read my entire manuscript on behalf of Stanford University Press. Your comments were insightful and quite helpful; my manuscript is better as a result of your care. I know the work that goes into such reviews, and I appreciate it.

The ideas in this project have been developing in fits and starts for the past ten years. Along the way, I have particularly benefited from the advice and support of the following people—Katelin Albert, Chas Camic, Hae Yeon Choo, Lis Clemens, Ivan Ermakoff, Myra Marx Ferree, Phil Goodman, Phil Gorski, Cinthya Guzman, Andreas Hoffbauer, Shamus Khan, Anna Korteweg, Vanina Leschziner, John Myles, Letta Page, Tricia Seifert, Dan Silver, Richard Swedberg, and Burin Yildiztekin. And I would be remiss if I did not acknowledge the students who read draft chapters of the book as part of an undergraduate seminar with me at the University of Toronto at Mississauga. Thanks to all of you—your efforts show that academic production truly requires a community.

Thanks to the scholars and other writers I cite in the book, particularly the biographers of Addams and Obama. Your careful historical research made my job much easier at times. And I very much enjoyed learning from you all.

I never would have tried to write a book in the first place had it not been for Mustafa Emirbayer. His instruction on pragmatism and the sociology of Pierre Bourdieu is what inspired me to pursue my research. As a mentor and friend, he poked and prodded at me, encouraging me in the development of my project. Mustafa, I put a few extra commas in the book, just for you.

Everyone needs cheerleaders. I have been fortunate to have several. My loudest and most spirited have been my parents, Cathryn and Paul Baird. Even at my most anxious and least productive moments, they never doubted my ability to finish the job. They also put up with my irritability and closed-mouth sulks—things I am sure they thought they had left behind. For this and more, I am grateful.

And then there are those who have had to live with the book every day, like it or not. I would like to thank my two children, Abby and Sam, and offer an apology: I am sorry that you had to spend an inordinate amount of your childhood hearing about Jane Addams. I promise to spend time in the future talking about the present. And I thank you for your consistent support as I went through the writing process. Your hugs and supportive questions kept me going during those lonely mornings of writing.

Finally, thank you to Frank Hammond, Pat Rude, John Rauh, and Mary Rauh for teaching me nearly everything I know about politics. I could not ask for better teachers and friends.

Notes

Chapter One

1. Addams (1961, 108–109).
2. Addams (1961, 83); Davis (1984).
3. Hunter (1902, 81–82); Davis (1984).
4. Scholars have exhaustively studied the emergence of the settlement house in the United States (see Carson 1990, Crocker 1992, Davis 1984, and Trattner 1999).
5. What do I mean by politics? Weber (1946, 77–79) is helpful here, pointing us to activities tied to the state and the relative distribution of power. Marx (especially writings in Tucker 1978, 70–93, 469–500) is also helpful, asking us to consider that politics is a reflection of class struggle. As capitalists control the system of production, they also become the dominant political group in society. Encouraged by Weber and Marx, then, we can think of politics as the struggle over the power to get things done (typically through state resources) in a context in which capitalist elites have a significant amount of control. This effort, following Weber, requires leadership. Since ambivalence implies powerlessness (an uncertainty as to what to do and how to do it), entering into the political sphere offers the chance to accrue power and break the log-jam. But this power typically comes through some sort of negotiated understanding with capitalist elites. Joining the political fray can be quite rough and tumble; it can require compromise and even result in dirty hands (calling to mind Sartre's (1985) *Les Main Sales*). Here we might draw on Michel Foucault's (1978, 93) understanding of politics as "war by other means," which ties to Carl Schmitt's (1996, 26) notion of politics as an exercise in confronting distinctions in society "between friend and foe." We get a sense of the political as a battle-ground, where you must quickly identify who your friends are and consider all others potential enemies. The political battle is fought through confrontation and compromise. In practical terms, I will focus primarily on electoral politics, considering how becoming political impacted the efforts of Addams and Obama to help others. But I will also consider the broader struggles each

faced in scaling up their efforts and effecting change while balancing the need to appease capitalist elites.

6. There are a number of terms one might use to describe the decisions that emerge out of moments of dilemma faced by Addams and Obama—times when they seem to have deviated from expressed principles. One might talk of cooperation, or compromise, or even selling-out. I prefer the less judgmental descriptor of their actions as "revisions." This takes us to the pragmatist ideas presented in the Appendix. We are never finished with the process of gaining social intelligence through trying different ways to move forward. True, we don't always see the consequences of our actions. And some decisions matter more than others. In the case of Addams and Obama, their increasing connections to Chicago elites and electoral politics impacted their work in helping others. They were able to do more of some things but had to leave other things behind.

7. Hewitt (1989, 13) considers individualism as "one pole of an axis of cultural variation" with the other pole loosely considered "communitarian" in terms of orientation. Stone (2008) sees the struggle in different terms, more as one internal to the "good Samaritan" who has to decide whether she should help or leave it to the government. Dionne (2012) presents the division in a political context, talking of our "divided political heart." The common denominator across these works is the idea of being pulled in different directions by our society's demands.

8. I use this turn of phrase deliberately. It is from a song written by Joe Hill in 1911. The song is a parody of the Salvation Army, which in Hill's mind was more focused on salvation than on helping. This song was likely sung in Chicago during Addams's time, with the following chorus:

You will eat, bye and bye,

In that glorious land above the sky;

Work and pray, live on hay,

You'll get pie in the sky when you die.

See *http://www.folkarchive.de/pie.html* for more information on the song.

9. James (1981, 26); Rorty (1982, 175).

Chapter Two

1. See Addams's "Cassandra" speech in *The Selected Papers of Jane Addams* (vol. 1), which will be cited with a reference to the appropriate volume and editors, in this case: Bryan, Bair, and De Angury (2003, 429). The SPJA contain nearly all of Addams's speeches and letters, along with background biography.

2. Brown (2004, 113); Bryan, Bair, and De Angury (2003, 427); Knight (2005, 113–114).

3. Letter dated September 6, 1881, in Bryan, Bair, and De Angury (2009, 59–60).

4. August 1881 letters from John Linn and Rev. Caverno in Bryan, Bair, De Angury (2009, 56–58).

5. See Sklar (1990) and Knight (2005, 117).

6. Bryan, Bair, and De Angury (2003, 428–430). See also Lengermann and Niebrugge (2007) and Brown (2004, 95).

7. See Brown (2004, 92–93) and Knight (2005, 107–108). See also Lengermann and Niebrugge (2007, 95–96), who observe that this kind of critical narrative was confined mainly to "upper-middle-class women—or working-class women who somehow fought their way to a college education." They point out that due to a lack of relative resources, black women were not able to pursue the settlement house as a career.

8. Bryan, Bair, and De Angury (2003, 469–472); Diliberto (1999, 31–32).

9. Brown (2004, 22–27); Knight (2005, 33).

10. Given that this recollection sets up Addams's autobiography *Twenty Years at Hull-House* (1961, 2), we should take this literary license with a grain of salt. But it is clear that she was aware of the inequality from an early age. On reading and the library, see Knight (2005, 50) and Polikoff (1999, 15).

11. Knight (2005, 20–22, 73); Brown (2004, 58–59); Addams (1961, 8).

12. Addams (1961, 9).

13. See Bryan, Bair, and De Angury (2009, 475) and Brown (2004, 27) on marriage; see Knight (2005, 43–53) on culture and education.

14. Addams (1961, 19–20); Knight (2005, 58).

15. Brown (2004, 39–40); Knight (2005, 70–75).

16. Addams (1961, 28, 33); Knight (2005, 81).

17. Knight (2005, 86–87; Addams (1961, 34–35, 24–25).

18. Knight (2005, 78, 85, 91, 101); Addams (1961, 25–26).

19. Knight (2005, 101).

20. Addams (1961, 40).

21. William James termed neurasthenia "Americanitis."

22. As Knight (2005, 117) points out, Addams would "spend much of her twenties testing her willingness to claim [her freedom]." Just over a decade after Jane went to Philadelphia, Charlotte Perkins Gilman would capture this dynamic in her famous *The Yellow Wallpaper*.

23. Knight (2005, 122).

24. Bryan, Bair, and De Angury (2009, 176–177, 198–203, 236, 287).

25. Ibid., pp. 270–271; Addams (1961, 49–50).

26. Letter dated January 4, 1883, in Bryan, Bair, and De Angury (2009, 187–189).

27. Addams (1961, 49–40).

28. Addams (1927) would later call Tolstoy's book *What to Do?* a "book that changed my life." Best known for his novels, such as *War and Peace* and *Anna Karenina*, Tolstoy was, in his time, a highly influential social activist and

public intellectual. Like Georg Simmel, Tolstoy envisioned the process of helping as a face-to-face relation that maintains the dignity of the poor:

> It is necessary that we should be in a condition to seat ourselves by the
> bunk of a tatterdemalion and converse earnestly with him in such a man-
> ner, that he may feel that the man who is talking with him respects and
> loves him, and is not putting on airs and admiring himself. And in order
> that this may be so, it is necessary that a man should find the meaning of
> life outside himself. This is what is requisite in order that good should be
> done, and this is what it is difficult to find. (Tolstoy 1887, 6)

(A tatterdemalion is literally a ragged or tattered person.) In essence, giving
money to a poor person seems like paying to maintain a distance. Tolstoy (1887,
6), writes, "But what is it you have given? It was only for the sake of getting
rid of him." So he, too, supported reciprocal interactions: One should come
into direct contact with the person, recognizing commonalities while pushing
through an uncomfortable barrier. He writes of a visit to a marketplace where
he could feel the looks of the poor. He felt questioned by their stares: "'Why
have you, a man from another world, halted here beside us?'" Tolstoy (1887,
14) says he stood still and unspeaking for some time, and gradually felt more
comfortable: "after the interchange of two or three glances we felt we were both
men, and we ceased to fear each other." Moving outside a habitual and comfortable social space—in effect, forcing a rupture that requires being inquisitive
and creative about how to move forward—was essential for Tolstoy. Addams
and Obama made similar moves in their efforts in Chicago.

29. Tolstoy (1887, 6).

30. Mill (1882); Knight (2005, 148).

31. Addams (1961, 50); Knight (2005, 149).

32. Bowker (1887, 158–159).

33. Addams (1961, 55); the data show that Addams definitely read the article—see Brown (2004, 169), Knight (2005, 453, n.63), and Wise (1963) for
evidence.

34. Knight, (2005, 150–151); Bryan, Bair, and De Angury (2009, 479–485).

35. Addams (1961, 55–57).

36. Jane Addams, "Outgrowths of Toynbee Hall," December 3, 1891 [ad-
dress delivered to the Chicago Woman's Club], from the Jane Addams Memorial Collection (JAMC), Special Collections, The University Library, University
of Illinois at Chicago, JAMC (reel 46–0480–0496); letter dated June 14, 1888,
from Jane Addams to Sarah Alice Addams Haldeman, Haldeman-Julius Family
Papers, JAMC (reel 2–0968–0973).

37. See Briggs and Macartney (1892) for in-depth discussion of the influences on Toynbee Hall. In a reverse of Jane Addams's story, the catalyst for
Barnett's career in helping others seems to have been a trip to America, where
he saw the influence of education on freed African Americans. See Meacham

(1987, ch. 2) for more detail; Nora Marks, "Two Women's Work: The Misses Addams and Starr Astonish the West Siders," *Chicago Daily Tribune*, May 19, 1890, pp. 1–2. This is one of the first substantive journalistic accounts of practice at Hull-House.

38. "Chicago's Toynbee Hall" *Chicago Daily Tribune*, June 21, 1891, p. 6.

39. Robert A. Woods, "The Social Awakening in London," *Scribner's Magazine* 11, no. 4 (April 1892): 401–424.

40. Addams (1961, 41, 57); Bryan, Bair, and De Angury (2009, 498).

41. Much of the history and discussion of pragmatism that follows is drawn from Schneiderhan (2011).

42. Hofstadter (1963, 2).

43. For a discussion of the terms "indoor" and "outdoor" relief, see McCarthy (1982, 54); see also Brown (1941) and Mayer (1978) for excellent overviews of mid-nineteenth-century charity in Chicago.

44. They were what McCarthy (1982, 23, 30–31) terms a "dedicated band of semiprofessional humanitarians." The idea of elites creating distance is reminiscent of Tolstoy and Simmel.

45. Founded as the Chicago Relief Association in 1850, it was created by rich businessmen who wanted to start a group like New York's Association for Improving the Condition of the Poor. The group was typical of American relief organizations—it emphasized the elimination of begging, the promotion of self-sufficiency, and the minimization of fraud through record keeping. In 1857, the organization added "aid" to its title to become the Chicago Relief and Aid Society (CRAS). This change was a response to widespread unemployment and financial panic, as well as to the perception that it had previously served primarily as a relief arm of the county and city government. See McCarthy (1982, 54), Sawislak (2004, 145), and Brown (1941, 40).

46. Sawislak (1995, 2); Flanagan (2002, 13–14); Chicago Relief and Aid Society Meeting Minutes, vol. 1, 1871–1887, p. 5, United Charities of Chicago Collection (UCCC), Chicago Historical Society. In the words of Sawislak (1995, 91), the CRAS became "a social welfare giant."

47. Sawislak (1995, 87, 119); Nelson (1966, 61); Johnson (1923, 61); McCarthy (1982, 70).

48. Mayer (1978, 57).

49. Chicago Relief and Aid Society Annual Reports, 1891–1908, pp. 18–22, UCCC.

50. Chicago Relief and Aid Society Board Meeting, April 7, 1883, p. 352; Chicago Relief and Aid Society Meeting Minutes, vol. 1, 1871–1887, UCCC.

51. This approach was not always well received; during the financial panic of 1873, some Chicagoans voiced displeasure with the CRAS by mobbing its headquarters and demanding that it relinquish its remaining Great Fire relief funds for disbursement to the poor. The superintendent of the CRAS was able

to diffuse the tension by offering jobs to some of the mob. The organization retained control and did not disburse any significant funds. See McCarthy (1982, 70) and Johnson (1923, 62).

52. See Johnson (1923) for a discussion of charity organization and the "Hamburgh Patriotic Society." See Steinmetz (1993) for a related discussion of charity in nineteenth-century Germany. For more on charity organization, see Wenocur and Reisch (2001), Watson (1971), and Katz (1996). For specifics on the Chicago case, see Kusmer (1973).

53. Trattner (1999, 95).

54. Ibid., p. 97.

55. Annual Report of the Directors of the Charity Organization Society of Chicago for the Year Ending October 1, 1886, UCCC. (note: no existing printed reports exist for prior years) Some scholars reject the optimistic view of the friendly visit, arguing that it was grounded in the premise of inequality of condition. Lubove (1980, 16) is skeptical of how "friendly" the visits actually were, seeing the interactions as more a process of "character reformation." And Katz (1996, 79) sees the friendly visitor as a "sympathetic friend, an official, a teacher, and a spy."

56. Johnson (1923, 54–55).

57. See Johnson (1899) and Mayer (1978, 83–85) for more. Of note is that in the shadow of the Relief and Aid Society, the Chicago Charity Organization Society had managed to develop ties to government, thereby becoming a viable player—maybe even the most important player—in helping people in Chicago.

58. Johnson (1923, 64–65).

59. 1886 Annual Report, Charity Organization of Chicago, pp. 10–11, UCCC.

60. Nelson (1966, 56–57). During the early 1830s, nearly the entire Cherokee nation had been forcibly relocated from Georgia and the Carolinas to poor-quality land in Oklahoma. The case was considered at a meeting of the Relief and Aid in April 1893. See Chicago Relief and Aid Society Meeting Minutes, vol. 2, 1887–1909, April 10 and May 8, 1893, UCCC.

61. See Rom (1958, 56), whose unpublished manuscript, a history of the United Charities of Chicago, is part of the UCCC.

62. See Brown (2004, 208) for the dilemma of choosing between family and the Chicago project. For the early Chicago scheme, see Bryan, Bair, and De Angury (2009, 499, 518 n.180), Linn(2000, 91), and Brown (2004, 210–220).

63. David Swing, "A New Social Movement," *Chicago Evening Journal*, June 8, 1889, p. 4. But, there are no data indicating that Addams made any initial efforts to connect her work at Hull-House to the Relief and Aid or to the remnants of the Chicago Charity Organization Society. Given the prominence of the Relief and Aid in Chicago social provision, the absence of any significant interactions between the Chicago Relief and Aid Society and Hull-House is remarkable. See Brown (2004, 208) on alumnae meeting.

64. Brown (2004, 217–221); Knight (2005, 195–196).

65. Addams (1961, 41).

Chapter Three

1. Obama (2010, 17).

2. Jane Addams's diary, 1889–1890, Swarthmore College Peace Collection, JAMC (reel 29–0101).

3. In particular, see Addams's letter to her sister of October 8, 1889, and Starr's lengthy letters to her family in November 1889, JAMC (reel 2–1085–1109); Jenny Dow, "The Chicago Toynbee Hall," *Unity*, March 15, 1890, *Hull-House Scrapbook I*, JAMC; For a discussion of the clubs and kindergarten see Knight (2005, 204).

4. Kelley (1986, 77).

5. Addams (1894, 107); Brown (2004, 233); Moore (1897, 632).

6. Jane Addams, "Outgrowths of Toynbee Hall," December 3, 1891, p. 15, JAMC (reel 46–0480–0496); Nora Marks, "Two Women's Work: The Misses Addams and Starr Astonish the West Siders," *Chicago Daily Tribune*, May 19, 1890, pp. 1–2.

7. Brown (2004, 240).

8. Jane Addams, "Outgrowths of Toynbee Hall," p. 13; Addams (1894, 99); Brown (2004, 233–235); Herndon (1892, 351–352); Knight (2005, 225).

9. Addams (2002, 14).

10. Ibid., pp. 12–13.

11. Briggs and Macartney (1984, 5).

12. Brown (2004, 246).

13. It is worth noting that the constellation of ethnicity was quite different then. Sharp social divisions between different groups of Europeans, some of which were not classified as "white" when they first immigrated to the United States, make it overly simplistic to say Addams worked "only" with whites.

14. Knight (2005, 237); Brown (2004, 238, 261); Sunderland (1893, 401).

15. Knight (2005, 247); Addams (1894, 102).

16. Sklar (1990, 95); Brown (2004, 258).

17. According to Knight (2005, 224–225), Hull-House's financial records for 1890–91 show that Addams was quickly running out of money.

18. See Residents of Hull-House (1895, 229).

19. Addams (1894, 106).

20. Ibid.; also see "What Hull House Really Is," *Chicago Daily Tribune*, April 28, 1895, p. 47; Residents of Hull-House (1895).

21. Just two years later, in 1892, Addams would join a group that was extremely critical of the Relief and Aid Society's practice of closing its doors during the summer. See the April 5, 1890, and March 7, 1892, CRAS Board of Directors meetings, UCCC.

22. Addams (1961, 72).

23. "Hull House Kitchen Opened," *Chicago Record,* August 24, 1893. Also see Addams (1894, 110). There appears to be some confusion as to when the Diet Kitchen actually began. An advertising flyer from the Rockford College Archives clearly shows that some form of the Diet Kitchen existed in 1891 (see Hull-House, Rockford College Archives, Hull-House Flyers, 1890s Box), but according to the newspaper account and Brown (2004, 261), it did not open until 1893.

24. Addams (1961, 87).

25. Ibid.

26. See Habermas (1989) for a discussion of the importance of the coffee-house in the historical development of the public sphere.

27. The origins of the Chicago Committee on Charity Organization (COCO) are not completely clear. See Knight (2005, 475 n.87) and the *Chicago Daily Tribune,* December 28, 1891, p. 6.

28. *Chicago Daily Tribune,* December 27, 1891, p. 18.

29. The data call into question the conventional story that Addams's ideas and work were generally at odds with the charity organization approach. See, for example, Agnew (2004), Lengermann and Niebrugge (2007, 109), Brown (2004), and Westhoff (2007). Mina Carson (1990) is one of the few scholars to avoid this line of thinking; she hints at early support by Hull-House residents for the Chicago Bureau of Charities.

30. Chicago Relief and Aid Society Meeting Minutes, vol. 2, 1887–1909, pp. 106–109, UCCC; see *The Daily Inter Ocean,* Tuesday morning, January 5, 1892, for a report on the meeting (originals at the Chicago Historical Society Library, Chicago). The article does not mention Addams as part of the delegation, but the meeting minutes indicate that she did attend.

31. *Chicago Daily Tribune,* January 19, 1892, p. 10; Chicago Relief and Aid Society Meeting Minutes, vol. 2, 1887–1909, pp. 110–121, UCCC.

32. For this exchange, see Chicago Relief and Aid Society Meeting Minutes, vol. 2, 1887–1909, pp. 124–133.

33. Letter dated July 26, 1892, Ellen Gates Starr to Mary Blaisdell, pp. 1–7, Ellen Gates Starr Papers, Sophia Smith Collection, Smith College, Northampton, Massachusetts, in JAMC, Special Collections, The University Library, University of Illinois at Chicago.

34. See Weekly Program of Lectures, Clubs, Classes, Etc. March 1, 1892, Hull-House, Rockford College Archives, Hull-House Flyers 1890s Box, p. 15.

35. Letter dated July 26, 1892, Ellen Gates Starr to Mary Blaisdell, pp. 1–7, Ellen Gates Starr Papers, Sophia Smith Collection, Smith College, Northampton, Massachusetts, in JAMC. Also see Addams (1961, 74–75), Knight (2005, 475 n.87), Diliberto (1999, 194), and Davis (2000, 92). On the Plymouth conference, see Davis (2000, 92) and Dilberto (1999, 191).

36. Letter dated May 24, 1896, Bernard Bosanquet to Jane Addams, JAMC

(reel 3–0176); letter dated September 4, 1895, Robert A. Woods to Jane Addams, JAMC (reel 2–1760); Woods (1892, 408).

37. Steeples and Whitten (1998, 48). Stead (1894) expanded upon his speech and published his thoughts in *If Christ Came to Chicago!*, which was read widely at the time.

38. "In Aid of Charity," *Chicago Daily Tribune*, December 27, 1891, p. 18.

39. On the Columbian Exposition, see Rydell (2004); Knight (2005, 269–270).

40. Moore (1897, 634); Knight (2005, 237).

41. See Knight (2005, 299–302) and Linn (2000, 162–164) for discussion of the events surrounding the creation of the Civic Federation. Also see the Chicago Civic Federation Papers Collection at the Chicago Historical Society.

42. Box 1, Folder 1, Minutes November 23, 1893, to June 9, 1898, Chicago Civic Federation Papers, Chicago Historical Society. The very first issue of the *American Journal of Sociology* contains an article dedicated to the social phenomenon of the Chicago Civic Federation. See Small (1895, 79–80).

43. Addams (1961, 171); Box 1, Folder "General Papers 1894–1941 and Articles of Incorporation, January 31, 1894," Chicago Civic Federation Papers, Chicago Historical Society; for information on Albion Small, see *http://www.asanet.org/about/presidents/Albion_Small.cfm*; letter to Jane Addams from Albion Small, dated December 26, 1893, Civic Federation Papers, Box 1, Folder "General Papers 1894–1941 and Articles of Incorporation, January 31, 1894," Chicago Civic Federation Papers, Chicago Historical Society.

44. Chicago Historical Society, Charity Organization Society, Chicago Relief Association and Chicago Bureau of Charities Minutes Books; Chicago Relief and Aid Society Meeting Minutes, vol. 2, 1887–1909, February 5, 1894, Chicago Relief and Aid Society Board Meeting, p. 219, UCCC. See also Mayer (1978).

45. Report of the Chicago Relief Association to the Civic Federation to its Contributors, June 20, 1894, pp. 11–12, Chicago Historical Society.

46. Chicago Relief and Aid Society Board Meeting, May 8, 1894, p. 231, Chicago Relief and Aid Society Meeting Minutes, vol. 2, 1887–1909, pp. 11–13, UCCC. Report of the Chicago Relief Association to the Civic Federation to its Contributors and the Public, June 20, 1894, Chicago Historical Society.

47. Addams (1961, 108–109).

48. Chicago Relief and Aid Society Board Meeting, May 8, 1894, p. 231, Chicago Relief and Aid Society Meeting Minutes, vol. 2, 1887–1909, pp. 248–251, UCCC.

Chapter Four

1. Addams (2002, 13).

2. Knight (2005, 195–196, 306–308); Brown (2004, 217–219, 255–258).

3. For a general overview of the strike, see Schneirov, Stromquist, and Salvatore (1999) and Smith (2004); see also Lindsey (1964).

4. Brown (1999, 133, 135).

5. Knight (2005, 316–318); Addams (1961, 151). Of interest is a passage from Addams's biography in which she recalls being roundly criticized by a man who said "You are all right now, but, mark my words, when you are subsidized by the millionaires you will be afraid to talk like this [things will be different]"(1961, 122–123).

6. Knight (2005, 321); Addams (1961, 172) mentioned her illness as a time for reflection: "I had time to review carefully many things in my mind during the long days of convalescence following an illness of typhoid fever which I suffered in the autumn of 1895."

7. Addams (1912); Knight (2005, 361).

8. Knight (2005, 243–244).

9. Chicago Civic Federation Central Council Meeting, June 21, 1894, Chicago Historical Society Collection; for background see Davis (2000, 120–121) and Knight (2005, 337–338). "Editorial: The `New Woman' Scavenger," *Chicago Daily Tribune,* March 21, 1895, p. 6, col. 3.

10. Addams (1961, 114) later acknowledged that Powers "did little to oppose the election to the aldermanic office of a member of the Hull-House Men's Club who thus became his colleague in the city council." Within a few months, Lawler and Powers were working closely together. See also Davis (2000, 122) and Davis (1984, 154); Knight (2005, 340–342).

11. Addams (1961, 105–106).

12. Ibid., p. 106.

13. Ibid., pp. 114–115; Knight (2005, 387).

14. Chicago Relief and Aid Society Meeting Minutes, vol. 2, 1887–1909, pp. 248–251, UCCC. In some of the meeting minutes and publications, the organization is referred to as the Chicago Bureau of *Associated* Charities (CBAC).

15. Box 5, Chicago Bureau of Charities Executive Committee Minutes, 1894–1903, p. 13, of volume of minutes from November 20, 1894–May 11, 1895, UCCC.

16. See corporation file number 07062397, Illinois Department of State.

17. See Knight (2005, 335–336); Addams also created a board of directors at this time, evidence of her need to create a pool of potential donors for fundraising.

18. Corporation file number 07062397, Illinois Department of State.

19. For the description, see pp. 30–31, *Palmer House Illustrated,* Chicago: J. M. Wing & Co., 1876. Chicago Historical Society Palmer House Collection; Box 5, 55c 1,448–Chicago Bureau of Charities Executive Committee Minutes 1894–1903. By 1895, Addams was giving speeches all over the country—for example, she spoke to United Charities in New York City in 1895. See Brown (2004, 2–4).

20. Box 5, Chicago Bureau of Charities Executive Committee Minutes 1894–1903, volume of minutes from November 20, 1894–May 11, 1895, UCCC. Ninth Annual Report of the Chicago Bureau of Charities for the Fiscal Year Ending May 31, 1903, p. 7.

21. Chicago Bureau of Charities Executive Committee Meeting Minutes, November 20, 1894, pp. 4–5, November 20, 1894–May 11, 1895; 1894, Chicago Bureau of Charities Executive Committee Meeting Minutes, November 20, 1894, pp. 1–2.

22. Sixth and Seventh Annual Reports of the Chicago Bureau of Charities, November 1, 1899–May 31,1901, UCCC (note: there was only one report for the two years); Fifth Annual Report of the Chicago Bureau of Charities, November 1, 1899–October 31, 1899; see both the Eighth Annual Report of the Chicago Bureau of Charities, for fiscal year ending May 31, 1902, and the Ninth Annual Report of the Chicago Bureau of Charities, for fiscal year ending May 31, 1903; the Chicago Bureau of Charities Condensed Report Year ending May 31, 1906; Ninth Annual Report of the Chicago Bureau of Charities, for fiscal year ending May 31, 1903, p. 38; 1898 pamphlet by West Side District of Chicago Bureau of Associated Charities entitled "Social Service."

23. Chicago Relief and Aid Society Board Meeting of January 7, 1895, pp. 240–243, in Chicago Relief and Aid Society Meeting Minutes, vol. 2, 1887–1909, UCCC; see pp. 248–251 of Meeting Minutes particularly. I quote extensively from this letter because of its importance for my argument and for the historical record. See Schneiderhan (2008) for a discussion of the importance of this data for Addams scholars.

24. As Knight (2005, 336) points out, Addams "was rarely seen to be angry when older" and was a firm believer in Tolstoy's approach to life as expressed in *My Religion*, which urges the avoidance of both physical violence and anger. See Westbrook (1991, 80–81) for evidence of a conversation between John Dewey and Addams in which she firmly opposed personal antagonism of any sort.

25. Letter dated December 26, 1893, from Albion Small to Jane Addams, Chicago Civic Federation Papers, Box 1, Folder of "General Papers 1894–1941 and Articles of Incorporation January 31, 1894."[continue]

26. "Relief vs. Charity. An Explanation of Charity Organization Work with Especial Reference to Administrative Expense" by Charles Frederick Weller, Bureau of Associated Charities Press, Chicago, 1899; Chicago Historical Society, Folder of Miscellaneous Pamphlets of Chicago Bureau of Charities, "Chicago Bureau of Associated Charities" West Side District report for activities between September 1, 1898 and September 1, 1899, UCCC; Report of General Superintendent to Executive Committee of the CBC, December 8, 1903, UCCC.

27. In early 1897, the bureau's board of directors decided to send a letter to the mayor's office asking him to issue a "proclamation requesting funds" for the bureau (January 22, 1897, CBC Executive Committee Meeting Minutes, 1894–

1903, UCCC). The bureau would then distribute the money to other social provision organizations. At a subsequent meeting, the bureau board asked Lyman Gage to sign a postscript at the bottom of the letter saying he agreed that the mayor should do this. Recall that Gage was a major figure in Chicago banking and was active in the Relief and Aid. He (along with two other men) complied with the board's request; the postscript, with separate signatures, reads like a stamp of approval, stating in essence "Yes, we agree with the above sentiments." It is clear from meeting minutes around this time that the bureau was low on funds (March 10, 1897, Chicago Bureau of Charities Executive Committee Meeting, UCCC).

28. March 20, 1897, Special Meeting of the Chicago Bureau of Charities Executive Meeting, UCCC.

29. March 31, 1897, Chicago Bureau of Charities Executive Committee Meeting, UCCC.

30. Addams (1961, 93); Knight (2005, 398).

31. Knight (2005, 368); Addams (1961, 105–106, 173).

32. Addams (1961, 176).

33. Ibid., pp. 181–182.

34. Addams (1894, 99).

35. Box 6, Folder 1 "CBC–Central District 1896–1902," UCCC. The note is written on the back of a piece of telegraph company paper.

36. Folder of Miscellaneous Pamphlets of Chicago Bureau of Charities, Chicago Historical Society; Chicago Bureau of Charities, West Side District report for activities between September 1, 1898 and September 1, 1899, Chicago Historical Society; 1898 pamphlet by West Side District of Chicago Bureau of Associated Charities entitled "Social Service," UCCC; Chicago Bureau of Charities Lower North District Annual Report, 1899, p. 7, UCCC.

37. Chicago Bureau of Charities, Fourth Annual Report, 1897–1898, Chicago Historical Society; Chicago Bureau of Charities Northwest District Annual Report, 1896–1897, p. 11, UCCC; Chicago Bureau of Associated Charities West Side District, 1898 pamphlet entitled "Social Service," UCCC; Addams (2002, 12).

38. In *Democracy and Social Ethics*, Addams (2002, 99) writes at length about her concerns with what she calls "the charity visitor." In the description, she clearly depicts the friendly visit as imbalanced. The typical friendly visitor existed in a state of "ethical maladjustment" that came from the reliance on an ethical frame "adapted to individual relationships."

39. Chicago Bureau of Charities pamphlet from 1897, "Touched at High Points," Folder of Miscellaneous Pamphlets Pamphlets of Chicago Bureau of Charities, Chicago Historical Society; Sixth and Seventh Annual Reports of the Chicago Bureau of Charities, November 1, 1899–October 31,1900–May 31, 1901, Chicago Bureau of Associated Charities Reports Book, Chicago Historical Society. Cybelle Fox (2012, 129–130) argues that Addams, at least later in life,

was an opponent of "targeted deportations." This is clearly not the case in the early part of Addams's career, as she was not just, in Fox's words "conspicuously silent" (like most social workers) but instead actively involved in supporting the deportation process.

40. In 1894, Addams began to write a scathing indictment of George Pullman, part of which she delivered in May 1895 as a speech in New York (1894). A later draft was published in 1912 as "A Modern Lear"; Chicago Bureau of Charities Third Annual Report, November 1896–October 1897, Chicago Bureau of Associated Charities Reports Book, Chicago Historical Society; Addams (1961, 92).

41. In fact, Addams was not the only Hull-House resident to develop ties with the Chicago Bureau of Charities. Julia Lathrop, a close friend of Addams as well as a resident, was a champion of charity organization efforts and did significant work for the CBC. Perhaps Lathrop was the impetus behind Addams's actions on behalf of charity organization. Addams (2004, 53) provides fodder for this notion when she writes that during the winter of 1893–94, "she [Lathrop] actually revived an interest in the Charity Organization Society which had experienced such hard sledding in Chicago, and started the movement all over again in a little office not so many blocks from Hull-House." The problem with this account is that we know that Addams herself (without Lathrop) had been involved in significant efforts to bring charity organization to Chicago. There is no question that Lathrop was involved with charity organization and was instrumental in bringing it to Hull-House (as we saw above). She was even suggested as a candidate to be superintendent of the Chicago Relief and Aid Society in 1903 (see November 5, 1903, Chicago Relief and Aid Society Board Meeting, p. 403). There is merit to the idea that Lathrop, given her connections to various economistic organizations and her friendship with Addams, might have had influence on what Addams did. But there is no record of her attempting to convince Addams that charity organization should come to Hull-House.

42. September 24, 1893, Residents Meeting, Sunday 9:15 p.m., Hull-House Collection, The University Library, University of Illinois at Chicago 32–295, Residents' Meetings Records Book, pp. 35–36.

43. See Chicago Relief and Aid Society Meeting Minutes, 1887–1909, pp. 240–243, UCCC; Addams (2004, 53–54).

44. Hull-House Collection, Special Collections, The University Library, University of Illinois at Chicago. Residents' Meetings Records Book (beginning January 1893), p. 7, for a microfilm copy, see JAMC (reel 50); February 16, 1895, Hull-House Residents' Meeting Records Book, p. 82.

45. *Hull-House Bulletin*, vol. 1, no. 1, January 1896, Charity Organization Society, Chicago Relief Association and Chicago Bureau of Charities Minutes Book; "Circular of Information Published by the Bureau of Charities, Operating Under the Civic Federation to Bring into Co-operation the Philanthropic Forces of the City," Chicago, February 1896, pp. 4–5.

46. *Hull-House Bulletin*, vol. 1, no. 7, December 1, 1896, p. 10; *Hull-House Bulletin*, vol. 2, no. 6, October 1, 1897, p. 10.

47. *Hull-House Bulletin*, vol. 1, no. 7, December 1, 1896, p. 4; Sixth and Seventh Annual Reports of the Chicago Bureau of Charities, November 1,1899–May 31, 1901 (note: there was only one report for the two years); Ninth Annual Report of the Chicago Bureau of Charities, for fiscal year ending May 31, 1903, p. 38; pamphlets of Chicago Bureau of Charities, West Side District Report, p. 7.

48. Lest one conclude this partnership was a smooth, benign one, perhaps the logical and inevitable consolidation of functions without any loss of service or quality, it is important to note that the Chicago Relief and Aid Society (CRAS) continued its business-style practices unabated. For example, at a May 1908 CRAS board meeting, there was discussion concerning the Crane Nursery. The CRAS was pleased to announce reaching over 150 families, but they heard a report from the principal of the Dore School who thought the children coming through the nursery were undernourished and needed a midday meal. The CRAS board was skeptical and thought the children were doing just fine. See the Chicago Relief and Aid Society Meeting Minutes, March 15, 1907, vol. 2, 1887–1909; Chicago Relief and Aid Society Board Meeting, December 7, 1905, p. 457; Chicago Relief and Aid Society Board Meeting, December 11, 1907, p 498; Chicago Relief and Aid Society Board Meeting, December 20, 1907, p. 499; Chicago Relief and Aid Society Meeting Minutes, Chicago Relief and Aid Society Board Meeting, May 6, 1908, p. 511.

49. Davis (2000, 94); Trattner (1999, 182); Chicago Relief and Aid Society Board of Directors Meeting, January 28, 1909, pp. 526–527, in Chicago Relief and Aid Society Meeting Minutes, 1887–1909, UCCC, Chicago Historical Society.

50. Addams (2002, 69); here Knight's (2005, 392–393) analysis of Addams as a cooperator rings most true: "[For Addams] cooperation meant stepping back, creating space, but also connecting with others' hopes, trusting, and moving forward on a collectively determined agenda." As Hall (1992, 129) points out, "although Addams never ceased to believe that 'scientific' philanthropy could be humanized, in her eagerness to be politically and organizationally effective she may have traded away those aspects of her work which made it so distinctive."

Perhaps the project that found Addams most in harmony with her individual and social goals was her involvement in the fight for women's suffrage as early as 1897. She saw early on that women's needs were not men's needs, and that they varied depending on standpoint. Addams took a leadership role:

. . . when I acted as chairman of the federation of a hundred women's organizations, nothing impressed me so forcibly as the fact that the response came from bodies of women representing the most varied traditions . . . by organizations of working women who had keenly felt the need of the municipal franchise in order to secure for their workshops the most rudimentary sanitation . . . by federations of mothers' meetings, who were interested in clean milk and the extension of kindergartens; by property-owning women, who had been powerless to protest against unjust taxation; by organizations of professional women, of university students, and of collegiate alumnae; and by women's clubs interested in municipal reforms. . . . A striking witness as to the need of the ballot, even for the women who are restricted to the most primitive and traditional activities, occurred when some Russian women waited upon me to ask whether under the new charter they could vote for covered markets and so get rid of the shocking Chicago grime upon all their food; and when some neighboring Italian women sent me word that they would certainly vote for public washhouses if they ever had the chance to vote at all.

The women of Chicago needed a voice that would be heard if they were to have their needs met. And the early part of the twentieth century would see Addams campaign doggedly for that voice. See Addams (1961, 221–222).

Chapter Five

1. Remnick (2010, 114).

2. Obama (2004, 134–138); see also Armstrong (2005) and Scott (2007).

3. Obama (2004, 135–137).

4. See Maraniss (2012, ch. 7) for details on Obama's time in Hawaii. (note: all page references in Maraniss are from the Kindle edition)

5. Maraniss (2012, 193–212, 231); Obama (2004, 43).

6. Maraniss (2012, 220); On "twoness" see Du Bois (1903); on the club, see Obama (2004, 47). The idea of being inside and outside of the group is reminiscent of Simmel's (1964) *The Stranger*, first published in 1950.

7. Lolo quote on saving is from Obama (2004, 38–39); on "being soft" see Maraniss (2012, 230).

8. Maraniss (2012, 264, 279, 302–303).

9. On Punahou, see Maraniss (2012, 264); quote is from PBS *Frontline* (2012) interview with Tom Topolinski (note: all PBS *Frontline* interviews cited in this book can be found at *http://www.pbs.org/wgbh/pages/frontline/oral-history/#choice-2012*)

10. Shamus Khan (2010) shows the cultivation of specialness in his book *Privilege*.

11. Obama (2004, 75).

12. Interview with Genevieve Cook, an Australian with connections to Indonesia, was conducted by Maraniss (2012, 420, 500).

13. Ibid., pp. 356–359.

14. Ibid., pp. 335, 345, 374.

15. Ibid., pp. 378–379.

16. Quote is from Remnick (2010, 111); Maraniss (2012, 385).

17. Maraniss (2012, 428); quote is from Remnick (2010, 112).

18. Maraniss (2012, 453); quote is from Remnick (2010, 112).

19. Maraniss (2012, 465–66); quote on "two years" is from Mendell (2007, 62); library quote is from Boss-Bicak (2005); Remnick (2010, 113).

20. Remnick (2010, 111–117).

21. Obama (2004, 120–121). The theme of "fracturing" resonates with the experience of Addams along gender lines in nineteenth-century Chicago.

22. Obama quote is from Maraniss (2012, 448); Maraniss (2012, 420–421).

23. Obama (2004, 1); Maraniss (2012, 454).

24. Obama (2004, 220–221).

25. Maraniss (2012, 452–454).

26. Remnick (2010, 117). This sense of being in two worlds runs parallel to Addams's experiences growing up on the eve of the women's suffrage movement. She, too, was pulled in different directions.

27. "His office didn't write back" is from Remnick (2010, 118); letter on Obama's plans is from Maraniss (2012, 466); Obama "conventional capacity" and "too low to survive" quotes are both from Maraniss (2012, 469). On being "broke" see Obama (2004, 139).

28. Maraniss (2012, 483).

29. Obama (2004, 135); Remnick (2010, 118–119).

30. Remnick (2010, 120).

31. Obama (2004, 76); "Q&A with Barack Obama," *The Crisis,* October 1995, vol. 102, no. 7. Cook kept a daily journal, which did not become part of the Obama historiography until it was published by Maraniss (2012). See ch. 17 of Maraniss (2012) for detailed excerpts from her journal.

32. On Obama and Business International, see Maraniss (2012, 471, 481–482) and Remnick (2010, 120); Lou Celi quote is from Maraniss (2012, 502).

33. Maraniss (2012, 424).

34. Lizza (2007, para. 14).

35. Quote is from Obama (2004, 139); Maraniss (2012, 502). In the wake of the 2008 presidential election, being a community organizer has become a bit of a dirty word. The basic premise is to empower community members to identify modifiable barriers that keep people from realizing their full potential, and then tear them down. This is not a new idea on one level, particularly given what we know of Addams's efforts in Chicago. But following the 1960s, there was a call for questioning authority and bringing power to everyday people. Community organizing was a way to give voice to the powerless, those who were overwhelmed by big business and the massive, seemingly intractable welfare state.

36. Maraniss (2012, 502–534) on PIRG; see Lizza (2007) on the recycling program. For background on NYPIRG, see *http://www.nypirg.org/about/history .html* and *http://www.nypirg.org/alumni/*; also see *Good Day New York* clip: *https://www.youtube.com/watch?v=0ThsZ8uOYik&feature=player_embedded*

37. Obama (2004, 140).

38. Lizza (2007) says Obama saw the ad in the *New York Times*; Maraniss (2012, 506); Remnick (2010, 130–131).

39. Kellman quote on Harold Washington is from PBS *Frontline* interview; *Chicago Tribune*, March 30, 2007.

40. Lizza (2007); Kellman interview PBS *Frontline* (2012).

41. For background on this period, see Mundy (2007); quote is from Remnick (2010, 114).

Chapter Six

1. Lizza (2007, para. 11).

2. Obama (2004, 144); letter from PBS *Frontline*: *http://www.pbs.org/wgbh/ pages/frontline/government-elections-politics/choice-2012/artifact-11–obamas-early -impressions-of-chicago/*; Mendell (2007, 64–65); Remnick (2010, 135–136).

3. *http://www.thecha.org/pages/altgeld_gardens_and_phillip_murray_homes /50.php?devID=254*; Obama (2004, 164–165).

4. Perhaps not surprisingly, the resident's web page (*http://altgeldgardens.com*) is a dead link. The descriptions of Altgeld come from Obama (2004, 164); the letter quote comes from PBS *Frontline* (2012): *http://www.pbs.org/wgbh/pages/front line/government-elections-politics/choice-2012/artifact-11–obamas-early-impressions -of-chicago/*

5. On separate neighborhoods, see Obama (1988, 3), see *http://www.lib.niu .edu/1988/ii880840.html*; "As I listened" quote from Obama (2004, 228).

6. Kellman from PBS *Frontline* interview, 2012: *http://www.pbs.org/wgbh/ pages/frontline/government-elections-politics/choice-2012/the-frontline-interview -gerald-kellman*

7. Kellman interview and letter to Boerner, 1985, are from PBS *Frontline* (2012).

8. First Kellman quote is from McClelland (2010, 9–10); on the CCRC, see Kellman interview from PBS *Frontline* (2012).

9. McClelland (2010, 12).

10. Obama (2004, 150).

11. Remnick (2010, 135).

12. Ibid.; McClelland (2010, 5–6, 11–12, 16).

13. Remnick (2010, 166); Obama (1988). Another influential guide for Obama was Reverend Jeremiah Wright (the activist preacher who would later officiate at Obama's wedding and was so much talked about in Obama's first presidential campaign). See Remnick (2010, 132). David Mendell, a journalist who covered Obama's campaigns, characterized Obama's mentoring as follows:

> At first I really bought into this father-figure kind of mentality, but these
> people seemed to pick him out. Rather than him always picking them out,
> they seem to find him. More than anything, Obama is such a political

creature that he has found people who can abet his political career along the way. [He's] been very good at selling himself to them or been very good at learning what he can from these individuals. And it's almost always a mutually beneficial relationship.

Mendell interview from PBS *Frontline* (2012): *http://www.pbs.org/wgbh/pages/ frontline/choice2008/interviews/mendell.html*

14. Kellman interview from PBS *Frontline* (2012).

15. On pastors, see McClelland (2010, 13); on Chicago and Rakove, see Remnick (2010, 136) and Rakove (1979); Kellman on churches from PBS *Frontline* (2012).

16. McClelland (2010, 44).

17. Kellman quote is from Remnick (2010, 136); Lizza (2007) calls Alinsky the "missing layer."

18. Alinsky (1971, 116–117); on Addams and Alinsky, see Hamington (2010, 255–274).

19. Kellman from PBS *Frontline* (2012); Secter and McCormick (2007).

20. Secter and McCormick (2007).

21. First two Kellman quotes from PBS *Frontline* (2012); on Obama wanting to be a novelist, see Mendell (2007, 64) and Remnick (2010, 135); final Kellman quote from Mundy (2007).

22. Remnick (2010, 137).

23. Obama (2004, 158–159).

24. Ibid., p. 159.

25. Lloyd quote is from Walsh (2007); Remnick (2010, 137); McClelland (2010, 10); Obama (2004, 158–159). Alinsky actually was a graduate student at the University of Chicago and did significant ethnographic research on the Al Capone gang.

26. Maraniss, (2012, 533).

27. Lizza (2007).

28. McClelland (2010, 15–16).

29. Ibid., pp. 19–20.

30. Remnick (2010, 179); McClelland (2010, 19–21).

31. McClelland (2010, 22).

32. Secter and McCormick (2007).

33. Kellman interview from PBS *Frontline* (2012); see McClelland (2010, ch. 3) for more on details on the asbestos campaign.

34. Kellman interview from PBS *Frontline* (2012).

35. Ibid.; Obama (2004, 238).

36. Walsh (2007).

37. Letter from PBS *Frontline* (2012).

38. McClelland (2010, 55–56).

39. Ibid., p. 56.

40. Ibid., pp. 56–57. Senator Jones would eventually become president of the Senate and Obama's patron in the state legislature. At the time, he had very little political power, which makes his success on behalf of the DCP more impressive.

41. Ibid., pp. 17–18.

42. Remnick (2010, 179). In fact, some tenants probably still have asbestos in their homes (Walsh, 2007).

43. Obama (2004, 159–162).

44. Ibid., pp. 159–160.

45. Ibid., p. 161.

46. Ibid.

47. Ibid., p. 162.

48. Secter and McCormick (2007).

49. Remnick (2010, 179–180).

50. Obama (1988).

51. Ibid.

52. Kellman interview from PBS *Frontline* (2012).

53. Obama (2004, 287).

54. The friend is Bobby Titcomb; on law degree quote, see Mendell (2007, 82); on politics, see Mundy (2007, 4).

55. Obama (2004, 158–159, 272–279). Kellman interview from PBS *Frontline* (2012).

56. Obama would eventually buy the house next door to Grimshaw's. See McClelland (2010, 47–48). While McClelland sees this as the start of "one of this country's greatest social climbs," one might see it as continuous uncertainty on Obama's part in the face of complicated dilemmas. He was trying to balance competing demands and often could make it work.

57. Kellman interview from PBS *Frontline* (2012).

58. Ibid.

59. Quote can be found here: *http://www.pbs.org/wgbh/pages/frontline/ government-elections-politics/choice-2012/artifact-three-listen-to-obama-make-the-case-for-activism/*

60. Kellman interview from PBS *Frontline*.

61. Obama (2004, 289–290).

Chapter Seven

1. Blum (2013, Kindle locations 132–145).

2. See Obama (2004, 299–323).

3. Obama (2004, 316–317, 374).

4. Ibid, pp. 334, 340; Maraniss (2012, 566–567).

5. Maraniss (2012, 570–572).

6. Obama (1988, 4).

7. Heilemann (2007).

8. Levenson and Saltzman (2007).

9. Kodama (2007); O'Shaughnessy (1990).

10. See PBS *Frontline* (2012) interview with Ken Mack; Levenson and Saltzman (2007).

11. Remnick (2010, 204); MacFarquhar (2007). For more on the law firm, see *http://www.sidley.com/chicago/*

12. Mundy (2007).

13. McClelland (2010, 73); Kellman interview from PBS *Frontline* (2012); Mendell (2007, 102).

14. Kantor (2007); quote from Obama (2004, 56); Scott (2008).

15. Kellman interview from PBS *Frontline* (2012). In terms of self-promotion, Obama even filmed a black history minute for TBS in 1991: *http://www.youtube .com/watch?v=liuGp32jkgc*

16. Levenson and Saltzman (2007).

17. Kodama (2007).

18. Remnick (2010, 267–268).

19. McClelland (2010, 65).

20. Ibid., 65–66; Mendell (2007, 103); Reynolds (2007); the Kruglik quote can be found at "Barack Obama and the History of Project Vote!": *http://www .youtube.com/watch?v=Px1Ut433xPU*

21. McClelland (2010, 66); "Q&A with Barack Obama," *The Crisis*, vol. 102, no. 7, October 1995.

22. Remnick (2010, 259).

23. Ibid., p. 272.

24. Ibid., pp. 268–269, 274.

25. McClelland (2010, 67–70); Reynolds (2007); for information on John Rogers, see *http://www.blackentrepreneurprofile.com/profile-full/article/john-w -rogers-jr/*; Schmidt quote on Project Vote! can be found at *http://www.youtube .com/watch?v=PxxUt433xPU;* Secter and McCormick (2007).

26. Quote from "Barack Obama and the History of Project Vote": *https:// www.youtube.com/watch?v=PxxUt433xPU*

27. The Banks quote is from *https://www.youtube.com/watch?v=PxxUt433xPU;* on the rallies, see McClelland (2010, 70).

28. McClelland (2010, 66–70); Reynolds (2007).

29. McClelland (2010, 67).

30. Ibid., p. 68; Whitfield quote is from the YouTube video: *http://www .youtube.com/watch?v=PxxUt433xPU;* Reynolds (2007).

31. The old way was buying votes, an approach that Obama rejected. The party would pay registrars a dollar for each new registered voter, but in the words of David Orr, former Cook County clerk, "Bounty systems don't really

promote participation. When the money dries up, the voters drop out." Obama knew this and wanted to find a different way. See also McClelland (2010, 68).

32. Mendell (2007, 103); on number of voters, see McClelland (2010, 72); Obama quote is from Reynolds (2007).

33. Reynolds (2007).

34. Kantor (2008); for Baird quote and information on Obama's uncle and the University of Chicago offer, see McClelland (2010, 79–80); Scott (2008).

35. Scott (2008); McClelland (2010, 80–81); Obama (2004, xiv).

36. McClelland (2010, 80–81); Remnick (2010, 266); for Obama quote see Mendell (2007, 103–104). The following is the University of Chicago's official position on Obama's relationship to the law school (*http://www.law.uchicago .edu/media*):

> From 1992 until his election to the U.S. Senate in 2004, Barack Obama served as a professor in the Law School. He was a Lecturer from 1992 to 1996. He was a Senior Lecturer from 1996 to 2004, during which time he taught three courses per year. Senior Lecturers are considered to be members of the Law School faculty and are regarded as professors, although not full-time or tenure-track. The title of Senior Lecturer is distinct from the title of Lecturer, which signifies adjunct status. Like Obama, each of the Law School's Senior Lecturers has high-demand careers in politics or public service, which prevent full-time teaching. Several times during his 12 years as a professor in the Law School, Obama was invited to join the faculty in a full-time tenure-track position, but he declined.

37. Davis is no longer part of the firm name. Morain (2008); quote is from Mendell (2007, 104–106); McClelland (2010, 63–65); Pallasch (2007).

38. McClelland (2010, 77); for Davis quote see Remnick (2010, 220); for Obama's time as lawyer and at University of Chicago see 260–61); Reynolds (2007); Morain (2008); Kellman interview from PBS *Frontline* (2012); Obama (2004, 438).

39. Shipps, Sconzert, and Swyers (1999).

40. Interview with Newton Minow from PBS *Frontline*: *http://www.pbs.org /wgbh/pages/frontline/choice2008/interviews/minow.html#2*

41. McClelland (2010, 97).

42. Maya quote is from Scott (2008, para. 20); Kellman interview is from PBS *Frontline*.

43. McClelland (2010, 100); "Friends of O," *Chicago Magazine*, June 2008; for review of the book, see the August 6, 1995, *New York Times*, "A Promise of Redemption" by Paul Watkins: *http://www.nytimes.com/1995/08/06/books/review /06obama-dreams.html*

44. Remnick (2010, 275–277).

45. Ibid., pp. 276–278, 283.

46. Quote from Michelle is from Remnick (2010, 277); Helman (2007).

47. Quote from Obama is from De Zutter (1995); Remnick (2010, 293–294).

48. Quote from Linda Randle is from Remnick (2010, 289); Hardy (1995).

49. On elections, see Remnick (2010, 290–292); Obama quote is from Jackson and Long (2007).

50. Reed's *Village Voice* piece is reprinted in his 2001 book, *Class Notes: Posing as Politics and Other Thoughts on the American Scene.*

51. Hardy (1995); Obama quote is from De Zutter (1995).

52. In fact, Kantor (2012, 164–165) does just that, calling Obama's exchange with Kellman "absurd on its face."

53. Kellman interview is from PBS *Frontline* (2012).

54. Lizza (2007, 11). The balancing act was one Addams (1921, 154) knew quite well: "Each generation of moralists and educators find themselves facing an inevitable dilemma; first, to keep the young committed to their charge 'unspotted from the world,' and, second, to connect the young with the ruthless and materialistic world all about them in such wise that they may make it the arena for their spiritual endeavor."

Chapter Eight

1. Addams (2002, 7).

2. Burns (1902); see Knight (2010) for the most comprehensive biography of Addams's later years.

3. One might even talk of their obstacles as part of what Patricia Hill Collins (1999) terms the "matrix of domination." Thanks to Tamara Beauboeuf for pointing this out to me.

4. Jeffries (2013) develops the idea of Obama's privilege, along race, gender, and class lines in his fantastic book *Paint the White House Black.* This is essential reading for anyone trying to understand Obama's biography through an intersectional lens. There are certainly gender dimensions of Obama's more clinical and "sensible" approach, influenced by Lolo's early teaching. Addams is seen as more compassionate, typically described as a more feminine virtue. My friend and colleague Hae Yeon Choo posed to me perhaps the most interesting question here: "Why is it when white men and men of color do the types of work described in the book, it is usually called political activism, but when women do it, it is called helping?"

5. The notion of multivocality and the potential for multiple lines of action is illustrated quite nicely by Padgett and Ansell (1993), using the case of Cosimo di Medici. Addams (1892, 229), too, saw her work at Hull-House in terms of lines of action: "The activities of Hull-House divide themselves into four, possibly more lines. They are not formally or consciously thus divided, but broadly separate according to the receptivity of the neighbors." The knowledge of both worlds evokes Hegel's "master-slave" dialectic. Whose knowledge of the world is

more true, asks Hegel (2013)—that of the master or the slave? The answer is the latter, as she needs to know both her own and that of the master. The reverse is not the case. In terms of the cultivation of privilege, the most comprehensive discussion of the social mechanisms involved is *Privilege*, by Shamus Khan (2010).

6. I use the idea of a guide deliberately here. The original Mentor, characterized by Homer in his epic works the *Iliad* and *Odyssey*, offered guidance to both Odysseus and his son Telemachus in moments of uncertainty.

7. We might even look to religion as underpinning the creation of these norms. Whether going to Christian heaven or moving along the eightfold path of Buddhism, at a personal level you help others in part to help with your own salvation. At the level of the social, there are a number of theories that might explain the connection between religion and habits of helping others. French sociologist Émile Durkheim thought of it in terms of collective effervescence. Religion might move beyond its symbols and rituals, whether the Cross or the Buddha, but Durkheim tells us "there can be no society that does not experience the need at regular intervals to maintain and strengthen the collective feelings and ideas that provide its coherence and its distinct individuality"(Durkheim 1995, 429). And as Emirbayer (2003, 15) tells us, for Durkheim these collective expressions of social solidarity are "potentially creative and dynamic moments. It was precisely in such moments, he felt, that one finds the wellsprings of human agency, of the capacity . . . to creatively reconfigure and transform the relational structures within which action unfolds."

8. As Sklar (1990, 95) points out, "Addams was able to act on impulse, confident that, through her own resources and this support network, she could find the means to match her imagination." She was able to engage in those activities at Hull-House that developed community and that provided help to neighborhood residents without paying much attention to the needs of the elites of Chicago. Addams is akin to French writer Gustave Flaubert, as described in Bourdieu's (1996) *The Rules of Art*. Like Flaubert (who was also quite wealthy), Addams possessed a remarkable degree of independence, particularly for a woman of her time: It is "money (inherited) that guarantees freedom with respect to money"(84). Flaubert was able to translate *his* financial independence into an independence from the market. He produced his art for its own sake, rather than for money. Addams, like Flaubert, was able to invert the economic world, in her case by engaging in activities that had tremendous social value to all involved in the settlement, but little commercial value. Like the avant-garde artist pursuing art for art's sake, Addams was able, in essence, to make the market disappear—and the weight of the market did not unduly influence considerations as to what to do. She and the other residents were able to focus on what was most important—helping other people without any particular ends forced on them by the need to raise money and cater to the wealthy elites of the city. We might understand Addams's early efforts at Hull-House as part of an avant-garde approach to social

provision that followed a logic of "help for help's sake" rather than "business is business." We are all familiar with the trope of the struggling artist, musician, or writer who does her work purely for the sake of the art and eschews any effort to make money from her efforts. But there is more going on than one person's refusal to produce for a particular audience. Following Bourdieu, what is at stake is "definition" in the field (a particular bounded social space of "play"), with each side trying to impose its rules and logic, influencing the way the game is played.

9. Thanks to one of the anonymous reviewers at Stanford for this idea.

10. Quote is from Remnick (2010, 114, Kindle edition).

11. Myrdal (1944); on the idea of cultural contradictions in American society, see Hitlin and Salisbury (2013), Jeffries (2013), Hewitt (1989), and Kloppenberg (2012).

12. See Bellah et al. (1985, ch. 2) for a detailed discussion of the historical origins of these cultural contradictions, an examination of which are beyond the scope of this book. The authors point to sources as varied as religion, Republicanism, Ben Franklin, entrepreneurship, psychotherapy, and economic integration driven by modernization. What is clear is that there are a number of different origins, not just one. What matters for this book is that these contradictions live on long after the conditions that made them possible and gave them initial meaning.

13. Sumner (1906).

14. Bauman (1996).

15. There is a vast literature on social citizenship, but most scholars anchor the use of the term in Thomas H. Marshall's (1950) work *Citizenship and Social Class*.

Appendix

1. See Linn (2000). It is worth noting that, as Anne Firor Scott (2000, xiv–xv) points out, Addams "had read and commented on the first eight chapters of Linn's manuscript and discussed his plans for the next three." Henry Steele Commager (1961, xiv), in the (now classic) foreword to the popular Signet edition of *Twenty Years at Hull-House*, published in 1961, famously characterized Addams as akin to the Red Queen in Lewis Carroll's *Through the Looking-Glass*: "More and more [Addams] came to feel like Alice with the Red Queen: no matter how fast she ran, she was still in the same place; the poverty, the slums, the crime and vice, the misgovernment, the illiteracy, the exploitation, the inhumanity of man to man—all these were still there."

While painting her as a heroic figure, Commager was perhaps one of the first to dwell on the limitations of Addams's work and the sheer daunting task faced by social reformers. In terms of gender, class, and culture, see Conway (1967), Lasch (1965), and Levine (1962). The general consensus at this time was that Addams had much to contribute to the radical political agenda of the 1960s, in terms of her struggles on behalf of organized labor, her efforts to empower women, and her understanding of the gap between her generation and the preceding one (a theme that still had resonance a hundred years after her birth). The point is that Addams scholarship increasingly became the site of contestation, with a plethora of publications in history and social work—for example, Lissak (1989), Lasch-Quinn (1993), and Mink (1995)—viewing Addams with a critical eye, particularly on matters of race. The work of two scholars—Mary Jo Deegan (1988 and 2002) and Charlene Haddock Seigfried (1996)—work over and against these critical assessments, presenting Addams as a "feminist pragmatist," emphasizing her advocacy for social citizenship and her efforts to bring racial equality to social relations in Chicago and beyond.

There are several recent biographies of Addams that provide a comprehensive overview and analysis of her life (see Brown, 2004; Knight, 2005 and 2010), while focusing on Addams's contributions to democratic theory and practice. These recent biographies should be the first stop for any reader interested in learning more about Addams.

Other recent work has picked up or paralleled the investigation of the nexus of Addams's democratic (and social) growth, engaging in reinterpretation or recovery of Addams's theory and practice. In terms of reinterpretation, Jackson (2001), for example, examines Addams's actions in terms of "lines of activity" that are creative and performative, taking a dramaturgical approach to Hull-House as a veritable performance hall of social provision. In terms of recovery, Westhoff (2007) sees Addams's ideas and practice as central to the development of what she terms "democratic social knowledge." The edited volume *Jane Addams and the Practice of Democracy* (Fischer, Nackenhoff, and Chmielewski, 2009) contains work in a similar vein. We see chapters that illuminate her cooperative spirit (Knight, 2009), highlight her ability to engage in "principled" compromise (Seigfried, 2009), and elucidate the ties between her democratic ideals and her spirituality (Brown, 2009). Deegan's (2010) forceful reclamation of Addams's reputation on race is the most recent and noteworthy in the literature, marking clear, empirically informed boundaries around Addams's theoretical and practical reputations.

2. See Tilly's (2002) work on stories for a good discussion of how we put narratives to work in the social world. See Vaisey (2009) on the challenges of using subjective data to make sense of culture.

3. I used the same coding strategy for both the Addams and Obama data. Following Miles and Huberman (1994), I used an *a priori* approach to coding (informed by categories tied to my conceptual framework), performing content analysis of all of the documentary evidence, both primary and secondary.

4. Jeffries (2013); Alexander (2010); Alexander and Jaworsky (2014).

5. See, for example, Bourdieu (1991, 1998) and Bourdieu, Chamboredon, and Passeron (1991) for the idea of looking at struggles.

6. Sartre (1975, 350–355).

7. Ibid., p. 358.

8. Merton (1976, 6).

9. Lynd (1967, 59, 60).

10. Wiebe (1967).

11. Lindblom (1959); Dewey (1991, 220); Addams (2002); Follett (1924, xv); Addams (1893, 44–45). A community itself can even experience perplexity as it grows and progresses—see Addams (2002, ch. 5).

12. Merton (1976, 10).

13. Sumner (1906).

14. See Tocqueville's (1990) *Democracy in America*. Bellah et al. (1985) extend these ideas of the "habits of the heart" in later work.

15. Addams (2002, 7).

16. Sumner (1906, 7, 22–26).

17. For a discussion of the idea of the "dynamo station" and relational creativity, see Follett (1924, 77–81, quote from 81).

18. For Follett's ideas on power, democracy, and community, see Follett (1942, 76–79).

19. See Dewey (1988, 181). Simmel (1965, 125) tells us that the development of community habits, or norm setting, allows helping to shift from a charitable donation "into an interaction, a sociological event." While we may feel good about dropping change into a box near a cash register, thinking our coins will help fight cancer or feed hungry children, Simmel asks us not to think of poor people in those terms. They are not boxes into which we throw donations. Instead, if both parties—the helper and person being helped—share an understanding of the interaction, they can help foster community. The kind of "paying forward" that Simmel is talking about is not money. Buying coffee for the next person in line at Starbucks or making a charitable donation to a cause are both fine things to do, but Simmel encourages bigger thinking. So, too, does the work of Addams and Obama demonstrate the value of face-to-face interactions of helping, over and above the value of writing a check.

20. Arendt (1994, 322).

21. Ibid.

Bibliography

Addams, Jane. 1892, October. "Hull House, Chicago: An Effort Toward Social Democracy." *Forum* 14:226–241.

Addams, Jane. 1893. "The Objective Value of a Social Settlement." In *Philanthropy and Social Progress* (pp. 27–56). New York: Thomas Y. Crowell & Co.

Addams, Jane. 1894. "Hull House as a Type of College Settlement." Wisconsin State Conference of Charities and Correction, Proceedings.

Addams, Jane. 1912, November 2. "A Modern Lear." *The Survey* 29 (5):131–137.

Addams, Jane. 1921. *The Spirit of Youth and the City Streets*. New York: Macmillan.

Addams, Jane. 1927, October 13. "A Book That Changed My Life." *Christian Century* 44 (41):1196–1198.

Addams, Jane. 1961. *Twenty Years at Hull-House*. New York: Signet Classic. Original edition, 1910.

Addams, Jane. 2002. "The Subtle Problems of Charity." In *The Jane Addams Reader* (pp. 62–75), edited by Jean Bethke Elshtain. New York: Basic Books.

Addams, Jane. 2002. *Democracy and Social Ethics*. Urbana: University of Illinois Press. Original edition, 1902.

Addams, Jane. 2004. *My Friend, Julia Lathrop*. Urbana and Chicago: University of Illinois Press. Original edition, 1935.

Agnew, Elizabeth N. 2004. *From Charity to Social Work: Mary E. Richmond and the Creation of an American Profession*. Urbana and Chicago: University of Illinois Press.

Alexander, Jeffrey C. 2010. *The Performance of Politics: Obama's Victory and the Democratic Struggle for Power*. New York: Oxford University Press.

Alexander Jeffrey C., and Bernadette N. Jaworsky. 2014. *Obama Power*. Malden, MA: Polity.

Alinsky, Saul D. 1971. *Rules for Radicals: A Practical Primer for Realistic Radicals*. New York: Vintage Books.

Arendt, Hannah. 1994. "Understanding and Politics (The Difficulties of Understanding)." In *Essays in Understanding, 1930–1954* (pp. 307–327), edited by Jermoe Kohn. New York: Shocken Books.

Armstrong, Dan. 2005. "Barack Obama Embellishes His Resume." *Analyze This,* last modified August 22, 2013. *http://www.analyzethis.net/2005/07/09/barack -obama-embellishes-his-resume/*

Bauman, Zygmunt. 1996. "From Pilgrim to Tourist—Or a Short Story of Identity." In *Questions of Cultural Identity*, edited by Stuart Hall and Paul du Gay. London: Sage Publications.

Bellah, Robert N., Richad Madsen, William M. Sullivan, Ann Swidler, and Steven M. Tipton. 1985. *Habits of the Heart: Individualism and Commitment in American Life.* New York: Harper & Row.

Blum, David. 2013. *President Barack Obama: The Kindle Singles Interview.* Amazon Kindle edition.

Boss-Bicak, Shira. 2005. "Barack Obama '83. Is He the New Face of the Democractic Party?" *Columbia College Today.* http://www.college.columbia. edu/cct_archive/jan05/cover.php

Bourdieu, Pierre. 1984. *Distinction: A Social Critique of the Judgment of Taste.* Cambridge, MA: Harvard University Press.

Bourdieu, Pierre. 1991. "Some Properties of Fields." In *Advances in Social Theory and Methodology: Toward an Integration of Micro- and Macro-Sociologies* (pp. 73–77), edited by K. Knorr-Cetina and A. V. Cicourel. Boston: Routledge & Kegan Paul.

Bourdieu, Pierre. 1996. *The Rules of Art: Genesis and Structure of the Literary Field.* Translated by Susan Emanuel. Stanford, CA: Stanford University Press. Original edition, 1992.

Bourdieu, Pierre. 1998. *Practical Reason.* Stanford, CA: Stanford University Press. Original edition, 1994.

Bourdieu, Pierre, Jean-Claude Chamboredon, and Jean-Claude Passeron. 1991. *The Craft of Sociology: Epistemological Preliminaries.* Edited by Beate Krais; translated by Richard Nice. New York: Walter de Gruyter. Original edition, 1968.

Bowker, R. R. 1887, May. "Toynbee Hall, London." *The Century: A Popular Quarterly* 34 (1):158–159.

Briggs, Asa, and Anne Macartney. 1984. *Toynbee Hall: The First Hundred Years.* London: Routledge & Kegan Paul.

Brown, James. 1941. *The History of Public Assistance in Chicago, 1833 to 1893.* Chicago: University of Chicago Press.

Brown, Victoria Bissell. 1999. "Advocate for Democracy: Jane Addams and the Pulllman Strike." In *The Pullman Strike and the Crisis of the 1890s. Essays on Labor and Politics* (pp. 130–158), edited by Richard Schneirov, Shelton Stromquist, and Nick Salvatore. Urbana and Chicago: University of Illinois Press.

Brown, Victoria Bissell. 2004. *The Education of Jane Addams.* Philadelphia: University of Pennsylvania Press.

Brown, Victoria Bissell. 2009. "The Sermon of the Deed: Jane Addams's Spiritual

Evolution." In *Jane Addams and the Practice of Democracy* (pp. 21–39), edited by Marilyn Fischer, Carol Nackenhoff, and Wendy Chmielewski. Urbana: University of Illinois Press.

Bryan, Mary Lynn McCree, Barbara Bair, and Maree De Angury, eds. 2003. *The Selected Papers of Jane Addams. Volume 1: Preparing to Lead, 1860–81*. Urbana: University of Illinois Press.

Bryan, Mary Lynn McCree, Barbara Bair, and Maree De Angury, eds. 2009. *The Selected Papers of Jane Addams. Volume 2: Venturing into Usefulness, 1881–88*. Urbana: University of Illinois Press.

Burns, Robert. 1902. "Persons in the Foreground: The Only Saint America Has Produced." Quoted in *Index of Current Literature* (pp. 377–379), edited by Edward J. Wheeler. New York: Current Literature Publishing Company.

Carson, Mina. 1990. *Settlement Folk: Social Thought and the American Settlement Movement, 1885–1930*. Chicago: University of Chicago Press.

Collins, Patricia Hill. 1999. *Black Feminist Thought: Knowledge, Consciousness, and the Politics of Empowerment*. New York: Routledge.

Commager, Henry Steele. 1961. "Foreword." In *Twenty Years at Hull-House* (pp. ix–xix), by Jane Addams. New York: Signet Classic.

Conway, Jill. 1967. "Jane Addams: An American Heroine." In *The Woman in America* (pp. 247–266), edited by Robert Jay Lifton. Boston: Beacon Press. Original edition, 1964.

Crocker, Ruth Hutchinson. 1992. *Social Work and Social Order: The Settlement Movement in Two Industrial Cities, 1889–1930*. Urbana: University of Illinois Press.

Davis, Allen F. 1984. *Spearheads for Reform: The Social Settlements and the Progressive Movement 1890–1914*. New Brunswick, NJ: Rutgers University Press. Original edition, 1967.

Davis, Allen F. 2000. *American Heroine: The Life and Legend of Jane Addams*. Chicago: Ivan R. Dee. Original edition, 1973.

Deegan, Mary Jo. 1988. *Jane Addams and the Men of the Chicago School, 1892–1918*. Reprint ed. New Brunswick, NJ: Transaction Books.

Deegan, Mary Jo. 2002. *Race, Hull-House, and the University of Chicago: A New Conscience Against Ancient Evils*. Westport, CT: Praeger.

Deegan, Mary Jo. 2010. "Jane Addams on Citizenship in a Democracy." *Journal of Classical Sociology* 10 (3):217–238.

De Tocqueville, Alexis. 1990. *Democracy in America*. 2 vols. New York: Vintage Books.

Dewey, John. 1988. "Reconstruction in Philosophy." In *John Dewey: The Middle Works, 1899–1924: Reconstruction in Philosophy and Essays* (pp. 77–201), edited by Jo Ann Boydston. Carbondale: Southern Illinois University Press. Original edition, 1920.

Dewey, John. 1991. "Theory of Valuation." In *John Dewey: The Later Works,*

1925–1953 (vol. 13, pp. 189–251), edited by Jo Ann Boydston. Carbondale: Southern Illinois University Press.

De Zutter, Hank. 1995, December 8. "What Makes Obama Run?" *The Chicago Reader.*

Diliberto, Gioia. 1999. *A Useful Woman. The Early Life of Jane Addams.* New York: Scribner.

Dionne, E. J. 2012. *Our Divided Political Heart: The Battle for the American Idea in an Age of Discontent.* New York: Bloomsbury Publishing USA.

Du Bois, William Edward Burghardt. 1903. *The Souls of Black Folk.* New York: Oxford University Press.

Durkheim, Émile. 1995. *The Elementary Forms of Religious Life.* Translated by Karen E. Fields. New York: Free Press.

Emirbayer, Mustafa. 2003. "Introduction." In *Émile Durkheim: Sociologist of Modernity* (pp. 1–28), edited by Mustafa Emirbayer. Malden, MA: Blackwell Publishing.

Fischer, Marilyn, Carol Nackenhoff, and Wendy Chmielewski, eds. 2009. *Jane Addams and the Practice of Democracy.* Urbana: University of Illinois Press.

Flanagan, Maureen. 2002. *Chicago Women and the Visions of the Good City, 1871–1933.* Princeton, NJ: Princeton University Press.

Follett, Mary Parker. 1924. *Creative Experience.* Toronto: Longmans, Green and Co.

Follett, Mary Parker. 1942. "Power." In *Dynamic Administration: The Collected Papers of Mary Parker Follett* (pp. 72–95), edited by Henry C. Metcalf and L. Urwick. New York: Harper & Brothers.

Foucault, Michel. 1978. *The History of Sexuality. Volume 1: An Introduction.* New York: Vintage Books.

Fox, Cybelle. 2012. *Three Worlds of Relief: Race, Immigration, and the American Welfare State from the Progressive Era to the New Deal.* Amazon Kindle edition. Princeton, NJ: Princeton University Press.

Habermas, Jürgen. 1989. *The Structural Transformation of the Public Sphere: An Inquiry into a Category of Bourgeois Society.* Cambridge: MIT Press.

Hall, Peter Dobkin. 1992. *Inventing the Nonprofit Sector and Other Essays on Philanthropy, Voluntarism, and Nonprofit Organizations.* Baltimore: Johns Hopkins University Press.

Hamington, Maurice. 2010. "Community Organizing: Addams and Alinsky." In *Feminist Interpretations of Jane Addams* (pp. 255–274), edited by Maurice Hamington. University Park: Pennsylvania State University Press.

Hardy, Thomas. 1995, December 19. "Jackson Foe Now Wants Old Job Back." *Chicago Tribune.*

Hegel, G. W. F. 2013. *The Phenomenology of the Mind: Volume 1.* New York: Routledge.

Heilemann, John. 2007, October 14. "When They Were Young." *New York Magazine.* http://nymag.com/news/features/39321/

Helman, Scott. 2007, October 12. "Early Defeat Launched a Rapid Political Climb." *Boston Globe.*

Herndon, Emily. 1892, February 20. "Hull House: A Swept-Out Corner of Chicago." *The Christian Union*, pp. 351–352.

Hewitt, John P. 1989. *Dilemmas of the American Self.* Philadelphia: Temple University Press.

Hitlin, Steven, and Mark H. Salisbury. 2013. "Living Life for Others and/or Oneself: The Social Development of Life Orientations." *Social Science Research* 42 (6):1622–1634.

Hofstadter, Richard. 1963. *The Progressive Movement: 1900–1915.* Englewood Cliffs, NJ: Prentice-Hall.

Hunter, Robert. 1902. "The Relation Between Social Settlements and Charity Organization." *Journal of Political Economy* 11 (1):75–88.

Jackson, David, and Ray Long. 2007, April 4. "Showing His Bare Knuckles." *Chicago Tribune.*

Jackson, Shannon. 2001. *Lines of Activity: Performance, Historiography, Hull-House Domesticity.* Ann Arbor: University of Michigan Press.

James, William. 1981. *Pragmatism.* Indianapolis: Hackett Publishing. Original edition, 1901.

Jeffries, Michael P. 2013. *Paint the White House Black: Barack Obama and the Meaning of Race in America.* Stanford, CA: Stanford University Press.

Johnson, Alexander. 1899. "Concerning Certain Wise Limits to Charity Organization Society Work." *American Journal of Sociology* 5 (3):322–328.

Johnson, Alexander. 1923. *Adventures in Social Welfare.* Fort Wayne, IN: Fort Wayne Printing Company.

Kantor, Jodi. 2007, January 23. "In Law School, Obama Found Political Voice." *New York Times.*

Kantor, Jodi. 2008, July 30. "Teaching Law, Testing Ideas, Obama Stood Slightly Apart." *New York Times.* http://www.nytimes.com/2008/07/30/us/politics/30law.html?pagewanted=all&_r=0

Kantor, Jodi. 2012. *The Obamas.* New York: Little, Brown and Company.

Katz, Michael B. 1996. *In the Shadow of the Poorhouse: A Social History of Welfare in America* (10th ed.). New York: Basic Books. Original edition, 1986.

Kelley, Florence. 1986. *The Autobiography of Florence Kelley*, edited by Kathryn Kish Sklar. Chicago: Charles H. Kerr Publishing Company.

Khan, Shamus Rahman. 2010. *Privilege: The Making of an Adolescent Elite at St. Paul's School.* Princeton, NJ: Princeton University Press.

Kloppenberg, James T. 2012. *Reading Obama: Dreams, Hope, and the American Political Tradition.* Princeton, NJ: Princeton University Press.

Knight, Louise W. 2005. *Citizen: Jane Addams and the Struggle for Democracy.* Chicago: University of Chicago Press.

Knight, Louise W. 2009. "Jane Addams's Theory of Cooperation." In *Jane Addams and the Practice of Democracy* (pp. 65–86), edited by Marilyn Fischer, Carol Nackenhoff and Wendy Chmielewski. Urbana: University of Illinois Press.

Knight, Louise W. 2010. *Spirit in Action: Jane Addams.* New York: Norton.

Kodama, Marie C. 2007, January 19. "Obama Left Mark on HLS." *Harvard Crimson.*

Kusmer, Kenneth L. 1973. "The Functions of Organized Charity in the Progressive Era: Chicago as a Case Study." *Journal of American History* 60 (3):657–678.

Lasch, Christopher. 1965. *The New Radicalism in America, 1889–1963: The Intellectual as a Social Type.* New York: Norton.

Lasch-Quinn, Elisabeth. 1993. *Black Neighbors: Race and the Limits of Reform in the American Settlement House Movement, 1890–1945.* Chapel Hill: University of North Carolina Press.

Lengermann, Patricia, and Gillian Niebrugge. 2007. "Thrice Told: Narratives of Sociology's Relation to Social Work." In *Sociology in America: A History* (pp. 63–114), edited by Craig Calhoun. Chicago: University of Chicago Press.

Levenson, Michael, and Jonathan Saltzman. 2007, January 28. "At Harvard Law, a Unifying Voice: Classmates Recall Obama as Even-Handed Leader." *Boston Globe.*

Levine, Daniel. 1962. "Jane Addams: Romantic Radical, 1889–1912." *Mid-America* 44 (4):195–210.

Lindblom, Charles E. 1959. "The Science of 'Muddling Through.'" *Public Administration Review* 19 (2):79–88.

Lindsey, Almont. 1964. *The Pullman Strike: The Story of a Unique Experiment and of a Great Labor Upheaval* (vol. 165). Chicago: University of Chicago Press.

Linn, James Weber. 2000. *Jane Addams: A Biography.* Urbana and Chicago: University of Illinois Press. Original edition, 1935.

Lissak, Rivka Shpak. 1989. *Pluralism & Progressives: Hull House and the New Immigrants, 1890–1919.* Chicago: University of Chicago Press.

Lizza, Ryan. 2007, March 19. "The Agitator." *New Republic*, pp. 22–30.

Lubove, Roy. 1980. *The Professional Altruist: The Emergence of Social Work as a Career, 1880–1930.* New York: Atheneum. Original edition, 1965.

Lynd, Robert S. 1967. *Knowledge for What? The Place of Social Science in American Culture.* Princeton, NJ: Princeton University Press.

MacFarquhar, Larissa. 2007, May 7. "The Conciliator." *The New Yorker.*

Maraniss, David. 2012. *Barack Obama: The Story.* New York: Simon & Schuster.

Marshall, Thomas H. 1950. *Citizenship and Social Class.* Cambridge UK: Cambridge University Press.

Mayer, John Albert. 1978. "Private Charities in Chicago from 1871 to 1915." Unpublished doctoral dissertation, University of Minnesota.

McCarthy, Kathleen D. 1982. *Noblesse Oblige: Charity & Cultural Philanthropy in Chicago 1849–1929*. Chicago: University of Chicago Press.

McClelland, Edward. 2010. *Young Mr. Obama: Chicago and the Making of a Black President*. New York: Bloomsbury Publishing USA.

Meacham, Standish. 1987. *Toynbee Hall and Social Reform, 1880–1914*. New Haven, CT: Yale University Press.

Mendell, David. 2007. *Obama: From Promise to Power*. New York: HarperCollins e-books.

Merton, Robert K. 1976. *Sociological Ambivalence and Other Essays*. New York: Free Press.

Miles, Matthew B., and A. M. Huberman. 1994. *Qualitative Data Analysis. An Expanded Sourcebook*. Thousand Oaks, CA: Sage Publications.

Mill, John Stuart. 1882. *On Liberty: The Subjection of Women*. New York: H. Holt and Company.

Mink, Gwendolyn. 1995. *The Wages of Motherhood*. Ithaca, NY: Cornell University Press.

Moore, Dorothea. 1897. "A Day at Hull House." *American Journal of Sociology* 2 (5):629–642.

Morain, Dan. 2008, April 6. "Obama's Lawyer Days: Brief and Not All Civil Rights." *Los Angeles Times*. http://web.archive.org/web/20080410065618/ http://www.latimes.com/news/politics/la-na-obamalegal6apr06,0,6774732 ,full.story

Mundy, Liza. 2007, August 12. "A Series of Fortunate Events." *Washington Post*. http://www.washingtonpost.com/wp-dyn/content/article/2007/08/08/ AR2007080802038.html. Accessed December 12, 2013.

Myrdal, Gunnar. 1944. *An American Dilemma: The Negro Problem and Modern Democracy* (2 vols.). New York: Harper & Bros.

Nelson, Otto M. 1966. "The Chicago Relief and Aid Society, 1850–1874." *Journal of the Illinois State Historical Society* 59:48–66.

Obama, Barack. 1988. "Why Organize?" *Illinois Issues* (August & September) :1–6.

Obama, Barack. 2004. *Dreams from My Father: A Story of Race and Inheritance*. New York: Three Rivers Press.

Obama, Barack. 2010. *Of Thee I Sing*. New York: Alfred A. Knopf.

O'Shaughnessy, Elise. 1990, June. "Harvard Law Reviewed." *Vanity Fair*.

Padgett, John F., and Christopher K. Ansell. 1993. "Robust Action and the Rise of the Medici, 1400–1434." *American Journal of Sociology* 98:1259–1319.

Pallasch, Abdon M. 2007, December 17. "Strong, Silent Type: Obama's Legal Career." *Chicago Sun-Times*.

Polikoff, Barbara Garland. 1999. *With One Bold Act: The Story of Jane Addams*. Chicago: Boswell Books.

Putnam, Robert D. 2000. *Bowling Alone: The Collapse and Revival of American Community.* New York: Simon & Schuster.

Rakove, Milton L. 1979. *We Don't Want Nobody Nobody Sent: An Oral History of the Daley Years.* Bloomington: Indiana University Press.

Reed, Jr., Adolph. 2001. *Class Notes: Posing as Politics and Other Thoughts on the American Scene.* New York: New Press.

Remnick, David. 2010. *The Bridge: The Life and Rise of Barack Obama.* New York: Vintage/Random House.

Residents of Hull-House. 1895. *Hull-House Maps and Papers: A Presentation of Nationalities and Wages in a Congested District of Chicago.* New York: Thomas Y. Crowell & Co.

Reynolds, Gretchen. 2007, July. "Vote of Confidence." *Chicago Magazine.*

Rom, Gudrun. 1958. *The United Charities of Chicago: Its History: 1857–1957.* Unpublished manuscript. Chicago Historical Society Archives.

Rorty, Richard. 1982. *Consequences of Pragmatism.* Minneapolis: University of Minnesota Press.

Rydell, Robert W. 2004. "World's Columbian Exposition." In *The Encyclopedia of Chicago* (pp. 898–902), edited by James R. Grossman, Ann Durkin Keating, and Janice L. Reiff. Chicago: University of Chicago Press.

Sartre, Jean-Paul. 1975. "Existentlialism." In *Existentialism from Dostoyevsky to Sartre* (pp. 280–374), edited by Walter Kaufman. New York: Plume. Original edition, 1946.

Sartre, Jean-Paul. 1985. *Les Main Sales.* London: Routledge.

Sawislak, Karen. 1995. *Smoldering City: Chicagoans and the Great Fire, 1871–1874.* Chicago: University of Chicago Press.

Sawislak, Karen. 2004. "Chicago Relief and Aid Society." In *The Encyclopedia of Chicago,* edited by James R. Grossman, Ann Durkin Keating, and Janice L. Reiff. Chicago: University of Chicago Press.

Schmitt, Carl. 1996. *The Concept of the Political.* Translated by George Schwab. Chicago: University of Chicago Press. Original edition, 1932.

Schneiderhan, Erik. 2008. "Jane Addams and Charity Organization." *Journal of the Illinois State Historical Society* 100 (4):299–327.

Schneiderhan, Erik. 2011. "Pragmatism and Empirical Sociology: The Case of Jane Addams and Hull-House, 1889–1895." *Theory and Society* 40 (6):589–617.

Schneirov, Richard, Shelton Stromquist, and Nick Salvatore. 1999. "Introduction." In *The Pullman Strike and the Crisis of the 1890s. Essays on Labor and Politics* (pp. 1–19), edited by Richard Schneirov, Shelton Stromquist, and Nick Salvatore. Urbana and Chicago: University of Illinois Press.

Scott, Anne Firor. 2000. "Introduction." In *Jane Addams: A Biography* (pp. ix–xxiii), by James Weber Linn. Urbana and Chicago: University of Illinois Press. Original edition, 1935.

Scott, Janny. 2007, October 30. "Obama's Account of New York Years Often Differs from What Others Say." *New York Times*. http://www.nytimes.com/2007/10/30/us/politics/30obama.html?_r=0&pagewanted=print. Accessed September 23, 2014.

Scott, Janny. 2008, May 18. "The Story of Obama, Written by Obama." *New York Times*. http://www.nytimes.com/2008/05/18/us/politics/18memoirs.html ?ref=thelongrun&pagewanted=all&_r=0

Secter, Bob, and John McCormick. 2007, March 30. "Barack Obama: Portrait of a Pragmatist" *Chicago Tribune*. http://www.chicagotribune.com/news/nation world/chi-0703300121mar30-archive-story.html#page=1

Seigfried, Charlene Haddock. 1996. *Pragmatism and Feminism*. Chicago: University of Chicago Press.

Seigfried, Charlene Haddock. 2009. "The Courage of One's Convictions or the Conviction of One's Courage? Jane Addams's Principled Compromises." In *Jane Addams and the Practice of Democracy* (pp. 40–62), edited by Marilyn Fischer, Carol Nackenhoff, and Wendy Chmielewski. Urbana: University of Illinois Press.

Shipps, Dorothy, Karin Sconzert, and Holly Swyers. 1999, March. *The Chicago Annenberg Challenge: The First Three Years*. Chicago: Consortium on Chicago School Research. *https://ccsr.uchicago.edu/publications/chicago-annenberg -challenge-first-three-years*. Accessed January 12, 2014.

Simmel, Georg. 1950. *The Sociology of Georg Simmel* (vol. 92892). New York: Simon & Schuster.

Simmel, Georg. 1965. "The Poor." *Social Problems* 13 (2):118–140.

Simmel, Georg, and Kurt Heinrich Wolff. 1964. *The Sociology of Georg Simmel*. Translated, edited, and with an introduction by Kurt H. Wolff. New York and London: Collier-Macmillan. Original edition, 1950.

Sinclair, Upton. 2006. *The Jungle*. New York: Signet Classic. Original edition, 1906.

Sklar, Kathryn Kish. 1990. "Who Funded Hull House?" In *Lady Bountiful Revisited: Women, Philanthropy, and Power* (pp. 94–115), edited by Kathleen D. McCarthy. New Brunswick, NJ: Rutgers University Press.

Small, Albion W. 1895. "The Civic Federation of Chicago: A Study in Social Dynamics." *American Journal of Sociology* 1 (1):79–103.

Smith, Carl. 2004. "Pullman Strike." In *The Encyclopedia of Chicago* (p. 666), edited by James R. Grossman, Ann Durkin Keating, and Janice L. Reiff. Chicago: University of Chicago Press.

Stead, William. 1894. *If Christ Came to Chicago!* London: The Review of Reviews.

Steeples, Douglas, and David O. Whitten. 1998. *Democracy in Desperation: The Depression of 1893*. Westport, CT: Greenwood Press.

Steinmetz, George. 1993. *Regulating the Social: The Welfare State and Social Politics in Imperial Germany*. Princeton, NJ: Princeton University Press.

Stone, Deborah. 2008. *The Samaritan's Dilemma: Should Government Help Your Neighbor?* New York: Nation Books.

Sumner, William Graham. 1906. *Folkways: A Study of the Sociological Importance of Usages, Manners, Customs, Mores, and Morals.* Boston: Ginn and Company, the Atheneum Press.

Sunderland, Eliza R. 1893, September. "Hull House, Chicago: Its Work and Workers." *The Unitarian.*

Swing, David. 1889, June 8. "A New Social Movement." Chicago Evening Journal, p. 4.

Tilly, Charles. 2002. *Stories, Identities, and Political Change.* Lanham, MD: Rowman & Littlefield.

Tolstoy, Leo. 1887. *What to Do? Thoughts Evoked by the Census of Moscow.* New York: Thomas Y. Crowell & Co. Trattner, Walter. 1999. *From Poor Law to Welfare State: A History of Social Welfare in America* (6th ed.). New York: Free Press.

Tucker, Robert C., ed. 1978. *The Marx-Engels Reader* (2nd ed.). New York: Norton.

Vaisey, Stephen. 2009. "Motivation and Justification: A Dual?Process Model of Culture in Action." *American Journal of Sociology* 114 (6):1675–1715.

Walsh, Kenneth T. 2007, August 26. "On the Streets of Chicago, a Candidate Comes of Age." *U.S. News & World Report.*

Watson, Frank Dekker. 1971. *The Charity Organization Movement in the United States: A Study in American Philanthropy.* New York: Arno Press. Original edition, 1922.

Weber, Max. 1946. "Class, Status, Party." In *From Max Weber: Essays in Sociology* (pp. 180–195), edited by H. H. Gerth and C. Wright Mills. New York: Oxford University Press.

Wenocur, Stanley, and Michael Reisch. 2001. *From Charity to Enterprise: The Development of American Social Work in a Market Economy.* Urbana: University of Illinois Press. Original edition, 1989.

Westbrook, Robert B. 1991. *John Dewey and American Democracy.* Ithaca, NY: Cornell University Press.

Westhoff, Laura M. 2007. *A Fatal Drifting Apart: Democratic Social Knowledge and Chicago Reform.* Columbus: The Ohio State University Press.

Wiebe, Robert H. 1967. *The Search for Order 1877–1920.* New York: Hill and Wang.

Wise, Winifred E. 1963. *Jane Addams of Hull-House.* New York: Harcourt, Brace & World.

"What Hull-House Really Is." 1895, April 28. *Chicago Daily Tribune*, p. 47.

Woods, Robert A. 1892, April. "The Social Awakening in London." *Scribner's Magazine* 11 (4):401–424.

Index